MARY SHELLEY

MARY SHELLEY
Portrait bust by the author, after contemporary portraits

MARY SHELLEY

AUTHOR OF "FRANKENSTEIN"

Elizabeth Nitchie

And Shelley, four-fam'd,—for her parents, her lord,
And the poor lone impossible monster abhorr'd.
   LEIGH HUNT, "Blue-Stocking Revels"

GREENWOOD PRESS, PUBLISHERS
WESTPORT, CONNECTICUT

Copyright 1953 by Rutgers University Press

Reprinted by permission
of Rutgers University Press

First Greenwood Reprinting 1970

Library of Congress Catalogue Card Number 72-100233

SBN 8371-3689-X

Printed in United States of America

Preface

A full century of alternating adulation and opprobrium has washed over the memory of Mary Wollstonecraft Shelley since her death in 1851. It seems fitting, therefore, to present a fresh evaluation of her as a woman and as a writer: as Shelley's wife, as a member of the Byron-Shelley circle, as an observer of her world, as an author who made a small name for herself in the literary life of the first half of the nineteenth century.

My investigations have led me to the chief repositories of printed and manuscript material: the British Museum, the Bodleian Library, the Huntington Library, the Pierpont Morgan Library, the Lord Chamberlain's collection of licensed plays, the Keats House and Museum in Hampstead, and the Keats-Shelley Memorial in Rome. They have opened to me the collections of Lord Abinger and the late Sir John Shelley-Rolls, joint heirs with the Bodleian of the Shelley papers belonging to Sir Percy and Lady Shelley. To them and to the Curators, Trustees, and Directors of the libraries and museums I am deeply indebted.

I have read and reread Mary Shelley's writings. I have explored the periodicals and annuals of her day and have discovered some hitherto unidentified work. I have found some new unpublished writings, finished and unfinished, among the manuscripts. None of them is of great literary value or importance. But they are often of biographical significance, adding to or modifying our knowledge of Mary and of Shelley, especially as Mary saw him and saw her relationship to him. In the books that are already familiar to scholars, there is room for further study of the fictional characters who represent Shelley, Byron, Trelawny, Claire Clairmont, Emilia Viviani, and Mary herself. Some erroneous identifications can be corrected. And there are other identifications and comparisons to be made. There is also much to be discovered about Mary Shelley's temperament and talent. The evidence of her own writing places her somewhere between the angel of her nineteenth century admirers and the devil of her twentieth century critics. We owe it to her, and to Shelley who chose her for his wife, to take her off the pedestal and to let her stand on her own two quite capable, far from clay, feet.

I wish to express my gratitude to the following: Lord Abinger and the late Sir John Shelley-Rolls for permission to examine and to quote from the unpublished material in their collections; the Curators of the Bodleian Library for permission to use and to quote from the reserved Shelley collection and other Mary Shelley manuscripts; the Trustees of the Pierpont Morgan Library for permission to use Mary Shelley's notes in their copy of the first edition of *Frankenstein*; the Keats House and Museum in Hampstead for permission to use the manuscript of *The Heir of Mondolfo* and for photographs of some of its pages; the Keats-Shelley Memorial in Rome for permission to examine and publish their unpublished Mary

PREFACE

Shelley letters and for photographs; Dr. Benjamin E. Powell, Librarian of Duke University, for the loan of the microfilms of Lord Abinger's papers and permission to quote from them; Lady Mander (R. Glynn Grylls), Mr. R. H. Hill (formerly Secretary of the Bodleian, now Librarian of the National Central Library), Professor Frederick L. Jones, Professor Leslie A. Marchand, Signora Cacciatore (Curator of the Keats-Shelley Memorial in Rome), and many other friends for innumerable acts of kindness: introductions, suggestions, criticism, sharing of minor discoveries and of microfilms, etc. I am saddened to think that two persons who helped and encouraged me are no longer living to read of my gratitude: Professor Newman Ivey White, whose friendly generosity to other scholars is well known, and Mr. Fred Edgcumbe, late Curator of the Keats House and Museum, kindly host and scholarly helper of all those interested in Keats and his contemporaries.

ELIZABETH NITCHIE

Goucher College
June, 1952

Contents

Introduction xi

1 The Self-Examiner 3
2 An Adverting Mind 22
3 Activity of Remembrance 49
4 The Godwins of Skinner Street 83
5 Albé and the Pirate 107
6 Friends, Foes, and Family 128
7 The Author: Eager Aspirant 141
8 The Author: No Idle Acclivity 165
9 The Keepsake of Mary Shelley 179

APPENDIX I Outline of Mary Shelley's Life 203
APPENDIX II List of Mary Shelley's Works 205
APPENDIX III Mary Shelley's *Mathilda* (reprinted from *Studies in Philology*) 211
APPENDIX IV The Stage History of *Frankenstein* (reprinted from *South Atlantic Quarterly*) 218

CONTENTS

APPENDIX V   Unpublished Poems
             by Mary Shelley   231
APPENDIX VI Persons Real and Fictitious
             Referred to in the Book   235

Bibliography   241

Index   245

Introduction

"To live with Mary Shelley," wrote Mrs. Marshall, under the spell of Mary's adoring daughter-in-law, "was indeed like entertaining an angel. Perfect unselfishness, *selflessness* indeed, characterized her at all times. . . . The influence of such a wife on Shelley's more vehement, visionary temperament can hardly be over-estimated. . . . He would not have been all he was without her sustaining and refining influence; without the constant sense that in loving him she loved his ideals also. We owe him, in part, to her." [1]

For many years this was the accepted judgment of Shelley's second wife. At that time there was "chatter about Harriet." Of late there has been much chatter about Mary. A recent writer accuses her of conniving with a forger—perhaps even of forgery—and of setting for her daughter-in-law an example in suppression of fact designed to create "the Shelley legend." [2] The partisans of John Howard

---

1. Marshall, *The Life and Letters of Mary W. Shelley*, II, 311, 324–325.
2. R. M. Smith, T. G. Ehrsam, et al., *The Shelley Legend* (N.Y., Scribner's, 1945), *passim*, especially pp. 79, 112. But see Mr. Ehrsam's

Payne have seen in her attitude toward him nothing but a desire for marriage with Washington Irving and for free opera tickets.[3] A biographer of Trelawny sneered at her "correct, genteel little soul,"[4] and insisted that she never truly loved Shelley. For Trelawny—that same Trelawny who had once tentatively proposed marriage to her—had written to Claire in the 1870's, "Mary Shelley's jealousy must have sorely vexed Shelley—indeed she was not a suitable companion for the poet—his first wife Harriett must have been more suitable—Mary was the most conventional slave I have ever met . . . she was devoid of imagination and Poetry—she felt compunction when she had lost him —she did not understand or appreciate him."[5]

But she deserves the sneers and innuendoes of Trelawny, Massingham, or Professor R. M. Smith as little as she does the blind adulation of Lady Shelley or Mrs. Marshall. She won the love of Shelley and at least a part of the fickle affections of Trelawny; she was courted by John Howard Payne and Prosper Mérimée; she was liked and respected by the Hunts, the Lambs, the Novellos, the Gisbornes, Bryan Procter, Sir John Bowring, Robert Dale Owen, and —at certain moments—Lord Byron. She proved herself a woman not only of charm but also of a liberal and independent mind. After Shelley's death, it is true, she slipped more easily into the ways of polite society. If this is slavery to convention, however, it must be remembered that Trelawny said of the whole Pisa circle, "Left to ourselves, we degenerated apace."

retraction: "Shelley's Letter to Mary Godwin," London *Times Literary Supplement*, Sept. 30, 1949.
  3. See *The Romance of Mary W. Shelley, John Howard Payne, and Washington Irving* (Boston, The Bibliophile Society, 1907).
  4. Massingham, *The Friend of Shelley*, p. 190.
  5. Trelawny, *Letters*, p. 229.

At the age of eighteen Mary Shelley wrote *Frankenstein,* a horror story which is at the same time a surprisingly mature study of loneliness and of the effect of environment. Stimulated by its success and encouraged by Shelley she continued to write during his life; after his death she wrote and published for twenty years more. Her first three novels are her best. Two of them were written while Shelley was still alive to hold her to a higher intellectual and creative standard than she could long maintain alone. The third was informed with her memories of him. The fact that Mary did most of her later literary work in order to earn money—for herself, for her father, for Percy—affected the quality of her last three novels and her short stories. She wrote *Frankenstein* and *Valperga* and even *The Last Man* out of a desire and a compulsion to write; she furnished tales for the purchasers of the "splendid annuals" and romantic novels for the readers of Bulwer and Disraeli, Lady Blessington and Mrs. Gore, with an eye to sales and checks. She fitted character and plot to the tastes of the public, especially the feminine public. For this very reason her books mirror the conventions of the times. Yet her own attitudes toward contemporary problems, not the conventional ones, often appear in satiric asides in her novels and tales or in thoughtful comments in her essays, biographies, and travel books. They show her the true daughter of William Godwin and Mary Wollstonecraft, the "suitable companion" of Shelley. Such comments as these, on social problems, on politics, on education, on science, on literature and the arts, give to her books an accidental value for the student of the nineteenth century, a value which she herself never guessed.

There is a further interest in her books. She could not help putting into her writing a large share not only of what she thought but also of what she experienced. Not gifted in invention, she turned to actuality for character and incident. Shelley, Byron, and Claire, Harriet and Eliza, Emilia and Trelawny appear and reappear. Situations in her married life are fitted into novels and fashioned into short stories. The realities of her existence furnish recurrent themes: loneliness, bereavement, the daughter-father relationship which parallels her own to Godwin. Her writing is highly autobiographical and self-revealing.

Modern critics, however, have too seldom cared to go beyond the obvious procedure of mere identity-hunting to find the real woman. They have sought her only in her letters or journals or accepted her at second hand from her contemporaries. But her contemporaries did not always see her as she saw herself, or as the sympathetic and inquiring modern reader sees her. There were contradictions between the woman they expected to see and the woman they saw; contradictions too between the woman they saw and the woman she was. Those who came to know her well sometimes—but not always—understood the nature of those contradictions; they acknowledged her merits and condemned or condoned her faults; but they placed the emphasis where their own characters pointed. It is, perhaps, small wonder that modern critics cannot agree about her.

What, then, was she really like? What sort of temperament did she have? What sort of mind? How did she look upon her husband, her family, her friends, her world? How successful and how good a writer was she? This book attempts to find, chiefly in her writings, the answers to these questions.

MARY SHELLEY

CHAPTER

1

𝒯he 𝒮elf-𝒞xaminer

Shortly after Shelley's widow returned to England from Italy in 1823, Crabb Robinson met her at Godwin's house. "She looks elegant and sickly and young," he reported. "One would not suppose she was the author of 'Frankenstein.'"[1]

Certainly there was nothing in Mary Shelley's physical appearance to remind an observer of monsters and presumptuous scientists.[2] She was of middle stature with slop-

1. Brown, *The Life of William Godwin*, p. 360.
2. A series of articles, "Lord Byron and His Contemporaries, by an Intimate Friend of His Lordship," appeared in the *Metropolitan Literary Journal* in 1836. In the third article (June 11) is an account of a call on Mrs. Shelley. The anonymous author was prepared to find her loud, masculine, daring; he found her low-voiced, feminine, and timid. In a note to the fifth article, the author owns to the name of Hunt. He may be John H. Hunt, who in the *Young Lady's Magazine* for 1838 published a story, "Luigi Rivarola: a Tale of Modern Italy," which uses many of the same details. In the story Mary, Byron, and Leigh Hunt are named Mrs. Godwin Percy, Lord Baron, and Mr. Huntley; in the article they are given their real names. But in inaccuracy and pure invention, honors are even.

ing shoulders, slender, even thin as a girl. The portraits of her whether at nineteen or at forty-four show the same features: the gray eyes, the broad, high forehead—her "great tablet of a forehead," as Hunt called it [3]—and the fair hair, "of a sunny and burnished brightness," falling "like a golden network round her face and throat" [4] or braided high on the crown of her head. The portraits bear out the never too reliable evidence of Medwin and Thornton Hunt that she grew better looking as she grew older. The somewhat awkward and carelessly dressed girl of Marlow days grew into the "sweetly pretty woman" whom Sophia Stacey saw in Florence and into the gracious lady with well-shaped head, marble-white shoulders, intellectually curved mouth, and delicate, flexible hands who won the adoration of young Mary Novello.[5] In her maturity she reminded one observer of a classical bust of Clytie, another of a Titian in the Louvre, a third of a portrait of Miss O'Neill. Owen wrote of her, "Her face, though not regularly beautiful, was comely and spiritual, of winning expression, and with a look of inborn refinement as well as culture." [6] Even churlish Trelawny admitted that she lighted up well at night. The only dissenting voice is that of William Rossetti's father, who, meeting Mrs. Shelley several times in the middle 1830's, "liked her well [but]

3. *Shelley and Mary*, II, 390.
4. Claire's description of Mary is in the memoranda which she headed "Reminiscences," one of the manuscripts in the Ashley Library in the British Museum, No. 2820. Printed from Ingpen's transcript in Grylls, *Claire Clairmont*, p. 254. The manuscript shows many revisions of the passage.
5. Charles and Mary Cowden Clarke, *Recollections of Writers* (London, Sampson, Low, 1878), pp. 37–38.
6. Robert Dale Owen, "Frances Wright, Lafayette, and Mary Shelley," *Atlantic Monthly*, October, 1873.

did not think her good-looking: indeed I have heard him say 'Era brutta.' "[7]

Shelley, however, thought her beautiful from the very start. "White, bright, and clear," as Christy Baxter remembered her, she must have been when he fell in love with her, a slender girl of sixteen, her fairness and poise standing out against the dark moodiness of Claire Clairmont and the gentle shyness of Fanny Imlay, and contrasting with the rosy bloom of Harriet. Her outward serenity must have soothed his inner turmoil over the domestic crisis which was separating him from Harriet. "Gentle and good and mild thou art," he told her in a poem written soon after she admitted her love for him. When separated from her he longed for a sight of her "redeeming eyes" and found consolation in her letters: "So soothing so powerful and quiet are your expressions that it is almost like folding you to my heart." Shelley's life was full of storms, and he was constantly needing green isles of serenity. "Love far more than hatred," he wrote to Mary in August of 1821, "has been to me, except as you have been its object, the source of all sort [sic] of mischief." When Mary herself was torn by storms, he found rest in the quietness of Jane Williams with her guitar music: "a sort of spirit of embodied peace in our circle of tempests"—until in the crowded joint kitchen of Casa Magni she began to long for her own saucepans.[8]

The young Mary he saw as

7. *The Diary of Dr. John William Polidori* (ed. by W. M. Rossetti, London, Elkin Matthews, 1911), p. 219.
8. Shelley, *Letters*, IX, 97–110, 248, 329; X, 346, 396. In this and in succeeding notes, references to Shelley's letters and prose works are to the Julian Edition, *The Complete Works of Percy Bysshe Shelley*, ed. by Roger Ingpen and W. E. Peck, 10 vols., London, 1926–1930.

lovely from thy birth
Of glorious parents, thou aspiring Child,

clothed in the radiance of her mother's glory, endowed by her father with an immortal name. They had endowed her with more than beauty or reflected glory or a name. It was her mind and understanding and her heritage of liberal ideas as much as her physical charm that convinced Shelley that he had found "an inestimable treasure." He was lost in admiration, he said, of her subtle and exquisitely fashioned intelligence, unequalled among women. "And I possess this treasure!" Hers was an understanding "made clear by a spirit that sees into the truth of things, free from vulgar superstition." [9]

> How beautiful and calm and free thou wert
> In thy young wisdom, when the mortal chain
> Of Custom thou didst burst and rend in twain,
> And walked as free as light the clouds among.[10]

Harriet, who had shown promise of a cultivated mind capable of development and molding, had abandoned the effort to keep up with Shelley. "Your thoughts alone," he told Mary in 1814, "can waken mine to energy; [my mind] without yours is dead and cold as the dark midnight river when the moon is down. . . . My understanding becomes undisciplined without you." She surpassed him in originality and simplicity of mind. "I believe I must become in Mary's hands what Harriet was in mine." [11] Although his early exuberance subsided, he retained always his respect for the powers of her intellect. Even when in 1822 he reluctantly admitted that Mary no longer understood him,

9. *Ibid.*, IX, 102.
10. *The Revolt of Islam,* Dedication, ll. 57–60.
11. Shelley, *Letters,* IX, 103.

he still spoke of her excellent powers and the purity of her mind.[12]

Shelley was not alone in feeling the attraction of Mary's personality. She enjoyed the warm, affectionate friendship of people as diverse as Leigh Hunt and Maria Gisborne. She was no insignificant part of the groups of friends in Florence, Rome, and Pisa during Shelley's lifetime. To John Howard Payne in 1825 she was "a being so beyond all others, that, even though her qualities are certainly 'images' of what is promised in 'heaven above' I can kneel down and worship them without dreading the visitation upon idolatry." In her he saw the "union of superior intellectual endowments with simplicity, fervour, and elevation and purity of character." [13] Less susceptible, and certainly not in love, Robert Dale Owen found her "gentle, genial, sympathetic, thoughtful and matured in opinion beyond her years; . . . essentially liberal in politics, ethics, and theology, indeed, yet devoid of stiff prejudice against the old or ill-considered prepossession in favor of the new; and, above all, womanly, in the best sense, in every sentiment and instinct." Few women, he said, had ever attracted him so much in so short a time: had he remained in London, they would surely have been dear friends and she would have had a salutary influence upon him.[14] To the young Mary Novello she was the object of "ceaseless admiration—for her personal graces, as well as for her literary distinction"; only Mrs. Norton and Lady Blessington equalled her in beauty or eminence. Vincent Novello held her in especial regard, and Edward Holmes and other young men of the circle "adored" her.[15]

12. *Ibid.*, X, 402–403.
13. Payne-Shelley Papers in the Huntington Library: HM 6773.
14. Owen, *loc. cit.*
15. Clarke, *op. cit.*, pp. 40–42.

Grace of carriage and charm of address won her many friends. Yet she too often set up a confusing and forbidding barrier of calm and apparent indifference: *placid* is an adjective applied to her again and again. Sometimes it made her seem secretive or indifferent. "Marina has been looking sideways," wrote Hunt, "and thinking it not worth speaking about." [16] After the dragoon episode in Pisa, when Shelley was sick from the blow he had received, the Countess Guiccioli was fainting, and Byron and Piero Gamba were "foaming with rage," Mrs. Shelley, Williams said, was "looking philosophically upon this interesting scene." [17] That very serenity which had soothed Shelley came at last to seem even to him like the light of "the cold chaste Moon." [18] Many others considered her cold. Trelawny thought it well for her that Percy had so much of her temperate blood, and commented caustically and ungrammatically, "When us three meet we shall be able to ice the wine by placing it between us." [19] Payne wrote to her out of his despair, "Is *ice* a non-conductor? But, if it is, how do you convey impressions?" [20] She seemed deficient in feeling, even for Shelley's memory. When Allsop met her at Lamb's house, he was puzzled: "She spoke of Shelley without apparent emotion, without regard or a feeling approaching re-

16. *Shelley and Mary*, II, 341.
17. *Journal of Edward Ellerker Williams* (London, Elkin Matthews, 1902), p. 43. A dragoon who insulted and assaulted a riding party of Byron and his friends had been wounded by one of Byron's servants.
18. *Epipsychidion*, l. 281. Cf. Mary W. Shelley, *Journal*, p. 182. In succeeding notes Mary Shelley's *Journal*, her *Letters*, and her works will be referred to without the use of her name.
19. Trelawny, *Letters*, p. 204.
20. Letter to Mary of May 28(?), 1825. Payne-Shelley Papers: HM 6781.

gret, without pain as without interest, and seemed to contemplate him, as everything else, through the same passionless medium." [21]

But like Allsop—and with more solid justification than he—we know that "this cannot be real." We have read her journals and letters and verses written after Shelley's death; we have read her poem, "The Choice." She kept her griefs and her regrets throughout her life, and she brooded over them. Twenty years after the death of little Clara, a visit to Venice recalled it vividly to a mind so sensitive to the association of place and emotion that the exact succession of objects on the journey, engraved on the memory, brought back pain and anguish.[22]

Indeed, the placid front which she displayed to the world and even to her friends seems to have been from the very first a protective covering for those moods of depression to which she was always subject. Godwin said that she had acquired "the practice of seeing everything on the gloomy side." She inherited not his cheerfulness but her mother's pessimism. "I am afraid you are a Wollstonecraft." [23] Her reserve was also a cloak for strong feelings not always perfectly controlled. Sometimes she temporarily dropped it and became, to use her own adjectives, gay and giddy and wild.[24] Yet she had no real sense of humor, neither Shelley's love of fun nor the saving sense of proportion. She took

21. T. Allsop, *Letters, Conversations and Recollections of S. T. Coleridge* (2 vols., London, Moxon, 1836), I, 224.
22. *Rambles in Germany and Italy*, II, 78–79.
23. Brown, *op. cit.*, p. 366.
24. Even as a child she apparently showed two faces. Coleridge wrote that Sara sent a kiss to "dear meek little Mary." But if, as is believed, she was the original of Marguerite in Godwin's *St. Leon*, she was subject to moods of inexhaustible vivacity as well as "enthusiastic" tenderness and grief. See Brown, *op. cit.*, pp. 181, 239.

herself too seriously for her own happiness.[25] Sometimes she could channel her passions through her letters and journals or through the emotional extravagance of her fiction. Consequently there was that other contradiction between the placid, reserved woman sitting in the corner of a conventional drawing-room sofa and the author of *Frankenstein* or *The Last Man* or *Lodore*. Lord Dillon once wrote to her: "I should have thought of you—if I had only read you—that you were . . . outpouring, enthusiastic, rather indiscreet, and even extravagant; but you are cool, quiet, and feminine to the last degree." [26]

Sometimes the controls slipped entirely. She could be passionate and jealous and bad-tempered, as witnesses interested and disinterested have testified: Medwin and Trelawny and Byron, Thornton Hunt and Dr. Furnivall, who attended her in Marlow. And well she knew it herself, that temper "at the same time quick and brooding," the irritability which, she said, often spoiled her as a companion and had vexed Shelley even in 1814 and which had put distance between them more than once thereafter. She mourned over it frequently in her letters and journals; she was, as she said, "much of a self-examiner." [27] Let one relatively unfamiliar passage from a letter to the Hunts of July, 1823, when she was on her dreary way back to England, suffice as illustration. She is sending messages to the children: "Thorny—you have not been cross yet— Oh my dear Thorny . . . do not let your impatient nature ever overcome you—or you may suffer as I have done—which God forbid! . . . remorse is a terrible feeling—and it requires a

---

25. Cf. her description of herself, "apt to be too serious, but easily awakened to sympathy." (*Rambles in Germany and Italy*, I, 9.)
26. *Shelley and Mary*, IV, 1122.
27. *Journal*, p. 204.

faith and philosophy immense not to be destroyed by the stinging monster." [28]

In her fiction she objectified her own traits, creating both morbidly reserved and bad-tempered characters. Once at least the two faults are combined in one person: not even her worst enemy could say harsher things about Mary than Mary says about herself in the obviously autobiographical *Mathilda*.[29] Written at the end of the tragic nine months during which both her children had died, this novelette was the fruit of the deep depression of spirits into which Mary fell. Her black moods had made her difficult to live with. In a fragment of verse, Shelley lamented that she had left him "in this dreary world alone."

> Thy form is here indeed—a lovely one—
> But thou art fled, gone down the dreary road,
> That leads to Sorrow's most obscure abode.
> Thou sittest on the hearth of pale despair,
>   Where
> For thine own sake I cannot follow thee.

Mary well knew what she was doing to him. In an effort, perhaps, to purge her own emotions and to confess her guilt in the late summer of 1819, she poured out on the pages of *Mathilda* the suffering and the loneliness, the bitterness and the self-recrimination of the past months.

Mathilda is certainly Mary herself. Like Mathilda's, Mary's mother died a few days after giving her birth. Like Mathilda's, her father had been, though dogmatic and self-centered, "a distinguished member of society; a Patriot; and an enlightened lover of truth and virtue," whom now his friends remembered "as a brilliant vision which would never again return to them." Like Mathilda, she spent part of her

---

28. *Letters*, I, 233.
29. For information about *Mathilda*, see Appendix III.

childhood in Scotland, roaming over the hills and moors, reading, dreaming, and recreating the romantic characters of fiction and drama. Like Mathilda, Mary met and loved a poet of "exceeding beauty"—although the fictitious Woodville, to be sure, was universally loved and his poem written at the age of twenty-three "was hailed by the whole nation with enthusiasm and delight. . . . There was not one dissentient voice."

And certainly Mathilda is the Mary of that sad year. She is the Mary who wrote to Miss Curran after William's death: "Let us hear also, if you please, anything you may have done about the tomb, near which I shall lie one day, and care not, for my own sake, how soon. I never shall recover that blow; . . . everything on earth has lost its interest to me."[30] Mathilda described herself as "one who had shut herself from the whole world, whose hope was death and who lived only with the departed."

Like Mary, Mathilda tortured herself and the poet she loved. "I had become captious and unreasonable," she wrote. "My temper was utterly spoilt. I called him my friend but I viewed all he did with jealous eyes. If he did not visit me at the appointed hour I was angry, very angry, and told him that if indeed he did feel interest in me it was cold. . . . I would fretfully say to him, '. . . I will not bear this; go. . . . You are cruel, very cruel, to treat me who bleed at every pore in this rough manner.' And then, when in answer to my peevish words, I saw his countenance bent with living pity on me . . . I wept and said, 'Oh, pardon me! You are good and kind but I am not fit for life.' . . . I was unreasonable and laid the blame upon him, who was most blameless, and peevishly thought that if his gentle soul were more gentle, if his intense sympathy were

30. *Letters*, I, 73–74.

more intense, he could drive the fiend from my soul and make me more human." These passages might well be transcripts of real encounters between Shelley and Mary.

Perhaps some of the other petulant and self-willed women in Mary's stories have a touch of their creator in them: Clarice the Mourner, Constance, who needed a nightmare to bring her to her senses, Cornelia in her attitude toward both Lodore and Horatio Saville. Perhaps into Katherine, with her devotion to Perkin Warbeck and to his memory, Mary was writing her own idealized self. In Ethel Villiers's unvarying sweet temper as she passed through experiences with her husband that were almost identical with those of the young Mary and Shelley in London,[31] she may have been picturing what she wished her own temper had been.

Undoubtedly her petulance and jealousy were closely linked with her need for companionship. When Shelley and Claire "walk out, as usual, to heaps of places,"[32] or when the Hunts, visiting at Marlow, leave Mary to take her first walk after her daughter's birth alone,[33] depressed and irritable spirits intensify and are intensified by loneliness. She was always, even from her girlhood, a lonely person. After Shelley's death her loneliness engulfed her. Naturally and inevitably she exaggerated it; but her suffering from it was a psychological fact.[34] Her reserve and placidity

31. In *Lodore*. See Chapter 3 of this book.
32. *Journal*, p. 28.
33. *Letters*, I, 30.
34. An unpublished sentence in the journal entry for December 2, 1834, reads, "Loneliness has been the curse of my life." And the entire entry (also unpublished) for April 16, 1841(?), the last entry in her journal except for a quotation from Burke in 1844 and a list of names and addresses, is an intentional misquotation from Coleridge:

of manner thickened the wall between herself and the human companionship which she needed. Sometimes her need drove her into foolish acts of trust and broke down her reserve with disastrous results. The reaction when she found that she had opened her heart too freely and confidingly, forced her, for a time at least, into renewed reserve and increased her sense of loneliness.

The theme of loneliness runs like a dark thread through much of her writing. Of it are woven her few, sentimental verses, published and unpublished. It often makes the pattern of pathos and tragedy in her novels and tales. With what is perhaps an attempt to disguise the subjectivity of the theme, she develops it most frequently and most effectively in the fortunes of her heroes. There are female recluses: Lady Lodore, Mathilda, Clarice, Rosina; most of them, however, are finally rescued from their retirement. It is the lonely men who really suffer. When Falkner, whose early years were marked by "solitude of the heart," decides that he must separate from his adopted daughter, it is he, not she, who is pathetic. "Surely," Mary writes in the maturity of her fortieth year,[35] "there is no object so sweet as the young in solitude. In after years—when death has bereaved us of the dearest—when cares, and regrets, and fears and passions, evil either in their natures or their results, have stained our lives with black, solitude is too sadly peopled to be pleasing." Lodore, self-exiled to "the Illinois," discovers that "Sensibility in such a situation is a curse: men become 'cannibals of their own hearts'; remorse,

> Alone—alone—all, all alone
> Upon the wide, wide sea—
> And God will not take pity on
> My soul in agony!

35. *Falkner* was published in 1837.

regret, and restless impatience usurp the place of more wholesome feeling: everything seems better than that which is; and solitude becomes a sort of tangible enemy, the more dangerous, because it dwells within the citadel itself."

Even for these lonely men a way out of their solitude opened. Lodore had only to go to New York to find companions—although he also found death. For Falkner there was a happy ending. But through Mary's two best novels, *The Last Man* and *Frankenstein*, move two figures whose loneliness is final and irreparable.

Lionel Verney, the narrator of the story of the plague that, in the closing years of the twenty-first century, destroyed the entire population of the earth except himself, is, in spite of the difference in sex and the superficial unlikeness of incident, Mary herself. "The last man!" she wrote in her journal on May 14, 1824. "Yes, I may well describe that solitary being's feelings, feeling myself as the last relic of a beloved race, my companions extinct before me." [36] In Verney's experiences, as he lost one after another of his friends, she was objectifying her own relations with Godwin, Byron, Claire, and especially Shelley. Adrian is a portrait of Shelley not only in his person and character and ideas, but also in his meaning for Lionel. "All that I possessed," said Mary-Lionel, ". . . I owed to him." His death by shipwreck left Lionel truly the Last Man on earth.

From the time when the plague began and especially after Verney's astonishing recovery from it, he was increasingly haunted by the loneliness which he foresaw for himself. Looking out of his window at midnight, after death had struck within his own household, he found the solitude unbearable: "Great God: would it one day be thus? One day all extinct, save myself, should I walk the earth

36. *Journal*, p. 193.

alone?" Symbols and images of solitude recur: the unpeopled streets of London, St. George's Chapel echoing to the step of the Countess of Windsor, the isolated cottage of Lucy Martin, Ryland's lonely death, the single mountain peaks, the organist in the deserted Alpine church, the doorbell tinkling through the empty vaulted rooms of a house in Ravenna, the tenantless palaces and libraries and public buildings of Italy, the solitary dog that attached himself to the solitary man on the Campagna. Verney finally entered Rome—"the desart ruins of Rome sleeping under its own blue sky . . . sheep were grazing untended on the Palatine, and a buffalo stalked down the Sacred Way that led to the Capitol. I was alone in the Forum; alone in Rome; alone in the world."

Lionel Verney was the symbol of Mary's lonely widowhood. Out of one of the happiest periods of her life came her most remarkable study of loneliness. *Frankenstein* is far more than a horror story based on presumptuous experiments in chemistry and biology. Its two themes of scientific curiosity and of loneliness run parallel to each other. Each is foreshadowed in the person of Robert Walton, the explorer whose curiosity about the North Pole is carrying him to the solitary ice fields of the Arctic regions. In the story itself, one becomes the motive of Frankenstein's life, the other the tragic fate of his monstrous creation. Here too are the symbols of solitude: Walton's solitary childhood, his lack of a friend on board his ship, the deserted graveyards, Frankenstein's lonely laboratory, the valleys of Servox and Chamounix, Mont Blanc dwelling apart, Montanvert "terrifically desolate," the isolated hut on "the remotest of the Orkneys," the ship caught in the endless fields of ice, the single dog-sled, the figure of the Monster disappearing into the unpeopled north.

The Monster, central symbol of loneliness, yearning for human intercourse, was set apart by the circumstances of his origin and by his deformity. There was always a barrier before him, like the wall which separated him in his hovel from the DeLaceys in their warm, social cottage. His every attempt to pass this barrier, to help others or to win affection, was repulsed with fear and horror. When Frankenstein, repenting of his reluctant promise to fashion a mate for him, tore his work apart, the Monster was doomed to a life of solitude and therefore of crime: his generous motives were changed to a desire for revenge on his creator and on the whole human race. "Evil thenceforth became my good," he said to Walton over the dead body of Frankenstein, ". . . the fallen angel becomes a malignant devil. Yet even that enemy of God and man had friends and associates in his desolation; I am alone." [37] That this monstrous being could be imagined by a young girl is due partly to the fact that he is the symbol of her own loneliness.

Mary has often been charged with so strong a desire for companionship that it led her into "a hankering after frivolous society" [38] and a growing conventionality. Well aware of the charges of worldliness which were made even by her friends, she wrote in self-justification in her journal in 1838: "I like society; I believe all persons who have any talent (who are in good health) do. The soil that gives forth nothing, may lie ever fallow; but that which produces

37. In 1819 Hunt wrote to Mary, "Polyphemus . . . always appears to me a pathetic rather than a monstrous person, though his disappointed sympathies at last made him cruel. What do you think of this Polypheme theory of mine?" (*Shelley and Mary*, II, 370.) Mary replied, "I have written a book in defense of Polypheme have I not?" (*Letters*, I, 66.)
38. Trelawny, *Letters*, p. 234.

—however humble its product—needs cultivation, change of harvest, refreshing dews, and ripening sun. Books do much; but the living intercourse is the vital heat." [39] She openly throve on social gatherings. She craved the affection and homage which many persons gave to her. She was excited by meeting new people, especially distinguished people. If she was a little of the lion hunter—after all, she had spent her youth in distinguished company.

Adjustment to the English environment, to which after Shelley's death she returned from the freer society of Italy, required certain concessions to convention. Yet she does not deserve Trelawny's phrase, "the most conventional slave I have ever met." If she was not as extreme a liberal as Shelley, if she did ask that Percy be sent to a school that would teach him to think like other people, if she did seek and find help for her father from the Conservatives, the necessities of her life drove her to take these positions.

She would undoubtedly have been a greater and nobler woman had she never compromised. But it was not in her nature to defy the world alone. She had run away with Shelley. She had fallen in with the plans of Shelley and Hogg for a triangular experiment in free love. Yet even then she must have felt relief when the scheme fell through. She soon became aware, not only because of her own experience but also because of the problem of explaining the anomalous position of Claire and little Allegra in her own household, of the difficulty of ignoring the laws of conventional society. She must have been honestly glad when, as she wrote to Byron, the "incident" of the marriage ceremony allowed her to sign herself "Mary W. Shelley." [40] Deprived by Shelley's death of his support, she shrank back

39. *Journal*, p. 205.
40. *Letters*, I, 18.

into herself, a process only too easy for one of her reserved temperament. She recoiled from publicity and from appearing conspicuously in public and indulged in what seems prudishness to the twentieth century. "She was," wrote Eliza Rennie, "almost morbidly averse to the least allusion to herself as an author." [41] She "could not make up her mind" to allow Murray to include a portrait of her in *Illustrations of Lord Byron*. She could not bring herself to go to the British Museum Reading Room, the only woman among men. She could not put herself forward, she said. "As well cast me from a precipice and rail at me for not flying." [42]

Mary knew that it was difficult, if not impossible, for men and women—especially a solitary woman, "the world's victim" [43]—to live in nineteenth-century England as if they were already "from custom's evil taint exempt and pure." Yet she never gave up her tolerance of unconventionality. Although she developed enough circumspection "to live among the lynx-eyed prudes of England" in spite of Hogg's fears,[44] she accepted the irregularity of Jane Williams's second union as easily as that of the first. She continued to believe that society, not the woman, was to blame. In 1837 she wrote that although Mme. de Monnier erred in leaving her husband for Mirabeau, she broke a social law that was nefarious and unnatural; subjecting herself to the misfortunes resulting from an attachment not sanctioned by convention, she was really a victim "of a depraved state of

41. Eliza Rennie, *Traits of Character* (2 vols., London, 1860), I, 113.
42. *Journal*, p. 206.
43. Mary Shelley's phrase in a review of "Loves of the Poets," *Westminster Review*, October, 1829.
44. *After Shelley* (ed. by Sylva Norman, London, Milford, Oxford Un. Press, 1934), p. 16.

society which set the seal of guilt on her attachment." [45]

Claire, in her bitter, sometimes cryptic, and often contradictory "Reminiscences," accused Mary of having "compromised all the nobler parts of her nature, . . . and exchanged the sole thought of [Shelley's] being for a share in the corruptions of society." [46] Far from abandoning the thought of Shelley's being, she was constantly measuring the men she met, especially the poets, against him. A passionate woman under her placid exterior, she attracted young men and she liked men. Her undeniable coquettishness in her conversations and her correspondence with them is, however, no proof that she was in flirtatious pursuit of a second husband. It was, like her "giddiness," the result of a not always wise, not always tasteful letting down of the bars of her reserve. When she realized that she had opened herself to misunderstanding, as with John Howard Payne, she was dismayed. She was not averse to marrying again; indeed, she often expressed her need and wish for masculine support and guidance. That she did not do so was largely due to a conviction, as she frankly told Payne, that she could never match Shelley. "Having once tasted Nepenthe, what is there left for me to hope for?" [47] She did not want an anticlimax in her life. She would not give one to her heroines: Cornelia married first Byron-Lodore and second—and happily—Shelley-Saville. She had known stimulating masculine society, Shelley, Byron, Godwin, Trelawny—too stimulating for her to settle down permanently, however attractive temporary friendship might be, with any second-rate intellect.

45. "Mirabeau," *Eminent Literary and Scientific Men of France* (in Lardner's *Cabinet Cyclopedia*), II, 222 and note.
46. Claire Clairmont, *Reminiscences*. See Note 4.
47. *The Romance of Mary W. Shelley, John Howard Payne, and Washington Irving*, p. 61.

Mary remained, therefore, a lonely woman. As Percy grew up, however, and repaid her sacrifices by his affection and his desire for her society, she began to feel a renewed happiness and security in the "good opinion of her child." When he married she relaxed into the comfort of the admiration and adoration of her daughter-in-law. She found in Percy and his wife not what she had lost at Shelley's death, but the kind of companionship of love and intellectual response that she needed in her last years.

CHAPTER

2

An Adverting Mind

If Mary sought the company of what Shelley might have called "adverting minds," she had reason. Her own intellect was good. Not, of course, as good as Shelley had thought it in the ardor of his early love: "the subtlest and most exquisitely fashioned intelligence, . . . among women there is no equal mind to yours." [1] But there are other witnesses, among them some of the severest critics of her temperament. Byron is reported to have said, "Mrs. Shelley is very clever—indeed it would be difficult for her not to be; the daughter of Mary Wollstonecraft and Godwin, and the wife of Shelley, could be no common person." [2] Trelawny wrote to Claire in 1835, "She has a fine intellect: her head might be put upon the shoulders of a Philosopher." [3] And Claire herself assured her, "If you would but know your own value and exert your powers you could give the men a most immense drubbing!" [4]

In spite of such tributes to her "masculine understanding," Mary had no illusions on the matter herself. She

1. Shelley, *Letters*, IX, 102.
2. Lady Blessington, *Journal of Conversations of Lord Byron* (London, 1893), p. 67.
3. Trelawny, *Letters*, p. 194.
4. Marshall, *Life and Letters of Mary W. Shelley*, II, 266.

wrote to Mrs. Gisborne: "You speak of women's intellect. We can scarcely do more than judge by ourselves. I know that, however clever I may be, there is in me a vacillation, a weakness, a want of single-winged resolution that appertains to my intellect as well as to my moral character. . . . In short, my belief is, whether there be sex in souls or not, that the sex of our material mechanism makes us quite different creatures, better though weaker, but wanting in the higher grades of intellect." [5]

It was, however, by men that her intellect was trained, by Godwin and by Shelley. Her mother, had she lived, might have planned and supervised a more formal education. But Mary had always been encouraged by her father to educate herself by extensive reading. And had not her mother written, in the chapter on reading in *Thoughts on the Education of Daughters*, "It may be observed, that I recommend the mind's being put into proper train, and then left to itself. Fixed rules cannot be given. . . . The mind is not, cannot be created by the teacher, though it may be cultivated, and its real powers found out."

In accordance with these parental principles, Mary read enormously—in her lonely childhood in Scotland, in the days when Shelley read with her (and above and all around her), and after his death when she found in books not merely a distraction but a way to return to companionship with him: "Greek shall lay this evil spirit; in the company of Homer I am with one of his best friends—and in reading the books he best loved I collect his acquaintance about me." [6] Although the lists she made of her reading in the years of her association with Shelley are in themselves extraordinary for their length, quality, and variety, they are

5. *Letters*, II, 98.
6. *Ibid.*, I, 277.

increased almost fifty percent by references in her journals to books read or read aloud in her hearing. The results of her reading are evident in her writing. Not a scholar, she contributed nothing new or original to the subjects which she treated. Yet she knew from Godwin's precept and example the difference between "simple reading" and "study." Full and careful investigation preceded the historical novels, some of her magazine articles, and the series of biographical studies which she wrote for Lardner's *Cabinet Cyclopedia*. Her knowledge of other languages, gained through study pursued under the encouragement of Shelley, shows in these accounts and criticisms of foreign writers and in her occasional translations from their works.[7] It was an intelligent woman who rambled through Germany and Italy with her son in the early 1840's. All her work shows her a literate, cultured person.

It bears witness also to the range and variety of her intellectual interests and tastes. Claire in the letter quoted above further assures her, "You could write upon metaphysics, politics, jurisprudence, astronomy, mathematics— all those highest subjects which [the men] taunt us with being incapable of treating, and surpass them." Extravagant as this list is, her interest in some of these and other subjects is very clear in her essays, her biographical studies, and her travel books. In her fiction, although that interest is obscured and overweighed by the conventional elements,

7. See her verse translation of a long passage from Boscan. (*Eminent Literary and Scientific Men of Italy, Spain, and Portugal*, III, 25–32.) Possibly some of the other unassigned translations in these volumes of Lardner's *Cabinet Cyclopedia* are hers. In the Shelley-Rolls papers in the Bodleian Library there are translations of a passage from Dante's *Convivio* and of the opening of Aeschylus's *Prometheus Bound*, both in Mary's handwriting. She is thought to have translated passages from Mérimée's *La Guzla*. See Jones, *Letters of Mary W. Shelley*, I, 376 n.

she frequently considers topics current in liberal, intellectual circles. Garnett was far from right when he said that the society around her did not interest her in the slightest degree.[8]

From any cultured woman one may expect awareness of the arts. Mary's full and intelligent comments will not disappoint a reader, although they will not impress him by originality or depth of perception.

The theater never failed to delight her, "a great treat quite exquisite enough, as of old, to take away my appetite for dinner." [9] As a girl she went frequently on the passes given to Godwin; in her poverty after Shelley's death she accepted freely the passes and tickets provided by John Hunt and—most lavishly and enthusiastically—by John Howard Payne. She had been greatly excited by the *improvisatore* Sgricci in Pisa, and by Kean in London. She tried her own hand at writing plays, though nothing has survived except *Proserpine* and *Midas*. Shelley had encouraged her, but Godwin's unfavorable criticism of her attempt at a tragedy made her throw all her "halting verses into the fire." [10]

The opera in Italy had been so much a part of her life that when she returned to England she went to hear it "sometimes merely for the sake of seeing my dear Italians and listening to that glorious language in its perfection." But in vocal and instrumental music she found great excitement and happiness. Paganini threw her into hysterics. Music was one of the strong links between Mary and Hunt. Her affection for Vincent Novello and his family was intensified by the music that always formed part of a social

8. *Tales and Stories by Mary Wollstonecraft Shelley*, p. x.
9. *Letters*, I, 22.
10. *Ibid.*, I, 287.

evening at their house. She found that his playing stimulated her imagination when she was at work on a novel. She took great pleasure in the fact that the composer Mignot dedicated a song to her. It may have been her ear for music that made her sensitive to voices. She could never hear Byron's without hearing Shelley's in answer to it. The plots of a number of her stories turn on the recognition of a voice rather than of a face.

Her own training in drawing and her genuine love for art took her to the galleries in London and on the continent. Her comments on painting and sculpture in her letters and her books of travel, usually not going much beyond the obvious, are occasionally unconventional, as when she calls the Venus de Medici "that plump little woman." It is significant of her aesthetic limitations, perhaps, that very little of her interest in literature, music, and art finds expression in her fiction. An occasional character is a poet, like Woodville in *Mathilda*, or a painter, like Marcott Alleyn in "The Bride of Modern Italy." But Mary makes no attempt to incorporate in any novel or tale aesthetic theory and criticism and none seriously to interpret the artistic—not even the literary—temperament. Adrian in *The Last Man*, her fullest portrait of Shelley, is not a poet.

On the other hand she makes frequent and extended use of her interest in science and of her liberal social and political ideas.

No young woman could have written so effectively of Frankenstein's scientific curiosity unless she had shared it to some degree. Absorbing from her reading (she had read Davy in October, 1816, while she was at work on *Frankenstein*) and from the conversation of Shelley some sense of what it meant to think at the same time scientifically and imaginatively, Mary set her lively mind to work on the possible results of research into the mystery of the life principle. It was the discussions at Diodati about the origins of life and the experiments in galvanism that furnished the stimulus for the story of *Frankenstein*.[11] The eager young people gathered in Byron's villa talked of Erasmus Darwin and his reputed success in imparting life to a piece of vermicelli, of his "speculations on the resemblance between the action of the human soul and that of electricity." "Perhaps a corpse would be re-animated; galvanism had given token of such things: perhaps the component parts of a creature might be manufactured, brought together, and endued with vital warmth." Between sleeping and waking one night Mary had a vision of "the pale student of unhallowed arts kneeling beside the thing he had put together," and of his creature. Endowed with life it frightened out of uneasy sleep both its creator and its creator's creator. She had found her "ghost story" to add to the abortive tales the others in the house party had already begun and abandoned. Mary's was to live in successive editions, in allusions, in stage plays, and even in moving pictures (which must "amuse" her in her grave) on through the first half of the twentieth century.[12]

Victor Frankenstein, the young Genevese student of natural philosophy, felt "the enticements of science," with its "continual food for discovery and wonder," comparing it with other studies in which the student goes only as far as others have gone before him. Always "embued with a fervent longing to penetrate the secrets of nature," he had his imagination first caught by the alchemists' search for

11. The material in this paragraph is based on Mary's introduction to the 1831 edition of *Frankenstein* in the Standard Novels series issued by Colburn and Bentley.
12. See Appendix IV, "The Stage History of *Frankenstein*."

the philosopher's stone and the elixir of life. He read avidly in the works of Cornelius Agrippa, Albertus Magnus, and Paracelsus. But modern science, as taught by Professor Waldman at Inglestadt, soon supplanted the ancient magic and put Victor's internal being into a state of turmoil. Waldman's opening lecture on chemistry concluded:

> The ancient teachers of this science promised impossibilities, and performed nothing. The modern masters promise very little; they know that metals cannot be transmuted, and that the elixir of life is a chimera. But these philosophers, whose hands seem only made to dabble in dirt, and their eyes to pore over the microscope or crucible, have indeed performed miracles. They penetrate into the recesses of nature, and show how she works in her hiding places. They ascend into the heavens: they have discovered how the blood circulates, and the nature of the air we breathe. They have acquired new and almost unlimited power; they can command the thunders of heaven, mimic the earthquake, and even mock the invisible world with its own shadows.[13]

Guided and advised by Waldman to pursue every branch of natural philosophy, including mathematics, Frankenstein progressed rapidly until he became the equal of his professors. In his interest in the nature and origin of life, he began to study anatomy and physiology. "To examine the causes of life," he concluded, "we must first have recourse to death." In the graveyards and charnel houses he observed the corruption and decay of the human body. "I paused, examining and analyzing all the minutiae of causation, as exemplified in the change from life to death, and death to life, until from the midst of this darkness a sudden light broke in upon me. . . . After days and nights of incredible labour and fatigue, I succeeded in discovering

---

13. Cf. Shelley, *Prometheus Unbound*, IV, ii 418-423.

the cause of generation and life; nay, more, I became myself capable of bestowing animation upon lifeless matter."

— And so Frankenstein, gathering the parts from graves, created his Monster. Finally "on a dreary night in November," he "saw the dull yellow eye of the creature open; it breathed hard, and a convulsive motion agitated its limbs." What the life-giving process was, Mary does not allow Frankenstein to tell us, whether it was galvanism or some chemical change. Her real reasons are obvious; the fictional reasons which she puts into the mouth of the discoverer are the result of his horrible experiences with the "Frankenstein Monster" which he had created and could not control. "I will not lead you on, unguarded and ardent as I then was, to your destruction and infallible misery."

The imaginations of later writers were stimulated by *Frankenstein* to use the theme of the creation of life. The Monster is the ancestor of many synthetic human beings and robots.[14] But what is more significant, however questionable the science, Mary had added a useful and pointed phrase to the English vocabulary. In an ironic sense it is easy to apply it to many of the recent inventions and discoveries of man's mind. Frankenstein's motives were not merely the disinterested motives of pure research: he saw himself as the benefactor of the world, creating a new and happy species and even restoring the dead to life. Instead he had created a monstrosity and brought death to the living. We hear almost daily in this Atomic Age the mourning voice of the scientist speaking the words of Frankenstein: "Alas! I had turned loose into the world a depraved wretch, whose delight was in carnage and misery; had he not mur-

14. For later books on the Frankenstein theme, see J. O. Bailey, *Pilgrims through Space and Time* (N.Y., Argus Books, Inc. [c. 1947]), pp. 29, 36, 62, 100–101, 158–159, 183, 281.

dered my brother?" And the creature used for destruction warns: "You are my creator, but I am your master."

Frankenstein did not exhaust Mary's use of ancient alchemy and contemporary science. She wrote a short story, "The Mortal Immortal," on the theme of Cornelius Agrippa's elixir of life. She told another "tale of impious tempting of Providence," in which the exchange of souls between two persons is effected by a mingling of their blood; "Transformation" is a short story of magic and presumption whose satisfactory denouement and impeccable moral won it entrance into the pages of the "splendid annuals." She left in manuscript and incomplete a story of an ancient Roman brought back to life in modern Italy. In her other novel of pure imagination, *The Last Man*, she speculated on the future progress in medicine, scientific farming, machinery, and aviation which determined her picture of a happy society nearly three centuries after her time.

By the time Mary was writing this novel, the papers and magazines had reported several attempts to transport passengers by air. In France in the eighteenth century, not long after the ascent of de Rozier, the Roberts brothers had sent up for a cruise of seven hours an "air galley" suspended from a silken balloon inflated with pure oxygen and propelled by silken oars handled by a crew of six. Lunardi's hydrogen balloon of 1784 had two wings for horizontal propulsion. In 1816 Sir George Cayley made rough designs for a navigable balloon, the ship depending from it being equipped with an engine driving two airscrews. *The Kaleidoscope* for April 30, 1822, records applications to the Governor of Bombay by Mr. Thomas Boyce and Mr. Charles Hudson for permission to carry mails from Bombay to London by means of balloon; and in the issue for June 18 the application of James Bennett of Philadelphia to Congress for exclusive privileges in air-navigation and the claim of D. B. Lee of the same city to priority of invention. In 1825 the *London Magazine* published an article on "Models of Switzerland" by W. S., who expressed a desire to float over the mountains of Switzerland in a "machine, somewhat resembling a boat, . . . with ten or twelve wings on each side, to be put in motion by steam." W. S. suggests the establishment of an Aerostation Company for the promotion of travel by air and the substitution of the balloon for the public diligence.

Mary had, therefore, models from which to draw the flying balloons which carried the characters in *The Last Man* from Windsor to Perth in forty-eight hours or from Ancona to Dieppe in six days. Lionel Verney describes his flight: "The balloon rose about half a mile from the earth, and with a favorable wind it hurried through the air, its feathered vans cleaving the unopposing atmosphere. . . . The pilot hardly moved the plumed steerage, and the slender mechanism of the wings, wide unfurled, gave forth a murmuring noise, soothing to the sense. Such was the power of man over the elements; a power long sought, and lately won."

On the sea, Verney and his friends traveled sometimes by sail, sometimes by steam. Mary could hardly have ignored the invention in which Henry Reveley and Shelley had been interested. But curiously enough, there is no sign of the railroad in *The Last Man*. The world of the twenty-first century apparently knew no intermediate mode of transportation between the horse-drawn carriage or diligence and the airship, as has actually been true of some South American countries in our own time. Mary travelled on railroads herself, recording her experiences in her *Rambles in Germany and Italy*, exclaiming over the great speed of Prussian trains, "very great, so that I heard passengers call out from the windows imploring that the speed might be lessened." She calls down blessings on steam, which has made England forget night travelling, "a traveller's blessing, who loves to roam far and free." [15]

In her travels she was always ready to turn aside to see some new marvel of man's inventive mind—cloth of glass in Milan (excellent for curtains and hangings because it would never fade and could easily be cleaned, but not good for clothes because it would chip [16]) or a "self-acting instrument" for the playing of music at Lenzkirch.[17] The sight of boiling metal in an iron foundry in Berlin fascinated her. In her biography of Pascal she presented a clear, interesting, and interested account of his geometric and physical studies and experiments.[18] In *The Last Man* she described vividly the tidal waves and the solar phenomena that accompanied the final stages of the plague. She was interested in theories about the polar regions. In her first novel she had created not only her presumptuous biochemist but also the explorer Walton, whose curiosity about the geographical and magnetic conditions at the North Pole was leading him on a search only less daring than Frankenstein's. Indeed, Mary believed, the power of man's mind was very great. "Farewell," cried Verney as the plague swept over the human race,

> Farewell to the giant powers of man,—to knowledge that could pilot the deep-drawing bark through the opposing waters of shoreless ocean,—to science that directed the

15. *Rambles in Germany and Italy*, I, 218, 5, 54.
16. *Ibid.*, I, 111.
17. *Ibid.*, I, 49.
18. In "Pascal," *Eminent Literary and Scientific Men of France* (in Lardner's *Cabinet Cyclopedia*), I, 185–195.

silken balloon through the pathless air,—to the power that could put a barrier to mighty waters, and set in motion wheels, and beams, and vast machinery, that could divide rocks of granite or marble, and make the mountains plain.

Like Godwin and her mother, Mary believed in the potentialities of man's mind and therefore in the supreme importance of education. She commented on various theories—Condorcet's, Rousseau's; she investigated the educational practice of the countries through which she travelled. Public education she approved of—the lack of provision for it she considered a defect in *Émile*—but not of exclusive governmental control. She found much to deplore in the failure in many places to educate the poor beyond the earliest stages and in restrictions, personal and intellectual, clamped upon students in Italy from elementary school to university.

Man, she believed, must be educated in liberal social and political thinking. Education was an important instrument which needed to be intelligently and morally handled to accomplish its end, the formation of the "character of social man." It might be dangerous, leading a Frankenstein to aspire "to become greater than his nature will allow." But if the teachers were men of good will, the results would be good.

When Guinigi and Castruccio became intimate, the youth would reason with him, and endeavour to prove, that in the present distracted state of mankind, it was better that one man should get the upper hand, to rule the rest. "Yes," said Guinigi, "let one man, if it be forbidden to more than one, get the upper hand in wisdom, and let him teach the rest: teach them the valuable arts of peace and love." [19]

19. *Valperga*, I, 49.

Mary puts her emphasis, whenever she speaks of education, on the power of the individual to influence the individual for good or ill either through direct contact or through books. Lady Lodore's faults were due to her bad bringing up. Falkner was made capable of dark deeds by father, uncle, and schoolmaster. Euthanasia learned to love "the very shadow of liberty" from her father, from a Greek patriot, from Dante and the ancient Latin authors. Lionel Verney's mind was trained and molded by Adrian. There was no room in Mary's philosophy for the doctrine of the noble savage. Nature does not necessarily ennoble: those of the Swiss, Mary says, who live deep in the rocky wilds are often brutish, stultified, and sullen; Lionel Verney, though brought up in contact with nature, was moved only by a desire for personal liberty, resentment against his betters, ambition, and passion until he met Adrian. Although she would not have accepted the materialism of Helvetius, she saw Frankenstein's Monster at his creation as a plain page on which could be written good or evil. Because his earliest extended contact with human beings was with the virtuous and high-minded family of Felix, the first writing on that page was good: "I felt the greatest ardour for virtue arise within me, and abhorrence for vice. . . . Induced by these feelings I was of course led to admire peaceable lawgivers, Numa, Solon, and Lycurgus, in preference to Romulus and Theseus. The patriarchal lives of my protectors caused these impressions to take a firm hold on my mind; perhaps, if my first introduction to humanity had been made by a young soldier, burning for glory and slaughter, I should have been imbued with different sensations." It was man's inhumanity to monsters that cancelled out those early lessons.

For the betterment of human society, more and more

persons must be educated to take their places nearer the greatest of mankind. In discussing Condorcet's doctrines Mary expressed doubt whether man can progress so that greater individuals than Homer or Socrates will appear. Philosophers, therefore, should aim not at removing the bounds of human perfection, but at bringing the many up to the level of the few great and good. In this interpretation of the theory of perfectibility, she was following Godwin and his disciple Shelley in their divergence from Helvetius, d'Holbach, and other radical thinkers.

Mary had been well trained in liberal thought. She had been brought up in the household of the author of *Political Justice*; she had elected at seventeen to become the "affectionate companion" of Shelley. She had early imbibed ideas of the superfluousness, in a reasonable and benevolent society, of positive institutions. When the many were great and good, there would result an ideal world whose foundations would be political freedom and a social order based on equality and justice.

Like Shelley, Mary eventually gave up any youthful illusions that Jerusalem could be built at once in England's green and pleasant land. Like him, she hailed every event that seemed a sign of promise for the future. Her letters and journals are full of the excitement and the hope of a brighter Hellas, symbol of a brighter world. The Greek struggle for independence was made actual for her first in the attractive figure of Prince Mavrocordato and later in the experiences of Trelawny, who stayed to serve under the chieftain Ulysses after Byron's death. She carried her interest over into her fiction, sending her heroes, like Byron and Trelawny, to fight for Greece—even Lord Raymond in *The Last Man*. It is a sign not only of her interest but also, perhaps, of a maturing realism and irony rather than of deficient imagination, that Greece should still be trying to win her independence from Turkey in the year 2092 and that Constantinople is conquered by the plague, not by the Greek armies.

Yet she never really lost the ideal and the hope. Although she regarded Chartism and the Revolution of 1848 with something approaching horror, it was the hardening of her social and political arteries that came with her declining strength. Until that time she remained true to her early teaching. When in 1842 she observed the change for the worse in the manners of the French people, she repudiated the common belief that the high were inevitably dragged down to the level of the low through the equalization of privileges and wealth. Certainly the very reverse should be the result of liberty, and "on that hope is built every endeavour to banish ignorance, and hard labour, from political society." She thought the more likely cause to be an attempt to imitate the English or the rubbing off of polish by universal military service.[20]

In 1826 Mary published her third novel, *The Last Man*, set in the future. In it twenty-first-century England, before the advent of the plague, is described as a country that in government, society, and intellectual life has made long strides toward the eradication of evil and the establishment of good. The change to a republican government with the abdication of the king had meant, politically, the amalgamation of the two houses of Parliament and the triennial election of a Lord Protector who might be, as was Ryland, a man of the people or, like Raymond, a member of the old nobility. The resulting society was a good society. Popular meetings could be held and the popular will expressed without fear of governmental or military interference, of

20. *Rambles in Germany and Italy*, I, 142–144.

another Peterloo. The arts of life and the discoveries of science had advanced incalculably: men travelled at amazing speed in flying balloons; "food sprung up, so to say, spontaneously—machines existed to supply with facility every want of the population." Towns were busy and fields were cultivated; harvests were plentiful; men, women, and children were active, healthful, and happy.

Yet this is no millennium. The picture of society is drawn, as a novelist's picture should be, in terms of the individuals who composed it and especially of those who controlled its destiny. Although England was a republic, it was not free from party strife, from the personal ambition of political leaders, from the discontent of the lesser nobility with a system which deprived them of hereditary power, from the threat of civil war, from commercialism in political elections. Society still was burdened with poverty and disease and labor and ignorance: when Raymond, as Lord Protector, visited the slums of London, he realized that he still had much to do before England became a Paradise.

The whole system, indeed, was as weak as the individual men who directed it, men who had not been educated so as to form "the character of social man." Raymond the aristocrat gave up his trust when a personal crisis arose. Ryland the republican resigned his high office in despair and terror when the plague reached England. Neither could have prevented the subsequent breakdown of society. By the time that Adrian, the "social man," took control, the plague was so far advanced that he could do nothing but exercise his talent for organization and his personal benevolence in an attempt, although a vain one, to save a small remnant of the English people.

The picture of England under the plague is curiously

modern in more than Adrian's title—Earl of Windsor. When the plague was ravaging the continent of Europe, thousands of refugees fled to England. England helped them as she helped the political refugees of the eighteenth century, and those of the twentieth, of whom Mary never dreamed. "The English spirit awoke to its full entirety, and, as it had ever done, set itself to resist the evil." Taxes were increased. Pleasure grounds and parks were ploughed up and planted, producing employment and food. Great estates became refuges for the poor and dispossessed. Trees were cut down for lumber to erect temporary dwellings. When the plague attacked England itself, London was evacuated by many of its population. In the desolate city, Verney passed St. Paul's—"much of what had in former days obscured this vast building was removed."

Yet this resemblance to the 1940's is purely fortuitous. Mary had no real power to look into the future and imagine what would happen in the course of the centuries. The virtues and the faults of Adrian's England were patterned after those of the England of George the Fourth, though the proportions were changed and the good outweighed the evil.

When Mary withdrew her eyes from the future and looked about her at her contemporary world, she found more to deplore than to praise. As she travelled from place to place in Germany and Italy in the early 1840's, she observed the effects of tyranny in government, whether in the Papal domains, or in the portions of Italy under Austrian control, or in Bohemia, whose peasants bore the marks of a conquered people, or in the Tyrol under Bavarian rule. The government of Leopold II in Tuscany was ostensibly mild; yet secret police, spies, and *agents provocateurs* created a situation which was almost worse than open tyranny.

"Tyranny," said one of her Tuscan acquaintances, "is, with us, a serpent hid among flowers." The better spirits among them pined for the intellectual food that was denied them. Many a young man, deprived of enlightened education, forbidden to travel, constantly watched, and barred from any career, fell into a state of lethargy "till at last the moss of years and hopelessness gathers over and deadens his mind." Vice flourished among the idle. Misrule and tyranny blighted the potential greatness of a people made to be free, active, and inquiring; their faults were those of an oppressed people—love of pleasure, disregard of truth, indolence, violence of temper. Their habit of deception was fostered by the bad use of the confessional in troubled times, by the system of secret police, and by the secret societies into which all those who refused to submit tamely were forced. "They fear a spy in the man who shares their oath; their acts are dark, and treachery hovers close. The result is inevitable; their own moral sense is tampered with, and becomes vitiated."

There was no possibility that art and literature should flourish when man's mind was enslaved. In seventeenth-century Spain, pretty, commonplace poetry had been the fashion. "Despotism and the inquisition gave the creative or literary spirit of Spain no other outlet. Thought was forbidden." And "latterly the state of the country has been too distracted for literature to gain any attention." The suppression of Amari's history of the Sicilian Vespers and the exile of Mme. de Staël by Napoleon were individual cases which elicited Mary's indignation; she welcomed such devotion to liberty as that of Alfieri or of Ugo Foscolo. The plans of Condorcet for a system of national education and for a national society of arts and sciences, though liberal in purpose, might, in Mary's opinion, have produced ill results had they been put in operation, for they would have given too much power to the government. She was criticizing, not any effort to improve the state of man, but "any endeavour of government to bind the intellect in chains."

Her hatred of tyranny extended to include its manifestations in the church, Protestant or Catholic. In the time of the plague in *The Last Man* the teachers of religion exerted a tremendous power, "a power of good, if rightly directed, or of incalculable mischief, if fanaticism or intolerance guided their efforts." The Methodist preacher was "an enthusiastic man with simple intentions"; his son preached "election, sin, and [the] red right arm of God." Mary found bigotry and intolerance and persecution in a highly placed Catholic family, the fictitious Rabys of *Falkner*, and in a real Pope who forbade scientific investigation and banned all liberal ideas and material progress in his domain, "fearful if the closed valves were opened, he should admit in one rushing stream, with industry and knowledge, rebellion." Except for the brief interval when, to Trelawny's and Hogg's disgust, she performed the neighborly act of attending Dr. Nott's services, she entered churches usually only to admire the architecture. The men and women in her novels do not go to church and there is only one clergyman, Francis Derham, and he a scholar rather than a preacher, who plays any part in her stories. Yet she found comfort in a faith in immortality that gave her hope of seeing Shelley again; and many of her characters professed a free, natural religion. Like Shelley, she admired the basic teachings of Jesus and respected true religious feeling. She found it in the young, like Clara, daughter of Lord Raymond; or in the Italian peasants and lower clergy who cared unselfishly for the sick and dying while the cholera raged in Rome in 1837. It was organized religion, where power over the many and the simple is centered in the few, that she distrusted.

Especially she feared power in the hands of one man. She saw the dangers of Raymond's dictatorship in *The Last Man* and of his plans for subduing all Asia under his rule. In speaking of the conscripting of mercenaries in Germany for foreign service (which she attacks' chiefly as an act of cruelty and tyranny against the mercenaries and their families), she expresses the hope that it will never happen again. "And yet," she adds, with another flash of what seems like prophecy of twentieth-century dictatorships, "what act of cruelty and tyranny may not be reacted on the stage of the world, which we boast of as civilised, if one man has uncontrolled power over the lives of many, the unwritten story of Russia may hereafter tell." [21]

Mary was aware of corruption in political life. Few statesmen had the respect for human nature and the enthusiasm for a cause which she thought necessary. Few lived up to the ideal of statesmanship which she pictured in Adrian. More of them fulfilled her cynical requirements for success in public life: a desire to triumph, a willingness to deface the worship of truth by "truckling to the many falsehoods and errors which demand subserviency in the world." [22] The leaders of England, whether in the actual nineteenth or in the fictional twenty-first century, Brougham, Ryland (who may be a composite of the popular leaders of her day, with Cobbett predominating), and Raymond, were neither dignified nor truly capable and devoted. "Party speeches were delivered, which clothed the question in cant, and veiled its simple meaning in a woven

21. *Ibid.*, I, 203–205.
22. In *Lodore*, Chapter XXXI.

wind of words." [23] She even looked as far as India and saw the results of empire. Falkner, who was in the British military service, tried to enlighten one or two native princes, whom "the English governors wished to keep in ignorance and darkness." He saved the life of one old Rajah and extricated him from a difficulty "in which the Europeans had purposely entangled him." In short, his views were diametrically opposed to those of the then Indian government.

Mary believed, with Blake, that war was the tyrant's gain and that

> the hapless soldier's sigh
> Runs in blood down palace walls.

War was the natural climate of palaces and castles, but not of humble cottages. It was the "companion and friend of monarchy," she wrote to Mrs. Gisborne in 1833, when there was a threat of war in America. "What is the use of republican principles and liberty, if peace is not the offspring?" [24] The only justifiable use of force was in self-defense or in a struggle for liberty, an exception to the rule of pacifism made by many of her liberal friends, including Shelley. The sympathy of young Mary Godwin on her "six weeks' tour" with Shelley and Claire had been called out by the sight of the desolation left by the Russians around Nogent, which "gave a sting to [her] detestation of war . . . this plague, which, in his pride, man inflicts upon his fellows." [25] She remembered the scene fifteen years later when in *Perkin Warbeck* she was describing the war-wasted villages along the Scottish border. Gui-

23. *The Last Man*, I, 120.
24. *Letters*, II, 73.
25. *History of a Six Weeks' Tour*, p. 19.

nigi, the Shelley-like character in *Valperga* who had "turned his sword to a ploughshare," pointed out to Castruccio the vast superiority of peaceful peasant ways to military life, a life of destruction and cruelty.

But while castles and cottages existed, men like Castruccio would choose the military life and the castle. Not even in Mary's republican England, nearly three hundred years in the future, was man

> Equal, unclassed, tribeless, and nationless,
> Exempt from awe, worship, degree, the king
> Over himself.

Yet there the evils of the division of society into classes were mitigated somewhat by the general benevolence of noble and common, and some of the leaders looked forward to a time when there would be no distinctions. In contemporary England and Europe, Mary looked upon the poor as pathetic victims of the social system and upon the rich and highborn—in spite of her alleged snobbery—with undisguised scorn and contempt. She deplored the extremes in English society, the gigantic fortunes and well-ordered luxury, the squalid penury, hard labor, and famine. Frankenstein's Monster heard with horrified astonishment of the "strange system of human society . . . of the division of property, of immense wealth and squalid poverty; of rank, descent, and noble blood." The Chaumonts, both father and son, in "The Swiss Peasant," oppressed, pauperized, and driven from their home, bitterly traced all human ills "to the social system, which made the few the tyrants of the many."

In her *Rambles* Mary noted the malnutrition and high infant mortality among the poor in Capri and in Sorrento, with its absentee nobles, where men worked night and day to send the staples of the place—fish, oranges, or hewn stone—to Naples and lived themselves chiefly on prickly pear and sour wine or water. She observed near Como the stunted, half-starved children and the young workers in the silk factories whose beauty soon faded under the stress of long hours and poor food. She saw the destitution and squalor in the villages along the Moselle and the Rhine, where the peasants, though more secure and even less poor than in former times, through lack of education still lived in the manner of their ancestors.

It is only too true, as Miss Norman has said, that in Mary's later novels "the rule of snobbery appeared to prevail; [the characters] must be highborn. . . . There was never again so humble a hero as the student 'Frankenstein.' "[26] There is an occasional minor character of plebeian origin who shows the strength of reality: old Martha who ministered to the sick in Marlow, Merrival the astronomer, Monna Gegia de' Becari, whose Ghibelline leg fixed her to her chair on the day of Guelph triumph. But too often her low-born maidens, a Lucy or a Fanny, are just what that sentimental term implies. Although she has much to say of the merits of the simple life, her words are usually a fairly conventional echo of romantic sentimentality. But not always. Even in her fiction she often speaks directly and sincerely or else ironically about the shams and artifices of high society and the condition of the poor under an unjust social system. It may well have been only the need of earning money that kept her novels and tales in the line that led straight to her readers' hearts—and pocketbooks.

On the life of the idle aristocracy of England she com-

26. Norman, "Mary Shelley, Novelist and Dramatist," *On Shelley*, p. 62.

mented caustically. The village woman on whose hands Elizabeth Raby was left by the death of her parents was proud to think that she had entertained under her roof the son "of somebody, who had younger sons and elder sons, and possessed, through wealth, the power of behaving frightfully ill to a vast number of persons." (From other passages in *Falkner* it is evident that Sir Tim was in Mary's mind.) She described the dullness of society life in the country, the "raking" of the highborn in the city. She saw what happened to a young man whose birth was too high for him to earn his living when his income was stopped: Edward Villiers, whose habits of expense and prodigality were implanted and fostered by his education and his position, fell into the hands of the money-lenders and had no hope of getting out of them save at his father's death. Yet his state troubled him little, for it was universal. "The idea of debt was familiar to him: every one—even Lord Maristow—was in debt." Of Edward's father Lady Lodore said, "He is keeping a carriage at this moment in Paris, and giving parties—however, I allow that is no proof of his having money."

The woman without husband or other natural protectors was in a very different situation. The Rights and Wrongs of Women were sharply outlined in Mary's mind. She had enough of the "woman's love of looking up and being guided" to keep her from any active crusade for women's rights. "If I have never written," she said, "to vindicate the rights of women, I have ever befriended women when oppressed. At every risk I have befriended and supported victims to the social system."[27] In her books she was often critical, as a daughter of Mary Wollstonecraft should be, of their wrongs and their dependence. Although

27. *Journal*, p. 206.

the nature of her plots and characters seldom allowed these victims to appear on the pages of her novels, there is Mrs. Raby, forced by her orphan state to earn her bread as a governess; there is Miss Jervis, who earned £80 a year at the profession to which she had been brought up from childhood. In fact, to be a governess was the only way in which a gentlewoman could earn her living and keep any vestige of her self-respect: Fanny Derham vainly imagined that she could enter service and yet possess her soul in freedom and power. Even with financial independence the unmarried woman on the continent had so much the worst of it that she usually married; and her sister in England was no better off, especially if she survived her parents. The English woman of social position was not trained to independence. Lady Lodore was always waited on. "She had never stept across a street without attendance; nor put on her gloves, but as brought to her by a servant." Only if a lady had been educated to act freely, like Elizabeth Raby, "beyond the narrow paling of boarding school ideas, or the refinements of a lady's boudoir," could she defy the proprieties and visit her father in jail. Only if she were Scotch, could she travel unattended on the continent without causing remark.[28] Indeed, according to Miss Jervis it was improper even to look out of a window in London.

Society, then, as Mary Shelley saw it, was far from perfect. The few signs of tolerance and freedom and social progress she warmly welcomed: the glimmerings of self-government in Tuscany, the amelioration of the state of the slaves in the West Indies, the increase in the influence of the masses except in Turkey and Russia, the encouragement of education for poor children even by Nicholas of Russia (a blessing whatever the motive), the sense of so-

28. *Rambles in Germany and Italy*, I, 127.

cial responsibility for the poor in Rome, the annual meetings of hundreds of scientists in northern Italy. To certain individuals in history she pointed as influential in spreading the ideas of freedom and progress: Luther in Germany, Condorcet in France. To some of the persons in her fiction she gave those characteristics of benevolence and a will for good which to her as to Shelley were necessary for the regeneration of society. "Guinigi . . . [laid] aside the distinctions of society, and with lovely humility recognized the affinity of the meanest peasant to his own noble mind." Fanny Derham and her father, like the Shelleys at Marlow, endeavored to relieve the distress of the cottagers. The heroine of "The Parvenue," brought up in poverty and married to a wealthy nobleman, was jarred by the thought of "how the rich could spend so much on themselves, when any of their fellow-creatures were in destitution." She felt that all had as good a right to comforts as herself or her husband and she regarded her so-called charities as merely the payment of her debts to her fellow-creatures. She dressed meanly: she declared warmly that she could not spend twenty guineas on a gown. She lost irrevocably her noble husband's affection.

When Mary was in Italy in 1842, she dreamed of living on Isola Bella in Lake Maggiore, with English friends arriving and Italians taking refuge there from persecution and oppression, creating "a little world of my own—a focus whence would emanate some light for the country round—a school for civilization, a refuge for the unhappy, a support for merit in adversity." [29] More significant, however, than this idyllic dream is the constant emphasis in her *Rambles through Germany and Italy* on every scene associated with liberty. The aim of the book, she said, was

29. *Ibid.*, I, 131.

to persuade English readers to attend to and sympathize with Italy's struggle for freedom. Englishmen in particular, she wrote in the preface, ought to sympathize, "for the aspiration for free institutions all over the world has its source in England. Our example first taught the French nobility to seek to raise themselves from courtiers into legislators. The American war of independence, it is true, quickened this impulse, by showing the way to a successful resistance to the undue exercise of authority; but the seed was all sown by us. The swarms of English that overrun Italy keep the feeling alive. An Italian gentleman naturally envies an Englishman, hereditary or elective legislator. . . . He sees that we enjoy the privilege of doing and saying whatever we please, so that we infringe no law." And he compares these liberties with the tyranny and persecution that he himself suffers.

Shelley too thought England, as he wrote to Peacock from Geneva in 1816, "a free country, where you may act without restraint, and possess that which you possess in security." He too found in the England of 1819, in need of reform as it was, an almost universal realization that a fundamental change in government was inevitable and a widespread hope for it except in those whose vested interests would be hurt. Whether in self-chosen exile in Italy or in reluctant residence under the pale English skies, Mary Shelley naturally shared his belief and his hope that from the graves of British tyranny and corruption

> a glorious Phantom may
> Burst to illumine our tempestuous day.

CHAPTER

3

Activity of Remembrance

On the evening of November 11, 1822, Mary Shelley sat by her sleeping baby and opened the cloth-bound notebook which she had entitled "Journal of Sorrow." Since the record of July 8, the date of Shelley's death, she had ceased to enter such brief daily notes as those that cover the years of her life with him. She was recording instead her reflections and feelings—her grief, her loneliness, her thoughts of the future, her wish to die, and her idealization of her husband: "brave, wise, gentle—noble-hearted—full of learning, tolerance, and love." "I shall write his life," she said, "& thus occupy myself in the only manner from which I can derive consolation. That will be a task that may convey some balm. What though I weep? [What though each letter costs a tear?] All is better than inaction and not forgetfulness—that never is—but an inactivity of remembrance." In the next entry, more than a month later, she continued:

And you, my own Boy!—I am about to begin a task, which if you live will be an invaluable treasure to you in after times. I must collect my materials, & then, in the commemoration of the divine virtues of your father, I shall fulfil the only act of pleasure there remains for me, & be ready to follow you, if you leave me, my task being fulfilled. [. . .] I have lived: Rapture, exultation—content, all the varied change of enjoyment have been mine. It is all gone [& the stream flows through a desart—] but still, [as by the shore of Messina] the airy paintings of what it has [passed] through float by—& distance shall not dim them. If I were alone, I had already begun what I had determined to do—but I must have patience, & for those events my memory is brass —my thoughts a never tired engraver—[& more time thus spent will only impress past scenes more indelibly—] France —Poverty—a few days of solitude, & some uneasiness—A tranquil residence in a beautiful spot—Switzerland—Bath —Marlow—Milan—The Baths of Lucca—Este—Venice—Rome—Naples—Rome & misery—Leghorn—Florence—Pisa—Solitude—The Williams—The Baths—Pisa—these are the heads of chapters—each containing a tale, romantic beyond romance.[1]

But these chapters were never completed. Eleven manuscript pages written by Mary were eventually included, with little indication of their limits, in Hogg's *Life of Shelley*.[2] When Mary prepared the volume of Shelley's *Posthumous Poems* in 1823 and 1824, Bryan Procter, one of the financial sponsors of the book, asked her to write a biographical notice. Mary suggested rather that Hunt revise for the purpose an article which he had written. Hunt delayed so long, however, that the book appeared with only

1. *Journal*, pp. 185–186. In the printed *Journal*, following *Shelley and Mary*, these two quotations are given as one entry. Actually they are parts of two entries, those for November 11 and December 19. Here and in other notes reference is made to the printed *Journal*. But the passages have been compared with the MS, which is in Lord Abinger's collection, and corrections and additions (indicated by square brackets) have been made in the text, except for those in which the MS differs from the printed version only in punctuation or in some quite immaterial change of phrase.
2. They may now be examined in the Shelley-Rolls collection in the Bodleian Library.

a brief appreciative preface by Mary including an account of the last weeks of Shelley's life and of his death. Sir Timothy Shelley ordered the suppression of the edition under the penalty of withdrawing his small but indispensable contribution to Mary's income and demanded a promise "not to bring dear S.'s name before the public again during Sir T.'s life." Since Sir Timothy was seventy years old and since three hundred copies of the book had already been sold and Mary felt disinclined to write a memoir at that time, she did not repine too much. But Sir Timothy lived for twenty more years, and although Mary edited Shelley's poetry and prose and included much biographical information in the notes for those volumes, she never carried out the intention recorded in her journal in 1822.

As the years went on, she grew less and less inclined to do so.[3] In 1829 Trelawny wrote from Florence that he was engaged on his autobiography and was beginning a book on Shelley's "life and moral character." "I always wished you to do this, Mary: if you will not, as of the living I love him and you best, incompetent as I am, I must do my best to show him to the world as I found him. Do you approve of this? Will you aid in it? . . . Will you give documents? Will you write anecdotes? . . . if you in the least dislike it, say so, and there is an end of it." [4] Mary did dislike it and said so, basing her objection on her dread of "rous-

3. She offered to write a brief outline of Shelley's life for the Galignani edition of the *Poetical Works of Coleridge, Shelley, and Keats*, published in Paris in 1829, stipulating that it must be printed anonymously and without alterations. Her pencil sketch of Shelley, after Miss Curran's portrait, was used (badly engraved, she thought), but Cyrus Redding wrote the memoir from material which she furnished.

4. Trelawny, *Letters*, p. 117. The editor's difficulty in construing the first sentence (see his footnote) seems uncalled for: "of the living" obviously modifies "I."

ing the slumbering voice of the public" against Shelley and of being dragged forward herself into public notice.[5] Trelawny spluttered to Claire, "Mary has written me a letter . . . with a good deal of mawkish cant . . . and a deal of namby-pamby stuff—as different from her real character and sentiments as Hell is from Helicon." [6] Although he did not reply directly on the subject to Mary, something in his letter made her repeat herself, but more calmly and less egotistically:

> Did you not receive a letter from me in answer to yours concerning Shelley's life. I sent one. I do not wish at present to renew the recollection of the past— Your recollections of our lost one will be precious as a record of his merit—but I am averse to having these mingled with a history which will be the subject of cavill. I hope one day to write his life myself —not to be published in my lifetime or even my child's. Meanwhile we neither desire the pity nor justice of the few attended as they would be by the barking and railing of his enemies, and the misjudgment of the multitude.[7]

Trelawny, convinced that, as he wrote Mary, "had Shelley's *detractor* and your very good *friend* Tom Moore— made the request . . . he would not have been so fobbed off," and sure that her reasons were mere evasion,[8] withdrew into hurt feelings. He had thrown down the gauntlet to Mary, he told Claire, and since she refused help he would do without her, speaking of her "according to her deserts." [9] Mary tried once more to explain her reluctance and to convince him that her objections to a biographer who would include mention of herself (and "I do not see

---

5. *Letters*, II, 13–14.
6. Trelawny, *Letters*, p. 126.
7. *Letters*, II, 18–19.
8. Grylls, *Mary Shelley*, p. 217.
9. Trelawny, *Letters*, p. 131.

what you could make of his life without me") extended to "all who have meddled with our Shelley," not excepting Hunt, who slurred over the real truth.[10] And so finally there was "an end of it," at least for Mary's lifetime. Many years later, after she was dead, Trelawny published his *Recollections of the Last Days of Shelley and Byron*, in the second edition of which, the *Records* of 1878, he allowed the wrath he had nursed through a long life to explode in the bitter comments which have been largely responsible for the modern blackening of Mary Shelley's character.

Mary persisted in her unwillingness to write Shelley's biography or to aid others to do so. In 1835, when Moxon was making his first suggestions that she bring out an edition of his works with a life and notes, she wrote to Mrs. Gisborne, "I am afraid it cannot be arranged yet at least —and the *life* is out of the question."[11] Sir Timothy's prohibition was relaxing sufficiently to make it possible in 1839 to publish Shelley's works. But Mary's reasons, as her letters to Trelawny show, were more deep-seated than mere conformity with her father-in-law's wishes. They were rooted in her own reluctance, part of her nature, to "put herself forward." They were also due to a dread of the attacks which she felt sure any full story of Shelley's life would bring upon his character and opinions. At the end of 1839 she responded in very much the old terms to a request for help that came to her through Leigh Hunt, probably from George Henry Lewes, who planned and advertised, but never published, a biography of Shelley.[12] And in her preface to the *Poems* she repeated her reasons not

10. *Letters*, II, 23–24.
11. *Ibid.*, II, 91.
12. See London *Times Literary Supplement*, January 12, 1946.

only for the delay in issuing "a perfect edition," but also for abstaining from recounting the events of his personal life except as they affected his poetry.

She could, however, even though she was "torn to pieces by memory," choose and interpret such material as would not be open to her objections in her notes on Shelley's poems and in her selection of his letters and prose works. The reviews of both editions recognized the biographical importance of Mary's notes and of the letters and essays made public for the first time. In the latter Mary included a reprinting of her *History of a Six Weeks' Tour*, the story of their "honeymoon" on the continent, which she had put together out of their journals—chiefly her own—and published in 1817. Although Shelley and Claire were thinly hidden under initials, the detailed story of the adventures of the trio, unpleasant and pleasant, near-tragic and wholly comic, furnished biographical information that Mary was willing to release.[13] It was the first chapter, "France," of her projected biography.

On the pages of her journal Mary was able to say what she pleased about Shelley and chiefly about her despairing sorrow with no fear of public reaction. She never expected them to be published: "White paper . . . I will trust thee fully, for none shall see what I write." [14] "It has struck me," she commented in the entry for December 2, 1834, "what a very imperfect picture (only *no one* will ever see it) these querulous pages afford of *me*. This arises from their being

13. The statement in *The Shelley Legend* (p. 28) that Mary sentimentalized the account of their tour by omitting all unpleasant details in the 1840 reprinting is completely mistaken. There are no changes except a few editorial ones and a few minor additions, as a comparison of the two books will show.

14. Grylls, *op. cit.*, p. 176. In entry for October 2, 1822.

the record of my feelings, and not of my imagination."[15] Little that she recorded has significance for our understanding of Shelley's life or of their relationship—it is too querulous, too self-pitying. But in her poems, of which some were printed in *The Keepsake*, some remained in manuscript,[16] though none is great and few are significant, her imagination exerted a measure of control over her feelings. In them the theme of loss and grief is constant, the imagery is repeated and reminiscent of Shelley.[17] The star, the ocean, the dream recur as the symbols of the influence of Shelley upon her ("How like a star you rose upon my life"), the sea-change that he suffered, the alluring visions that gave her hope only to end in waking disappointment. Sensitive always to voices, she heard in her sleeping or waking dreams the voice of Shelley. About two weeks after Shelley's ashes were buried in Rome she wrote in her journal: "A storm has come across me; . . . I was reading; I heard a voice say 'Mary!' 'It is Shelley,' I thought; the revulsion was of agony. Never more—"[18] One of the two poems with the most explicit biographical material, an unpublished poem dated 1833, develops a similar illusion.[19]

Most important, earliest, and best of all her verses is the long poem, *The Choice*.[20] Although it begins with and

15. *Journal*, p. 203.
16. For hitherto unpublished poems by Mary, see Appendix V.
17. Especially of *Adonais* and of the epigram from Plato which Shelley used for the motto of his elegy on Keats and translated under the title "Stella."
18. *Journal*, p. 187.
19. See Appendix V. Cf. Mary's poem "On Reading Wordsworth's Lines on Peel [sic] Castle," in Grylls, *op. cit.*, pp. 202–203.
20. *The Choice* was composed apparently only a few weeks after Shelley's death, but it was never printed until H. Buxton Forman edited it from a manuscript among Leigh Hunt's papers in 1876. See

often returns to the emotional first person singular, it is a fairly objective and genuinely moving reflection of her life with Shelley in Italy. Her sad recognition of her own failure is there, but the agonizing self-flagellation of *Mathilda*[21] is gone.

> My heart was all thine own,—but yet a shell
> Closed in its core, which seemed impenetrable,
> Till sharp-toothed misery tore the husk in twain,
> Which gaping lies, nor may unite again.
> Forgive me! let thy love descend in dew
> Of soft repentance and regret most true.

Her memory goes back to the sharing of common hopes and fears, to "our best companionship," to the loss of their children, especially of William whose "spirit beats within his mother's heart," to her anxiety over Shelley's fluctuating health, to his happiness among Italian scenes, and to the final catastrophe.

> No more! no more!—what though that form be fled,
> My trembling hand shall never write thee—dead—
> Thou liv'st in Nature, Love, my Memory,
> With deathless faith for aye adoring thee,
> The wife of Time no more, I wed Eternity.[22]

It was in her fiction, when her imagination shone upon her and lightened the "weight of deadly woe," [23] that she found the way to write of Shelley without fear of attack from his critics or of reprisals from Sir Timothy. She could ease her heart and at the same time tell the public what

Grylls, *op. cit.*, pp. 297–301, for readings from another version of the poem on leaves torn from the journal of 1822–1824.

21. See Chapter 1 and Appendix III.
22. Cf. *Journal*, p. 183; *Letters*, I, 178.
23. *Journal*, p. 203. This whole passage is a somewhat garbled summary of the MS entry.

she wished it to know under cover of the events and characters in her novels and short stories. She had done so even in Shelley's lifetime, in the unpublished novelette *Mathilda* and in the novel *Valperga*. Leigh Hunt's son Thornton was convinced that in Mary's writings he could trace allusions to many facts in Shelley's life, familiar and obscure. He concluded that Mary knew him best, and that her writings plus Shelley's own contain the best materials for an estimate of his character, although she lacked the power of "distinct, positive, and absolute portraiture." [24]

She attempted only two full-length portraits of Shelley, Woodville in *Mathilda* and Adrian in *The Last Man*. For the rest she distributed his physical, intellectual, and moral traits among the persons of her stories; she assigned his voice, his eyes, his slight frame, his puckish love of fun, his gentleness, his opinions, his ideals to one or another of her imagined men and women. In this way she could tell the story of some events in his life: his schooldays at Eton; his trials with Eliza Westbrook; their experiences shortly after their elopement, experiences which would have come under the chapter headings of "Poverty—A few days of solitude and some uneasiness"; his care for the poor and sick at Marlow; his chivalrous "rescue" of Harriet from school and his attempt to rescue Emilia Viviani from the convent; his death. She could echo his ideas and his phrasing; she could put into a new setting some of the unpublished fragments of his prose and verse. She could draw before his death a picture of her sins of commission and omission toward him and after his death one of their "best companionship."

Shelley does not appear in *Frankenstein* except as his

[24]. "Shelley, by One Who Knew Him," *Atlantic Monthly*, February, 1863.

ideas and ideals are expressed. Probably he played no part in Mary's still earlier, apparently unfinished and lost story, *Hate*. Her earliest extant picture of him is in the unpublished story, *Mathilda*.[25] The Shelley here portrayed in the person of Woodville is virtually perfect, "glorious from his youth," like "an angel with winged feet"—all beauty, all goodness, all gentleness. Mathilda has treated him badly and he may not love her, but nothing can lessen the nobility of his character, his unselfishness, his idealism. Woodville has all Shelley's personal beauty, the charm of his conversation, his poetic ideals, his high moral qualities.

> I was struck by his exceeding beauty, and as he spoke to thank me the sweet but melancholy cadence of his voice brought tears into my eyes. . . . His personal beauty; his conversation which glowed with imagination and sensibility; the poetry that seemed to hang upon his lips and to make the very air mute to listen to him were charms that no one could resist. . . . His own mind was constitutionally bent to a firmer belief in good than in evil and this feeling . . . ever shone forth in his words. He would talk of the wonderful powers of man; of their present state and of their hopes: of what they had been and what they were, and when reason could no longer guide him, his imagination as if inspired shed light on the obscurity that veils the past and the future. He loved to dwell on what might have been the state of the earth before man lived on it, and how he first arose and gradually became the strange, complicated, but, as he said, the glorious creature he now is. . . . The poetry of his language and ideas . . . held me enchained to his discourses.

And Woodville's response to Mathilda's invitation to join her in drinking laudanum is highly characteristic of Shelley —in thought if not always in phrase:

25. See Appendix III.

Listen I entreat you to the words of one who has himself nurtured desperate thoughts, and longed with impatient desire for death, but who has at length trampled the phantom under foot, and crushed his sting. . . . We know not what all this wide world means; its strange mixture of good and evil. But we have been placed here and bid live and hope. I know not what we are to hope; but there is some good beyond us that we must seek; and that is our earthly task. . . . Whether this prospect of future good be preparation for another existence I know not, or whether that it is merely that we, as workmen in God's vineyard, must lend a hand to smooth the way for our posterity. If it indeed be that; if the efforts of the virtuous now, are to make the future inhabitants of this fair world more happy; if the labours of those who cast aside selfishness, and try to know the truth of things, are to free the men of ages, now far distant but which will one day come, from the burthen under which those who now live groan, and like you weep bitterly; if they free them but from one of what are now the necessary evils of life, truly I will not fail but will with my whole soul aid the work. . . . Believe me, I will never desert life untill this last hope is torn from my bosom, that in some way my labours may form a link in the chain of gold with which we ought all to strive to drag Happiness from where she sits enthroned . . . to inhabit the earth with us. Let us suppose that Socrates, or Shakespeare, or Rousseau had been seized with despair and died in youth when they were as young as I am; do you think that we and all the world should not have lost incalculable improvement in our good feelings and our happiness thro' their destruction. I am not like one of these; they influenced millions: but if I can influence but a hundred, but ten, but one solitary individual, so as in any way to lead him from ill to good, that will be a joy to repay me for all my sufferings, . . . and that hope will support me to bear them. . . . The inhabitants of this world suffer so much pain. In crowded cities, among cultivated plains, or on the desart mountains, pain is thickly sown, and if we can tear up but one of these noxious weeds, or, if in its stead we can sow one seed of corn, or plant some fair flower, let that be motive sufficient against suicide. Let us not desert our task while there is the slightest hope that we may in a future day do this. . . . Indeed I dare not die. I have a Mother whose support and hope I am. I have a friend who loves me as his life, and in whose breast I should infix a mortal sting if I ungratefully left him. So I will not die.

In *Julian and Maddalo*, written earlier in this same sad year, Shelley had said:

> We are assured
> Much may be conquered, much may be endured
> Of what degrades and crushes us. We know
> That we have power over ourselves to do
> And suffer—what, we know not till we try;
> But something nobler than to live and die.

And the Madman said to the scornful Lady:

> Do I not live
> That thou mayst have less bitter cause to grieve?
> I give thee tears for scorn, and love for hate;
> And that thy lot may be less desolate
> Than his on whom thou tramplest, I refrain
> From that sweet sleep which medicines all pain.

In writing of Shelley's death Newman White says, "In poems, letters, and conversation he had shown for several years that he regarded death primarily as a release and an opportunity and that his desire to live was based mainly upon his personal obligations." [26] In Woodville Mary was drawing a portrait of the Shelley who wore a ring inscribed *"Il buon tempo verrà,"* and who had so strong a sense of his mission and of his responsibility.

About a year after the completion of *Mathilda*, Mary was at work on her second novel, a historical tale about Castruccio, Prince of Lucca. The scenery of *Valperga* Mary

26. White, *Shelley*, II, 378.

knew well from her own residence in Tuscany. The facts she had found in many books she read and consulted. The characters, although costumes belonged to the thirteenth century, took on the familiar appearance of Mary's contemporaries. There is no full portrait of Shelley here, but his characteristics appear in more than one person.

There is certainly much of Shelley in the benevolent Guinigi, Castruccio's mentor. His heart was warmed to see his fellow creatures happy; he "thought only of the duty of man to man"; his overflowing affection could not confine itself to son or country, or be "spiritualized into a metaphysical adoration of ideal beauty"—which may be Mary's answer, based on intimate knowledge of Shelley's actions, to those of his own day who denied him a realistic concern for mankind. In her 1839 note to *The Revolt of Islam*, telling of Shelley's personal service to the poor of Marlow, she said, "I mention these things—for this minute and active sympathy with his fellow-creatures gives a thousandfold interest to his speculations, and stamps with reality his pleadings for the human race."

Like Shelley, Guinigi thought of kings and military leaders as "the privileged murderers of the earth." But it is another character, Beatrice, Castruccio's mistress, who, defying convention in both action and thought, reflects in her "creed" and final "anathema" the even more daring Shelleyan imputation of war, tyranny, cruelty, pain, disease, and domestic "strife, hatred and uncharitableness" to the God of human orthodoxy, the spirit of Evil. Mary expected more severe public attacks than she received: *Blackwood*'s review alone, though largely favorable, grieved over the thought "that any English lady should be capable of clothing such thoughts in such words," eloquent though they were, and blamed "the writers of that school, with which this gifted person has the misfortune to be associated." [27]

Into the person of her heroine, Euthanasia, Mary put her idealization of the qualities she most loved in Shelley. Claire recognized her: "Euthanasia is Shelley in female attire, and what a glorious being she is!" Her generosity, her gentleness, her love of beauty, her hatred of war, her belief that a corrupt clergy had falsified the teachings of Christ, her absorption in the classic authors—all are Shelleyan.[28] Her understanding of history from her study of the ancient classics, like that of our own contemporary, Professor Arnold J. Toynbee, would be approved by the poet of *Hellas:* "She did not acquire that narrow idea of the present times, as if they and the world were the same, which characterizes the unlearned; she saw and marked the revolutions that had been, and the present seemed to her only a point of rest, from which time was to renew his flight, scattering change as he went." [29] The catastrophe of the book—Euthanasia's death by drowning in a boat caught in a storm—is, as Mary herself said, "strangely prophetic," resembling those apparent premonitions in Shelley's poems. "Is not the end of [my book] wondrous," she asked Jane Williams, "the fate—the shore—how miserably foretold —it is very st[range]." [30] Like Captain Roberts, a countryman stands watching Euthanasia's vessel until it fades from sight. It is caught in a fierce scirocco, and nothing

27. *Blackwood's Edinburgh Monthly Magazine* (March, 1823), XIII, 290.
28. She echoes Shelley's words in "To a Skylark": "Oh! could I even now pour forth in words the sentiments . . . that then burst upon my soul . . . the whole world would stand and listen."
29. Cf. Arnold Toynbee, "My View of History," *Civilization on Trial* (New York, Oxford University Press, 1948).
30. From an unpublished letter in Lord Abinger's collection. Used by his kind permission.

more is known of it until wreckage is washed ashore. Unlike Shelley's, Euthanasia's body is never found.

The death of Shelley intervened between the completion of *Valperga*[31] and its publication. When Mary turned again to writing, she found in the activity therapeutic value. Yet she could not for a good many months seek the relief she later found in objectifying her memories and her sorrow. Her first ventures—contributions to *The Liberal* and *La Belle Assemblée* [32]—add nothing to our knowledge of Shelley. But in 1824 she published in the *London Magazine* three unsigned contributions, all of which have Shelleyan interest. They are the result of her gleanings from the manuscripts which she was turning over in preparation for her edition of Shelley's *Posthumous Poems*.[33]

The first, which appeared in the January issue, has never before been identified as Mary's. It is a sketch called "Recollections of Italy." The writer, on one of the few bright days in midsummer, wanders out to the bank of

---

[31]. There are in *Valperga* traces still of the unhappiness of the year before, especially of Mary's grief over her two dead children. Euthanasia too suffered "many losses, following swift one upon another." Beatrice, parting from Castruccio, "was as a mother, who reads the death-warrant of her child on the physician's brow, yet blindly trusting that she decyphers ill, will not destroy the last hope by a question." Mary and Shelley both had felt "parental tenderness, the strongest of all passions, but often the most unfortunate."

[32]. See Appendix II.

[33]. Only two of them have been identified. See *The Letters of Mary W. Shelley* (1944), I, 272 n. Professor Jones there speaks of "On Ghosts" and "The Bride of Modern Italy" as "hitherto unidentified." The present writer too, in 1938, thought that she had made a discovery. But she soon found that the identification of these two articles —but not of "Recollections of Italy"—had been made in a letter in April, 1824, by Thomas Lovell Beddoes to Thomas Forbes Kelsall and published in 1935. See Beddoes' *Works*, ed. by H. W. Donner (Oxford and London, 1935), p. 586.

the Thames. There she meets Edmund Malville, who is a warm lover of Italy, especially Tuscany. He describes an expedition from the Baths of Pisa to Vico Pisano on September 15, 18—. As the climbers sat before the church above Vico Pisano, Malville's "best and now lost friend" cried, "Look, behold the mountains that sweep to the plain like waves that meet in a chasm; the olive woods are as green as a sea and are waving in the wind; the shadows of the clouds are spotting the bosoms of the hills; a heron comes sailing over us, a butterfly flits near; at intervals the pines give forth their sweet and prolonged response to the wind; the myrtle bushes are in bud, and the soil beneath us is carpeted with odoriferous flowers." These are Shelley's words, with only a few changes to fit them into the narrative. They were first published as his in 1862 by Garnett in *Relics of Shelley* as one of three prose fragments. In 1823 only Mary could have had access to Shelley's papers. If any further proof were needed that she wrote this article, it would be furnished by her journal entry for Saturday, September 15, 1821: "Trip to Vico Pisano with the Williams'."

Malville too, as well as his lost friend, is Shelley, both in his love for Tuscany and in his appearance: his dark blue eye, his slight person, seeming to take on when he talked "the aspect of an etherial substance . . . , and to have too little of clay about it to impede his speedy ascent to heaven."

In the third of Mary's contributions, a tale called "The Bride of Modern Italy," a younger, more earthy Shelley appears in the person of Marcott Alleyn, the young English artist who acts as messenger between his friend Giacomo and Giacomo's beloved, Clorinda Saviani, who is immured in a convent in Rome. Clorinda is an obvious representation of both Harriet (for Alleyn was only seventeen) and Emilia Viviani. She falls in love with her Giacomo's John Alden and in no uncertain terms asks him to speak for himself and to help her escape from the convent. Alleyn is at first enchanted. But when from Clorinda's letters he learns that she wishes him to take her to England, he hesitates. Giacomo and Clorinda together plot to drug the Mother Superior, steal her keys, and make wax impressions of them.[34] Alleyn refuses to be a party to the plot: he puts the wax impression, which has been entrusted to him, against a sunny wall outside the convent gate. Clorinda finally (like Emilia) yields to the inevitable and marries her elderly, family-approved suitor. Alleyn goes off to paint his picture, "The Profession of Eloisa." Shelley wrote his *Epipsychidion.*

In personality Alleyn was less like Shelley than in his adventures. He had a soft voice and expressive eyes. He was easily won to compassion for Clorinda as a victim of organized society. He was young and idealistic and also fond of fun. The older Shelley fell in with Allegra's mischief when he visited her at Bagnacavallo: she made him run with her all over the convent like a mad thing, scattering the nuns to their beds and then ringing the bell to call them out again. The younger Alleyn furnished the mischief himself: he took rum and sweets to the nuns, kissed some of the least ugly, and "introduced a system of English jokes and hoaxes, at which the poor Italians were perfectly aghast, . . . and then, when their loud voices pealed through the arched passages in wonder and anger, they were appeased by soft words and well-timed gifts."

34. Perhaps this was part of the mad scheme which Claire concocted for getting Allegra out of the Convent of Bagnacavallo and which Shelley refused to consider. See Shelley, *Letters,* X, 365.

This, Mary's earliest treatment of Shelley's "Italian Platonics," is only a faint attempt to tell the story. Clorinda herself is faintly drawn, and Alleyn is a mere shadow of a youthful Shelley. Ten years later, in her novel *Lodore*, a more mature Shelley-Saville rescued from a convent and married another Emilia-Clorinda. But before Mary could draw those richer portraits, she needed the perspective of years and other writing.

"On Ghosts,"[35] which had appeared in the *London Magazine* a month before "The Bride," includes, almost verbatim from the journal, ghost stories told by Hogg, the Chevalier de Mengaldo, and Monk Lewis and refers to one of the tales read at the time of the inception of *Frankenstein*. But this article adds nothing to Mary's portrait of Shelley except one reference to the willingness of "the person of the most lively imagination I ever knew" to suspend disbelief in ghosts, surely the Shelley who in the journal, in answer to the skepticism of Byron and Lewis, expressed his conviction that many people are at least "admonished by the approach of loneliness and midnight to think more respectably of the world of shadows."[36]

With the *Posthumous Poems* in the press, Mary began in the spring of 1824 to write her next novel, *The Last Man*. The calling up of memories by her work with the papers associated with Shelley and their life together, congenial as the task was, stirred her deepest emotions and intensified her loneliness. She felt that her imagination was dead, her energies asleep; nothing she wrote pleased her. Immured

---

35. In *The Pocket Magazine* for 1830 (Vol. II, 29–34, 132–138) appeared two articles signed "Anselm" which borrowed liberally and without acknowledgment from Mary's article.
36. *Journal*, p. 57.

in London, she was bereft not only of Shelley's encouragement but of the inspiration she had felt in Genoa, even after his death. "To be here without you is to be doubly exiled, to be away from Italy is to lose you twice." [37] The news of the death of Byron in Greece broke another link with the past. "Byron had become one of the people of the grave—that miserable conclave to which the beings I best love[d] belong. . . . At the age of twenty-six I am in the condition of an aged person. All my old friends are gone." [38]

In this mood she was quick to seize upon the theme of the wiping out of civilization by a plague, leaving one man alive. This theme, already popular and later almost done to death—only to be revived in our own times—gave her an opportunity to present those old friends and her loss of them, especially Shelley, and to interpret their relationship. For the fanciful Introduction she chose as setting one of their happy expeditions in Italy, that of December 8, 1818, to the Elysian Fields, Avernus, and the Bay of Baiae, made memorable by Shelley's descriptions in his letters and in his "Ode to the West Wind." It was in an inner chamber of the cave of the Cumaean Sibyl that the author and her "companion" found the leaves and pieces of bark, on which, in languages ancient and modern, were inscribed the poetic rhapsodies, prophecies, disconnected hints of events in the far future that she later shaped into her "narration of misery and change." Together they studied the inscriptions, and then, after the loss of "the selected and matchless companion of my toils," the author alone employed her time in deciphering them. "My labours have cheered long hours of solitude, and taken me out of

37. *Ibid.*, p. 193.
38. *Ibid.*

a world, which has averted its once benignant face from me, to one glowing with imagination and power."

"I have endeavoured, but how inadequately," wrote Mary of Shelley to Sir John Bowring, "to give some idea of him in my last published book—the sketch has pleased some of those who best loved him—I might have made more of it but there are feelings which one recoils from unveiling to the public eye." [39] Granting at once the truth of Mary's adverb, *inadequately*, those today who best love Shelley may still find pleasure in the sketch of Adrian.

Adrian was the heir to the throne of England in the last years of the twenty-first century. But his father abdicated and England became a republic. Adrian was in full sympathy with republican ideas, even though he retained his title of Earl of Windsor. He first appears as a boy still in his teens, a tall, slender, fair boy, with a thrilling voice and "a physiognomy expressive of the excess of sensibility and refinement," vivacious and intelligent, deeply read and imbued with the spirit of high philosophy. Lionel Verney, the narrator, who represents Mary herself, confronted by Adrian's active spirit of benevolence, "felt the influence of sweet benignity sink upon [his heart]." "In person, [Adrian] hardly appeared of this world; his slight frame was overinformed by the soul that dwelt within; he was all mind; . . . but the might of his smile would have tamed an hungry lion, or caused a legion of armed men to lay their weapons at his feet." After their first conversation, in which Adrian had talked "of the old Greek sages, and of the power which they had acquired over the minds of men, through the force of love and wisdom only," Verney sought the hills, and as he ran he thought, "This is power! Not to be strong of limb, hard of heart, ferocious, and daring; but

39. *Letters*, I, 341.

kind, compassionate and soft." And, as if in answer to Shelley's youthful vow recorded in the Dedication of *The Revolt of Islam* to Mary, Verney vowed, "Doubt me not, Adrian, I also will become wise and good."[40]

Their companionship knew happy years when Verney, having married Adrian's sister, was living in Windsor Castle, devoting himself to reading and writing under his friend's encouragement, as Mary herself had been encouraged by Shelley. It continued through the events of the last years of the twenty-first century: the development of England as a republic, the plots to restore the monarchy, the Turco-Greek wars which took the life of the Byronic Raymond, the plague which devastated the world causing not only widespread death but the breakdown of society— a society for which Adrian had had high hopes and which he tried in vain to save.

Like Shelley, Adrian was for a time considered mad by those who had no sympathy with his liberal ideas. His early plans for England, for diminishing the power of the aristocracy, effecting a greater equalization of wealth and privilege, and converting the government into a perfect republican system, ran directly counter to his mother's schemes to re-establish the House of Windsor on the throne. He was sent to Dunkeld to remain in seclusion, and the physical and nervous illness which attacked him as the result of both the opposition to his plans and a frustrated love affair was very close to a mental breakdown. When he recovered and returned to active life, he was urged by Raymond and Verney to be a candidate for election as Lord Protector of England on the ground that he would

40. Cf. Shelley's lines:
    So, without shame, I spake:—'I will be wise,
    And just, and free, and mild . . .'

then be able to carry out his plans. But the visions of his boyhood—visions as bright and schemes as quixotic as some of Shelley's—had faded, he said, in the light of reality: "I know now that I am not a man fitted to govern nations; sufficient for me, if I keep in wholesome rule the little kingdom of my own mortality." That this was no narrow doctrine of withdrawal into self is proved by Adrian's subsequent actions and by his prototype Shelley's repeated insistence that self-knowledge, self-rule, and self-esteem are central to any philosophy of human brotherhood and any program for human betterment. Adrian was not a poet; his direct efforts to bring about political reform may be compared to Shelley's political poems and prose treatises. Professor Carlos Baker has said of Shelley's "experiences with the mythology of politics,"

> When these failed, only direct personal participation, such as he once tried as a boy in Dublin, remained to him. Although he dreamed of going to Spain in 1820, and although, after the manner of Aeschylus, he celebrated the military prowess of the Greeks, he was too much a believer in gradualism and too deeply the proponent of brotherly love to place any strong faith in bloodshed as a means to human progress. Thought, rather than direct political action, was becoming for him the sole reality, and in the realm of thought he lived and worked.[41]

Adrian went, not to Spain, but to Greece, content to serve under Lord Raymond in the Greek war of independence. A hater of war and violence like Shelley, he felt, also like Shelley, that so great an end justified the means. He was later to lead a band of armed men to repel an invasion from Ireland; but his more characteristic act was to step be-

---

41. Carlos Baker, *Shelley's Major Poetry* (Princeton, Princeton University Press, 1948), p. 189.

tween the warring groups and persuade them, by the power of his love, to lay down their arms. He suffered intensely with the suffering of friend and enemy.

> I shall not be suspected of being averse to the Greek cause; I know and feel its necessity; it is beyond every other a good cause. I have defended it with my sword,[42] and was willing that my spirit should be breathed out in its defense; freedom is of more worth than life, and the Greeks do well to defend their privilege unto death. But let us not deceive ourselves. The Turks are men; each fibre, each limb, is as feeling as our own, and every spasm, be it mental or bodily, is as truly felt in a Turk's heart or brain, as in a Greek's. . . . Think you, amidst the shrieks of violated innocence and helpless infancy, I did not feel in every nerve the cry of a fellow being? They were men and women, the sufferers, before they were Mahometans, and when they rise turbanless from the grave, in what except their good or evil actions will they be the better or worse than we?

When Adrian assumed the leadership of England in its fight against the plague, he felt that he was undertaking a task not merely of rule but of mercy, free from political intrigue, in which "my *would*, . . . for ever enchained by the *shall not* of these my tyrants" was freed to serve and if possible to save. Owning affinity with all mankind and all nature, he proved under stress more practical and steady than Raymond, whose view of the world was centered in himself. He was a capable leader, with the same practical wisdom linked with determination and kindly patience that made Shelley's friends turn to him in emergencies. Yet he met many discouragements, and, like Shelley, he was subject as he had always been to moods of depression, for from his childhood "aspiring thoughts and high desires [had]

---

42. Mary did not foresee the "progress" in weapons of destruction to come in the next centuries.

warred with inherent disease and overstrained sensitiveness."

In spite of frail health, Adrian survived the plague, together with Verney, Verney's little son Evelyn, and Clara, the daughter of Raymond and Perdita (Byron and Claire), whom Adrian and Verney loved, as Shelley and Mary had loved Allegra. Evelyn died, like the real Clara, William, and Allegra, of a fever. The fictitious Clara and Adrian drowned when their little boat was wrecked in a storm off the coast of Italy. "I shall never see them more," said Verney. "The ocean has robbed me of them. . . . I was an untaught shepherd-boy, when Adrian deigned to confer on me his friendship. The best years of my life had been passed with him. All I had possessed of this world's goods, of happiness, knowledge, or virtue—I owed to him. He had, in his person, his intellect, and rare qualities, given a glory to my life, which without him it had never known. Beyond all other beings he had taught me, that goodness, pure and single, can be an attribute of man."

Although the "best companionship" of Shelley and Mary is shown in that of Adrian and Verney, Mary had not forgotten some of the rifts in it. Evadne, the Greek girl whom Adrian loved, "thought he did well to assert his own will, but she wished that will to have been more intelligible to the multitude." She failed Adrian. Mary was perhaps remembering that she had, in 1820, been urging Shelley to consider more practically the average intelligence of the public and the reviewers. She would have liked him to win popular acclaim for his poetry, as had Mathilda's Woodville, and she continued to believe, as she said in her note on *The Witch of Atlas*, that he would have attained even greater mastery over his powers and greater happiness in his mind if he could have created a link of appreciation and sympathy with the public.

It is not only in the depiction of events in Adrian's life and the portrayal of his character that Mary brings Shelley before us in this book. His habits are there: his pleasure in playing with children, his love of boats, and his fondness for setting afloat paper boats, leaves, or bits of bark. His thought of withdrawing with Mary and their child to a Greek island is reflected in Raymond's similar plan. His phrasing is often echoed: "the painted veil of life," "gay as a lark carolling from its skiey tower," the boat and stream image with tones of *Alastor*, descriptions of the Alps which remind one of *Mont Blanc*—Arveiron, white and foaming, the yellow lightning playing silently about the great peak.

It is possible that Mary, just as she incorporated a prose fragment by Shelley in her article, "Recollections of Italy," has preserved here another otherwise unpublished passage from his manuscripts [43]—perhaps even two. A "writing" of Adrian's fell into Perdita's hands:

> Life is not the thing romance writers describe it; going through the measures of a dance, and after various evolutions arriving at a conclusion, when the dancers may sit down and repose. While there is life there is action and change. We go on, each thought linked to the one which was its parent, each act to a previous act. No joy or sorrow dies barren of progeny, which for ever generated and generating, weaves the chain that make[s] our life:
>
> > Un dia llama à otro dia
> > y ass i llama, y encadena
> > llanto à llanto, y pena à pena.

43. Mr. H. Buxton Forman, in a letter to the *Athenaeum* in 1887, raised the question about the first passage. As far as I know, the second one has never been considered.

> Truly disappointment is the guardian deity of human life; she sits at the threshold of unborn time, and marshals the events as they come forth. Once my heart sat lightly in my bosom; all the beauty of the world was doubly beautiful, irradiated by the sun-light shed from my own soul. O wherefore are love and ruin for ever joined in this our mortal dream? [44] So that when we make our hearts a lair for that gently seeming beast, its companion enters with it, and pitilessly lays waste what might have been a home and a shelter.

This passage has never turned up among the Shelley papers. But it is possible that it is by Shelley. It reflects Adrian's mood when Evadne had deserted him. Did it touch Mary too nearly, so that when she had used it for her novel she destroyed it?

Possibly Adrian's long apostrophe to earth after his recovery from illness may also, with some changes by Mary, have been taken from his papers. The final paragraph at least expresses so many of his ideas, with echoes from *Prometheus Unbound, Julian and Maddalo, Adonais,* and his letters, that it might well be by Shelley's hand:

> Oh, that death and sickness were banished from our earthly home! that hatred, tyranny, and fear could no longer make their lair in the human heart! that each man might find a brother in his fellow, and a nest of repose amid the wide plains of his inheritance! that the source of tears were dry, and that lips might no longer form expressions of sorrow. Sleeping thus under the beneficent eye of heaven, can evil visit thee, O Earth, or grief cradle to their graves thy luckless children? Whisper it not, lest the daemons hear and rejoice! The choice is with us; let us will it, and our habitation becomes a paradise. For the will of man is omnipotent, blunting the arrows of death, soothing the bed of disease, and wiping away the tears of agony. And what is each hu-

---

44. Cf. "Though Ruin now Love's shadow be," and other songs by the Spirits in *Prometheus Unbound*, Act I, ll. 763 ff.

man being worth, if he do not put forth his strength to aid his fellow-creatures? My soul is a fading spark, my nature frail as a spent wave; but I dedicate all of intellect and strength that remains to me, to that one work, and take upon me the task, as far as I am able, of bestowing blessings on my fellow-men.[45]

During the following years before the editing and publishing of Shelley's poetry and prose, Mary was writing constantly and industriously. By 1839 she had published three novels, sixteen stories, half a dozen more articles, and most of the biographical sketches in five volumes of Lardner's *Cabinet Cyclopedia*. But for about ten years she seemed largely to have satisfied, in the great effort of *The Last Man*, her need to write at length about Shelley. In all her work there were brief glimpses of him. The conventionally idealized figure of Richard in *Perkin Warbeck* slightly—but only slightly—resembles Shelley. Katherine's fears for his safety at sea and her grief for him after his death are like those of Mary for her husband. The Princess's lament in the final chapter for the "beloved outcast" whose wanderings she shared, that most "single-hearted, generous, and kindly being," sound like pages from Mary's journal. Here and in other works, as in *The Last Man*, there are echoes of his poetry as well as many direct quotations.[46] The backgrounds Mary and Shelley had shared appear in both novels and short stories: the France of their elopement, Naples, Albano, the Swiss Alps, Virginia Water, Marlow,

45. Cf. Woodville's speech quoted on pp. 59–60 above.
46. Ludovico, the Heir of Mondolfo, like Shelley in dejection near Naples, "sat on the beach watching the monotonous flow of the waves; they danced and sparkled; his gloomy thoughts refused to imbibe cheerfulness from wave or sea." The image of the painted veil is quoted or alluded to twice in *Perkin Warbeck* and four times in *Lodore*. Falkner alludes to "The Indian Serenade" and the Actaeon passage in *Adonais*.

Bath, cheap London lodging houses. She wrote two articles that utilized her knowledge of Italy, another that followed their expeditions around the Lake of Geneva. In one of her short stories Mary made use of facts from Shelley's early life. Horace Neville, who at the beginning of "The Mourner" is introduced to the reader in a boat on Virginia Water and who slightly resembles Shelley, at the age of eleven entered Eton, where he suffered so bitterly under the fag system that he ran away. In a review of *The Loves of the Poets,* she quoted freely from Shelley's translation of the *Symposium* and from his *Essay on Love,* and she defined a poet in terms of her own poet.

> What is a Poet? Is he not that which wakens melody in the silent chords of the human heart? A light which arrays in splendour things and thoughts which else were dim in the shadow of their own insignificance? His soul is like one of the pools in the Ilex woods of the Maremma, it reflects the surrounding universe, but it beautifies, groups, and mellows their tints, making a little world within itself, the copy of the outer one; but more entire, more faultless. But above all, a poet's soul is Love; the desire of sympathy is the breath that inspires his lay, while he lavishes on the sentiment and its object, his whole treasure-house of dependent imagery, burning emotion, and ardent enthusiasm. He is the mirror of nature, reflecting her back ten thousand times more lovely; what then must not his power be, when he adds beauty to the most perfect thing in nature—even Love.[47]

"Have you read Lodore?" Mary asked Mrs. Gisborne in 1835. "If you did read it, did you recognize any of Shelley's and my early adventures—when we were in danger of being starved in Switzerland—and could get no dinner at an inn in London?"[48] All modern readers of *Lodore* and

---
47. Mary Shelley's review of "The Loves of the Poets," *Westminster Review,* October, 1829.
48. *Letters,* II, 108–109.

of Shelley's life recognize those adventures, so closely do they follow fact. On their honeymoon in Naples, Edward Villiers and Ethel are in debt because of the delay of remittances from England, as were Shelley and Mary in Switzerland and in Paris; and Villiers finds that Ethel, as Shelley said of Mary, "seems insensible to all future evil. She feels as if our love would alone suffice to resist the invasions of calamity." [49] "I cannot fear," says Ethel; "you are in health and near me." The young couple return to London to experience separation and furtive meetings at coffee houses to escape the bailiffs, for Villiers as well as Shelley has raised money on annuities and can not pay the interest. Their Sundays spent together are happy times, devoted, as Mary had said, "to love in idleness," even when their landlady refuses to send up dinner. "People want their money," Mary had written in her journal; "won't send up dinner, and we are all very hungry." [50] Both young couples finally took refuge at Salt Hill, beyond the jurisdiction of bailiffs. But Villiers's expeditions to London ended more dramatically than Shelley's: he was arrested; Ethel joined him in lodgings near the prison, living "within the rules"; and Lady Lodore finally swallowed her pride and sacrificed her jointure to save her daughter's husband.

The story of Villiers and Ethel is the tale "romantic beyond romance" which would have filled the early chapters of that biography of Shelley which Mary had planned so many years before. She included in the same novel a part of the first Pisa chapter, her second version of the Emilia Viviani episode. Villiers's cousin, Horatio Saville, was taken by an acquaintance to see a beautiful girl in a con-

49. *Journal*, p. 6. The entry, like several in the first year, is by Shelley.
50. *Ibid.*, p. 24.

vent in Naples, shut up there to wait until her parents found a suitable husband for her. Filled with pity, admiration, and tenderness, he called upon her often, trying to comfort and offering to serve her. "He visited her frequently, he brought her books, he taught her English. They were allowed to meet daily in the parlour of the convent, in the presence of a female attendant." So far the story follows the familiar facts. Clorinda (her name is the same as that of the bride of modern Italy) fell passionately in love with Horatio. He felt for her "a brother's regard," pity, and tenderness. But believing that he could rescue her from an unworthy fate and make her happy, he acted, his sisters said, "with his usual determination and precipitancy" and married her. Their married life, in spite of her strong love and his patience and affection, was a tragedy. Clorinda was subject to almost insane jealous rages. She died as they were returning to England, "a victim of uncontrolled passion," in a spasm induced by jealousy of Lady Lodore, Saville's first and real love.

Would this or its reasonable facsimile have been the course of events on that Elysian isle to which Shelley invited his Emily? If Shelley's Juno had not proved a cloud would this life of stormy, tragic emotion have been theirs instead of the idyllic companionship and passionate union of the closing lines of *Epipsychidion?* Perhaps Mary thought so. At least she thought she knew her Emilia and her Shelley.[51]

In spite of her abundant use of biographical fact in *Lodore,* Mary did not ask Shelley to sit for any of the characters, as he had for Adrian. There are echoes of Shelley's education and of his first marriage and its disaster in the events of Lodore's life, but none of Shelley's personal-

51. See Chapter 6 for a discussion of Mary's two pictures of Emilia.

ity in Lodore himself. She distributed his traits among three men in her story, endowing Saville most generously. Edward Villiers was Shelley as a gay young wooer, blue-eyed and silver-voiced. Francis Derham at Eton was like Shelley with his slender frame and fair countenance. "The boy was unlike the rest; he had wild fancies and strange inexplicable ideas. . . . He could discourse with eloquence, and pored with unceasing delight over books of abstrusest philosophy." He refused to learn his allotted tasks; like Horace Neville he refused to fag; "he was the scoff, the butt, and victim, of the whole school." He resembled Shelley also in his fascination by ghosts and spirits as a boy, in his gentleness, in his philosophical scholarship and his philanthropy.

Horatio Saville was not another Shelley. He was "often cold in seeming, because he could not always master his passion"—like Mary herself, rather than like Shelley; he was distinguished at college by the energy with which he pursued his studies; he was timid and diffident. He had deep-set gray eyes and he dressed well. But the Shelleyan characteristics are strong. Physically he was frail, with sparkling eye, flushed cheek, and languid step, "tokens that there burned within him a spirit too strong for his frame." When Ethel met him in Naples, she at first thought him plain; then, as he talked, "His features were delicately moulded, and his fine forehead betokened depth of intellect; but the charm of his face was a . . . smile, which diffused incomparable sweetness over his physiognomy. . . . His voice was modulated by feeling, his language was fluent, graceful in its turn of expression, and original in the thoughts which it expressed. His manners were marked by breeding, yet they were peculiar. They were formed by his individual disposition and under the dominion of sensibility. Hence they were often abrupt and reserved." [52] He had an ardent mind whose energies he spent on the study of abstruse metaphysics. He loved learning and the pursuit of truth. He abhorred strife. He devoted himself to the service of others. He was "distinguished by every excellence; to know that a thing was right to be done, was enough to impel Horatio to go through fire and water to do it; he was one of those who seem not to belong to this world, yet who adorn it most."

In *Falkner*, Mary's last novel, Shelley appears only briefly as Edwin Raby, the son of an aristocratic county family who had rebelled against their bigotry and had been disowned. He married a girl of whom his family could not approve—because of her humble birth, however, rather than because of radical parents or unconventional conduct. The young couple, like Shelley and Mary—and like Villiers and Ethel—went through difficult times. "You know," wrote Mrs. Raby to a friend, "what our life in London was—obscure, but happy." After Edwin's early death, she tried like Mary to secure financial aid for herself and her child from her father-in-law. He proposed the terms proposed to Mary by Sir Timothy—terms to which she could not agree and which she refused to accept. With this refusal the Shelley story disappears from the pages of *Falkner*, unless the exhumation of Alithea's body recalls its last scene on the beach near Via Reggio. A few flashes of Shelley's character can be seen in the humanitarian and liberal ideas of Falkner, in the generous spirit of Gerard Neville. But there is no Woodville or Adrian, not even a Villiers or a Saville. It is the spirits of Byron and Trelawny that darken this tale of passionate crime and retribution and, *per contra* perhaps, give point to its theme of fidelity.

52. Cf. White, *Shelley*, I, 557.

Mary's final published word on Shelley as man and as poet was said in the Preface and Notes of her collected editions of his works in 1839 and 1840. Now, no longer behind the veil of fiction or in the privacy of her journal, she could show the world what she believed to be the true Shelley, man, poet, and lover of beauty and of mankind. Although she erred in her critical estimate of certain poems, she recognized that in all his work "is that sense of mystery which formed an essential portion of his perception of life—a clinging to the subtler inner spirit, rather than to the outward form—a curious and metaphysical anatomy of human passion and perception." His "conception of love was exalted, absorbing, allied to all that is purest and noblest in our nature." He endeavored "to ally the love of abstract beauty, and adoration of abstract good . . . with our sympathies with our kind." "Whatever faults he had ought to find extenuation among his fellows, since they prove him to be human; without them, the exalted nature of his soul would have raised him into something divine."

As she speaks, we can see the model from which she drew Woodville and Adrian. Her Shelley is idealized but not legendary. Allowing for the "light of love" and sorrow that shone upon her model and her canvas, we can see also the Shelley of modern critics—at least of those sympathetic to him.

> The qualities that struck anyone newly introduced to Shelley were,—First, a gentle and cordial goodness that animated his intercourse with warm affection and helpful sympathy. The other, the eagerness and ardour with which he was attached to the cause of human happiness and improvement; and the fervent eloquence with which he discussed such subjects. His conversation was marked by its happy abundance, and the beautiful language in which he clothed his poetic ideas and philosophical notions. To defecate life

of its misery and its evil was the ruling passion of his soul; he dedicated to it every power of his mind, every pulsation of his heart. He looked on political freedom as the direct agent to effect the happiness of mankind; and thus any new-sprung hope of liberty inspired a joy and an exultation more wild than he could have felt for any personal advantage. . . . He had been from youth the victim of the state of feeling inspired by the reaction of the French Revolution; and believing firmly in the justice and excellence of his views, it cannot be wondered that a nature as sensitive, as impetuous, and as generous as his, should put its whole force into the attempt to alleviate for others the evils of those systems from which he himself had suffered. Many advantages attended his birth; he spurned them all when balanced with what he considered his duties. He was generous to imprudence, devoted to heroism.

These characteristics breathe throughout his poetry. The struggle for human weal; the resolution firm to martyrdom; the impetuous pursuit, the glad triumph in good; the determination not to despair;—such were the features that marked those of his works which he regarded with most complacency, as sustained by a lofty subject and useful aim.

CHAPTER

4

The Godwins of Skinner Street

When Mary Godwin was ten years old, her father moved to the shop and dwelling house on Skinner Street which was to be his home until he was evicted in 1822. It was a strange and complex household: Godwin and his second wife; Fanny, natural daughter of Mary Wollstonecraft and Gilbert Imlay, and Mary, daughter of the same mother and of Godwin; Jane [1] and Charles Clairmont, children of Godwin's second wife; William, the only child who belonged to both parents. There the three girls grew up together. From the doors of Number 41 they escaped, Mary to elope with Shelley, Jane to go with them and to make her home with them intermittently until Shelley's death, and Fanny to take her own life in a Swansea inn.

The two boys were sent to school; but the girls were educated at home. Most of the time they had a governess; at intervals they had daily language lessons. But Godwin himself did most of the teaching. In the first edition of *Frankenstein* there is a passage which must be based on Mary's educational experiences. "Our studies," said Victor Frankenstein, "were never forced; and by some means

[1]. Later called Claire.

we always had an end placed in view, which excited us to ardour in the prosecution of them. . . . We learned Latin and English, that we might read the writings in those languages. . . . Perhaps we did not read so many books, or learn languages so quickly, as those who are disciplined according to ordinary methods; but what we learned was impressed the more deeply on our memories."

In 1812 Godwin wrote to an unknown correspondent:

> Your enquiries relate principally to the two daughters of Mary Wollstonecraft. They are neither of them brought up with an exclusive attention to the system and ideas of their mother. I lost her in 1797, and in 1801 I married a second time. One among the motives which led me to chuse this was the feeling I had in myself of an incompetence for the education of daughters. The present Mrs. Godwin has great strength and activity of mind, but is not exclusively a follower of the notions of their mother; and indeed, having formed a family establishment without having a previous provision for the support of a family, neither Mrs. Godwin nor I have leisure enough for reducing novel theories of education to practice, while both of us honestly endeavour, as far as our opportunities will permit, to improve the mind and characters of the younger branches of our family.[2]

Mary Wollstonecraft's "system" would have insured loving, rational, personal care for her two little girls from the very beginning. She presented her ideas—which seem today sensible rather than novel—in *Thoughts on the Education of Daughters*, and she gave a sample of their application in the manuscript "Lessons" which she left at her death, "the first book of a series which I had intended to have written for my unfortunate girl." Fanny and Mary would not have been sent to school: "If a mother has

---

2. Paul, *William Godwin: His Friends and Contemporaries*, II, 213–214.

leisure and good sense, and more than one daughter, I think she could best educate them herself." Above all Mary Wollstonecraft would have trained them to combine systematically and carefully those ideas presented to them by their mother-teacher. "I wish them to be taught to think." The training would not have been entirely of the mind: "A woman may fit herself to be the companion of a man of sense, and yet know how to take care of his family." Accomplishments such as painting, music, and even dancing would not be discouraged, provided they involved "employment of the mind." Education would be planned but not rigid. "Fixed rules cannot be given. . . . The mind is not, cannot be created by the teacher, though it may be cultivated and its real powers found out." [3]

Had her mother lived, Mary might have received a more systematic education, with more personal supervision. But Godwin's richly stored and active mind served as a spur to those of his children. He encouraged Mary to read and to listen to his conversations with his friends. Mary Wollstonecraft would have added brilliance to those discussions in the library and would have seen to it that her daughters were never kept from them by household tasks in the kitchen or the storeroom—tasks such as were imposed upon them by their somewhat jealous stepmother.

The second Mrs. Godwin, in spite of Godwin's professed motive in marrying her, was disqualified by her inferior intellectual gifts as well as by her prejudice in favor of her own daughter Jane. Godwin, however, although his one experiment in systematic teaching was a failure, not only attracted young people but also was able to present information so that they were interested in it. His histories

3. Quotations from *Thoughts on the Education of Daughters* (London, 1787), pp. 57, 22, 54.

of England, Rome, and Greece and his *Fables, Ancient and Modern*, published under the name of Baldwin by him and his wife, were "so printed as to be agreeable and refreshing to the eye of a child" [4] and well adapted to his understanding. He had tried them out on his own children and had won their approval—"How easy this is! Why, we learn it by heart almost as fast as we read it!" Mrs. Godwin contributed to the joint publishing venture her business ability and a few translations of French books for children. To the education of Mary Wollstonecraft's daughters she contributed little except practical training. So it devolved upon the father to practise upon the girls his "system of sentimental education" based upon Helvetius, and Shelley found Mary a girl with an eager and lively mind, ready for his own further teaching.

Mary recognized her father's part in her upbringing, its strength and its weakness. "There is a peculiarity," she wrote in her novel *Lodore*, "in the education of a daughter, brought up by a father only, which tends to develop early a thousand of those portions of mind, which are folded up, and often destroyed, under mere feminine tuition." In this novel two girls had been brought up by their fathers: Ethel, the daughter of Lord Lodore who had been separated from his wife, and Fanny Derham, whose mother, like Mary's stepmother, would have been inadequate to the task. The two girls, though Fanny Imlay certainly sat for her portrait in Fanny Derham, perhaps exemplify two parts of Mary's own education.

Ethel, reared in the solitude of the Illinois by a father who had steeped himself in books to compensate for the absence of his equals in culture, was patterned after Milton's Eve. Though trained (as if under Godwin's Spartan

4. Preface to *History of England*. See Paul, *op. cit.*, II, 123.

regime) to be fearless and scornful of pain, she was taught to be in spirit "ductile and dependent" and to surround herself by a barrier of "womanly reserve." Like Mary, she occupied herself with books and music and with drawing, a study which her father deemed especially conducive to happiness. Fanny Derham, on the other hand, had been instructed by her father "in the dead languages, and other sorts of abstruse learning, which seldom make a part of a girl's education. Fanny . . . loves philosophy, and pants after knowledge, and indulges in a thousand Platonic dreams." Mary, too, according to Godwin, was "active of mind. Her desire of knowledge is great." And she was quite ready to share Shelley's Platonic dreams.

So the two girls had been educated by their fathers—both men of superior qualities of mind which united those of Godwin and Shelley, Mary's two teachers—to opposite results. Ethel had been trained to be a yielding, devoted wife, guided by her tender heart, Fanny to be independent and self-sufficing, guided by her understanding. They were alike in their honesty and their sense of duty. They were alike in a certain intellectual similarity to Godwin's daughter and Shelley's wife. Some of Mary's other heroines show the same training. By her adopted father, who used the Godwinian system of praise, Elizabeth Raby was taught "the uses of learning"; Euthanasia was made a scholar by her father, Euphrasia by her guardian.

Mary had planned, in accordance with the request in Godwin's will, to select and edit his manuscripts, knowing, as she wrote Trelawny, that "his passion was posthumous fame," although she dreaded the attacks from the orthodox that might follow. She intended also to carry on the story of his life from the end of his own autobiographical notes. The book was announced as in the press in 1836, but it was never published.[5] In her fragmentary notes for this biography she included an estimate of her father.

Most of the fragments are character sketches of Godwin's friends, with incidental comments on Godwin himself, comments which are often shrewd and revealing. She speaks of James Marshal:

> In a thousand ways he was useful to Godwin, who, sensitive, proud, and shy, whose powers of persuasion lay in the force of his reasoning, often found the more sociable and insinuating manners of his friend of use in transacting matters of business with editors and publishers. . . . Godwin, whose temper was quick, and, from an earnest sense of being in the right, somewhat despotic on occasions, assumed a good deal of superiority and authority.[6]

In writing of Holcroft's treatment of his difficult runaway son, she says:

> . . . it is certain that Holcroft carried further than Godwin a certain unmitigated severity, an exposition of duty and truth, and of the defalcation from these in the offender, conceived in language to humiliate and wound, a want of sympathy with the buoyant spirit of youth. . . . Something of this Godwin detected in himself in his conduct toward Cooper.[7]

She tells of Godwin's domestic and literary habits; she comments on his enthusiasm for political liberty as the source of virtue, adding, however, that "no man was a more strenuous advocate for the slow operation of change, no one more entirely impressed with the feeling that opinions should be in advance of action."[8] She writes fully of

---

5. The reason apparently is unknown.
6. Paul, *op. cit.*, I, 47.
7. *Ibid.*, I, 64.
8. *Ibid.*, I, 76.

his support of the defendants in the political trials of the 1790's.

Even though she recognizes some of Godwin's faults in these passages, she presents him always as a great man. Probably there would have been no different emphasis if she had completed and published the book. But in her fiction the emphasis is reversed. She knew the earlier Godwin largely by hearsay; she knew the later Godwin in person. She was aware that he was no longer the brilliant, influential political philosopher, the idol of young liberals, whose *Political Justice* had seemed to Shelley a revelation of truth which, if only it had been as widely read as the Bible, would have brought in the millennium. She knew his inability to make or to keep money. She knew his vanity and egotism as well as his generosity. She experienced his abrogation of his theories in his disapproval of her union with Shelley, in his refusal to see them or to permit any intercourse between the two households in London, and in his smug satisfaction when the marriage ceremony was finally performed. She was aware of his constant demands on Shelley for funds. She was deeply hurt by his lack of sympathy with her over the loss of her children.

Yet all his life long she gave to him all that a daughter in her financial circumstances could give. She turned over to him the entire profits of *Valperga*. She contributed to his needs out of her meager income. She pulled what strings she could to secure and continue for him his small government post. And her love for him did not falter. In 1822 she wrote to Jane Williams, "Until I met Shelley I [could?] justly say that he was my God—and I remember many childish instances of the [ex]cess of attachment I bore for him." [9] That attachment, she told Mrs. Gisborne

9. From an unpublished letter in Lord Abinger's collection, quoted

in 1834, had always been excessive and romantic.[10] Her sense of the tragedy of his deterioration was proportionately strong and sad.

In her fiction she presented Godwin in his strength and in his weakness through two characters: the father of Mathilda and the father of Lionel Verney.[11] Of both the circumstances are so modified that Godwin probably would not have recognized himself or been recognized by his contemporaries.

Drawing in Mathilda's father what is perhaps an exaggerated picture of the Godwin of 1819, she ascribes the change in him mainly to the death of his wife Diana, whom he had lost as Godwin had lost Mary Wollstonecraft. Yet, interested as always in the effects of education, she finds also in his early training and in his character and habits the seeds of his degeneration. It is here, as well as in the main events of the story, that she substitutes invention for fact. Mathilda's father in his early years was very different from Godwin. He was a man of rank, brought up by a weak, indulgent mother. At Eton and at college he spent money lavishly, gratifying every whim. He cared little for study, concerned only to make others happy—and thereby himself, for he was self-centered and egotistical. The circumstances of this boy were very different from those of the young Godwin, with his Calvinistic upbringing, his education at Hindolveston School and Hoxton College, his thirst for knowledge, his seriousness. But they produced very similar men, each extravagant, generous, vain, dogmatic,

by his kind permission. In an unpublished journal entry for June 7, 1836, she wrote, "I have lost my dear darling Father." Godwin had died on April 7.
   10. *Letters*, II, 88.
   11. For *Mathilda* see Appendix III. Lionel Verney is in *The Last Man*.

and rigid in holding to "the only feelings he could consider orthodox"—however differently they might define orthodoxy.

Marriage to Diana matured the young spendthrift of *Mathilda*. He learned to understand the true ends of life and through her influence "he cast off his old pursuits and gradually formed himself to become one among his fellow men; a distinguished member of society; a Patriot; and an enlightened lover of truth and virtue." Upon his strongly susceptible nature her death had a disastrous effect.

> All outward things seemed to have lost their existence relatively to him. . . . Thus this towering spirit who had excited interest and high expectation in all who knew and could value him, became at once, as it were, extinct. He existed from this moment for himself only. His friends remembered him as a brilliant vision which would never again return to them. The memory of what he had been faded away as years passed; and he who before had been as a part of themselves and of their hopes was now no longer counted among the living.

There is more of Godwin in this tale than the account of a great man ruined by character and circumstance. This is the story of a relationship between father and daughter which, except for its morbid and unnatural basis, has its parallel in the relation between Godwin and Mary. Mary Shelley often used as a theme in her later fiction the love of a daughter for her father: Euthanasia's for the blind Adimari, Clarice's for Lord Evesham, Elizabeth Raby's for her foster father, Ethel's for Lodore—all of them motherless girls. And Fanny Derham, although her mother was alive, found only in her father the intellectual companionship she needed. These relationships, however, were normal and happy; they did not come out of the bitter year of 1818.

The main theme of *Mathilda*, the father's unnatural love for his daughter, reflects the interest which Mary and Shelley were taking in the subject of incest in 1818 and 1819. They both regarded it as a dramatic and effective subject.[12] But Mary may also have been recording, in Mathilda's sorrow over her alienation from her father and her loss of him by death, her grief at a spiritual separation from her own father through what could only seem to her his cruel lack of sympathy. After Clara's death Godwin wrote to her about this "first severe trial of your constancy and the firmness of your temper," adding, "You should, however, recollect that it is only persons of a very ordinary sort, and of a pusilanimous [sic] disposition, that sink long under a calamity of this nature. . . . We seldom indulge long in depression and mourning, except when we think secretly that there is something very refined in it, and that it does us honour."[13] Mary may have needed such Spartan advice, but that need made it no easier to take. Godwin's letter on William's death came after *Mathilda* was finished, but the expostulations for which he claimed the privilege of a father and a philosopher must have seemed only a confirmation of her feeling that she had lost him:

> What is it you want that you have not? You have the husband of your choice, to whom you seem to be unalterably attached, a man of high intellectual attainments, whatever I and some other persons may think of his morality. . . . You have all the goods of fortune, all the means of being

---

12. About a year earlier Shelley had been urging upon Mary a translation of Alfieri's *Myrrha*. In August of 1819 he completed *The Cenci*. During its progress he had talked over with Mary the arrangement of its scenes; he had even suggested at the outset that she write the tragedy. See Mary Shelley's note on *The Cenci* in her edition of Shelley's *Poems*.

13. *Shelley and Mary*, II, 338A.

useful to others, and shining in your own proper sphere. But you have lost a child: and all the rest of the world, all that is beautiful, and all that has a claim upon your kindness, is nothing, because a child of two years old is dead.[14]

He could not even, she might well have thought, remember how old William was! Yet had she not recognized and recorded in the manuscript which she had just finished the truth of his final admonition? "Remember too," he wrote, "though at first your nearest connections may pity you in this state, yet that when they see you fixed in selfishness and ill humour, and regardless of the happiness of every one else, they will finally cease to love you, and scarcely learn to endure you."[15] These words came too close for comfort to her reading of her own character in the picture of the selfish, ill-humoured Mathilda.

Moreover, for some time Godwin had been repeatedly demanding money from Shelley and violently attacking his moral character. In a letter to Mary, Shelley wrote Leigh Hunt, he "called her husband (me) 'a disgraceful and flagrant person' tried to persuade her that I was under great engagements to give him *more* money (after having given him £4,700), and urged her if she ever wished a connection to continue between him and her to force me to get money for him. . . . He heaps on her misery, still misery."[16] No wonder if Mary felt that, like Mathilda, she had truly lost a beloved but cruel father.

On her return to England after Shelley's death Mary's love for her father became tempered by a kind of protective affection that changed somewhat their relationship but only increased her loyal devotion. He turned to her

14. Marshall, *Life of Mary W. Shelley*, I, 255.
15. *Ibid.*, I, 255–256.
16. Shelley, *Letters*, X, 69.

for companionship and for literary as well as financial help. He had been evicted from the Skinner Street house and was living in the Strand. His self-confidence and vanity were still strong in spite of failures and losses. Mary wrote ironically to Leigh Hunt in 1825: "My father's complicated annoyances, brought to their height by the failure of a very promising speculation, and the loss of an impossible-to-be-lost lawsuit, have ended in a bankruptcy—the various acts of which drama are now in progress. That over, nothing will be left him but his pen and me." [17]

It was almost inevitable that this pathetic ruin should form part of the landscape of the novel which Mary was then writing, *The Last Man*, and that Mary's father should become the father of Lionel Verney. Yet many modifications must be made to protect Godwin from recognition. The elder Verncy, prodigally endowed with wit and imagination, the center and leader of a group whose admiration he craved and won, lacked reason and judgment in the management of his affairs. Through his extravagance and lack of self-control he fell into debt, lost his high-placed friends, and betrayed the generosity of the king who had forgiven him in Biblical measure.

> Ashamed to apply again to the king, he turned his back upon London, its false delights and clinging miseries; and with poverty for his sole companion, buried himself in solitude among the hills and lakes of Cumberland. His wit, his bon mots, the record of his personal attractions, fascinating manners, and social talents, were long remembered and repeated from mouth to mouth. Ask where now was this favorite of fashion, this companion of the noble, this excelling beam, which gilt with alien splendour the assemblies of the courtly and the gay—you heard that he was under a cloud, a lost man; not one thought it belonged to him to repay

17. *Letters*, I, 317–318.

pleasure by real services, or that his long reign of brilliant wit deserved a pension on retiring.

In his exile he repined, fell ill, and married his nurse, the daughter of a poor cottager. Not long after the birth of his second child, he died.

Substitute in this narrative the radical intellectual élite for the world of fashion, unprofitable business projects and mistakes about leases for gambling, and a government post for a royal pension; make the man dogmatic and reserved instead of frank and confiding; change the poor cottager's daughter into a buxom widow; read the account of his death figuratively—and you have a not too distorted picture of William Godwin.

Mary's love for her living parent was complemented by her devotion to the memory of her mother. Mary Wollstonecraft, the most famous of the women who bore the name of Godwin, never lived in Skinner Street. She died a few days after Mary was born. Yet her brilliant and charming spirit must have followed her husband and her two little girls. Although Godwin scarcely mentioned her after his second marriage—Mary Jane Godwin offered too sharp a contrast to the first Mary—he could never have lost the memory of "the treasures of her mind, and the virtues of her heart." Her death, he said (even though he philosophically called it "a fatal event, hostile to the moral interest of mankind"), "ravaged from me the light of my steps, and left to me nothing but the consciousness of what I had possessed, and must now possess no more!" [18]

Although Mary never knew her mother, her sense of her heritage and of what she had lost was strong and abiding. She had a vivid realization of her personality. From God-

18. Godwin, *Memoirs of the Author of a Vindication of the Rights of Women*, 2nd ed. (London, 1798), pp. 200, 205.

win, silent and reserved though he was, she must have learned something. Perhaps Fanny retained a few faint memories which she shared with her little sister. In later life Mary found friends who could talk with her about her mother: Mrs. Mason, who in her girlhood had been a pupil of Mary Wollstonecraft in Ireland, and especially Mrs. Gisborne, who with her first husband had known Mary and William Godwin well. She treasured mementoes: a ring, a portrait, locks of her mother's hair, and especially her books. With Shelley and by herself she read and reread her mother's works. She frequently visited her mother's grave in St. Pancras Churchyard, a spot that came to have two-fold association, for it was there that her romance with Shelley began and prospered. At the age of twenty-six she considered the most flattering thing that anyone could say of her a friend's remark that she had grown very like her mother in manner.

In her fiction Mary shows that she was very conscious of the plight and of the emotions of the motherless child. There are many orphans and half-orphans among her heroes and heroines. The characters who most resemble Mary herself, Elizabeth Raby, Ethel Fitzhenry, Mathilda, and Lionel Verney, all lost their mothers early, either by death or by separation. Elizabeth, lonely and unloved, like Mary made daily visits to her mother's grave. Ethel, taken to America by her father at the age of three, kept vague memories of "being kissed and caressed by a beautiful lady," memories such as three-year-old Fanny Imlay might have had; and her longing to be reunited to her mother probably reflects Mary's own sense of loss. Yet Mary Wollstonecraft resembles Mrs. Raby and Lady Lodore not at all. She resembles Mathilda's mother slightly, in her intellect and in the circumstances of her death: Diana had "an understanding that receives the name of masculine for its firmness and strength while in her feelings she was gentle and susceptible"; she died a few days after Mathilda was born. Although Gosse thought Lionel Verney's mother "as like Mary Wollstonecraft as one pea is like another," [19] she had nothing of the brilliance, the passionate nature, and the tendency to melancholy which characterized Mary's mother. Mrs. Verney had, however, known poverty in her childhood; she was sweet and patient in adversity; she died leaving two little orphan children. But she is really only another of Mary Shelley's peasant girls.

In Mary's novels and tales, then, there is no real portrait of Mary Wollstonecraft, perhaps because Mary had no personal, immediate knowledge of her mother. It is only in the notes for her projected biography of her father that we find the conclusions that she drew from her own reading and from talks with her mother's friends and probably with Godwin himself.

> Mary Wollstonecraft was one of those beings who appear once perhaps in a generation, to gild humanity with a ray which no difference of opinion nor chance of circumstances can cloud. Her genius was undeniable. She had been bred in the hard school of adversity, and having experienced the sorrows entailed on the poor and the oppressed, an earnest desire was kindled within her to diminish these sorrows. Her sound understanding, her intrepidity, her sensibility and eager sympathy, stamped all her writings with force and truth, and endowed them with a tender charm that enchants while it enlightens. She was one whom all loved who had ever seen her. Many years are passed since that beating heart has been laid in the cold still grave, but no one who has ever seen her speaks of her without enthusiastic veneration. Did she witness an act of injustice, she boldly came forward

19. Edmund Gosse, *Silhouettes* (London, Heinemann, 1925), p. 234.

to point it out, and induce its reparation. Was there discord among friends or relatives, she stood by the weaker party, and by her earnest appeals and kindliness awoke latent affection and healed all wounds.[20]

Her desertion by Gilbert Imlay, her struggles against despair and poverty, her acquaintance with Godwin, when, as he said, friendship melted into love—on these experiences, seemingly so made for a novelist,[21] Mary merely touches in her notes and otherwise is silent. They could scarcely have been disguised. And they were to Mary so intimate and precious that to use them without disguise would doubtless have seemed like betrayal.

Mary gives scant attention in her novels to Godwin's second wife. Mrs. Baker, the village woman in *Falkner* on whom the care of the orphan Elizabeth devolved, may have treated the child as Mary's stepmother treated her. There is no other resemblance between them. But Mrs. Derham, in *Lodore*, was certainly suggested by Mary Jane Clairmont. Godwin's second wife astutely appealed to his vanity and took advantage of his helplessness when he desperately needed a woman to care for Mary Wollstonecraft's two little girls and all his wooings had ended in refusals. "Is it possible that I behold the immortal Godwin?" she exclaimed from her balcony—and Godwin was caught. Handsome, capable, determined, somewhat vulgar, unintellectual but shrewd, she managed not only the publishing business but also the mixed family with a strong hand and little understanding of its intellectual and psychological needs. As Mary grew up she must often have thought how different the household would have been if her own

---

20. Paul, *op. cit.*, I, 231–232.
21. Mary Wollstonecraft had used many incidents from her own earlier life in her novel *Mary, a Fiction* (London, 1788).

mother had lived. When she needed for her story an unsuitable wife for Francis Derham and mother for his daughter Fanny, she chose a woman cut after the pattern, a little degraded, of her stepmother: "She was illiterate and vulgar—coarse-minded though good-natured." But—perhaps prudently—she did not develop this character.

This ill-matched pair had two daughters, Sarah, who resembled her mother, and Fanny, who was like her scholarly father. The prototype of Fanny Derham is Fanny Imlay, who until almost the time of her suicide believed herself to be Fanny Godwin [22] and gave to her supposed father a strong devotion like that of Fanny Derham for her father. The relation between Fanny Derham and Edward and Ethel Villiers, her sisterly affection, her service to them when they were in debt, is undoubtedly Mary's interpretation of Fanny Imlay's relation to herself and Shelley. It is corroborative evidence that Mary at least saw nothing alarming in Shelley's feeling for Fanny, or in hers for him; she showed no sign of jealousy. In anticipation of her marriage she wrote to Shelley: "Poor dear Fanny if she had lived until this moment she would have been saved for my house would then have been a proper asylum for her." [23] The statement imputed to Godwin that Fanny's suicide was due to hopeless love for Shelley has little support.[24]

Certainly Fanny Derham did not fall in love with Edward Villiers, or he with her. Indeed, "Such a woman as Fanny was more made to be loved by her own sex than by the opposite one. . . . Fanny could not be the rival

[22]. See White, *Shelley*, I, 472, and Paul, *William Godwin*, II, 243–244.
[23]. *Letters*, I, 16.
[24]. See White, *op. cit.*, I, 719.

of women, and, therefore, all her merits were appreciated by them."

Her merits were many; and they were Fanny Imlay's also: an unusual intellect, a thirst for knowledge, benevolence, frankness, fearlessness, common sense, practicality, integrity, independence, and courage, which, however "little in accord with masculine taste," would have made her a worthy daughter of a nobler mother than she had, of a mother like Mary Wollstonecraft. She was probably prettier than the real Fanny. About the latter, although she was considered to have potentialities for beauty, Godwin could only say that she was "by no means handsome, but in general prepossessing." [25] Godwin, however, never flattered his women-folk; Fanny Imlay may, as her sister saw her, have been very like Fanny Derham. When Ethel first met her in America, "She was pale and fair; her light golden hair clustered in short ringlets over her small, well-formed head, leaving unshaded a high forehead, clear as opening day. Her blue eyes were remarkably light and penetrating, with defined and straight brows." What Godwin recognized as Fanny Imlay's disposition to "exercise her own thoughts and follow her own judgment" [26] showed in Fanny Derham's face and manner: "Intelligence, or rather understanding, reigned in every feature; independence of thought, and firmness, spoke in every gesture."

Fanny Derham, however, although she represented in fiction the elder daughter of Mary Wollstonecraft, did not share her inherited tendency to melancholy. In spite of the death of her father and the uncongeniality of her mother and her sister, she was not unhappy or depressed. As long as she could study and be of service to others she was

25. Paul, *op. cit.*, II, 214.
26. *Ibid.*, II, 214.

content. She would never have committed suicide or written the note found by Fanny Imlay's body.

Her material fortune changed, for her proud, hostile grandfather, finding that she was consorting with persons of rank, relented (unlike Sir Timothy Shelley) and settled money on his son's widow and their two daughters. *Lodore* closes with a rather cryptic paragraph on Fanny's subsequent experience, which may be a kind of parable of the fate of Fanny Imlay. "She continued for some time among her beloved friends, innocent and calm as she was beautiful and wise; circumstances at last led her away from them, and she entered upon life." By this phrase with its overtones of the New Testament, this familiar euphemism for death, Mary may be reminding herself of the bottle of laudanum at Swansea. She had shared Shelley's shock at the news of Fanny's suicide and at the revelation of unhappiness in her farewell note:

> Her voice did quiver as we parted,
> Yet knew I not that heart was broken
> From which it came, and I departed
> Heeding not the words then spoken.

It is pleasant to think that the final words of *Lodore* are Mary's tribute to her sister, some compensation though belated for a youthful thoughtlessness that failed to appreciate Fanny's shy unselfishness and to understand her depression. In them it is possible to read either the story of what might have happened to Fanny had she lived to join Shelley and Mary at Marlow, or else a veiled vision of Fanny in Heaven:

> One who feels so deeply for others, and yet is so stern a censor over herself—at once so sensitive and so conscientious—so singleminded and upright, and yet open as day to charity and affection, cannot hope to pass from youth to age

unharmed ... still she cannot be contaminated—she will turn neither to the right nor left, but pursue her way unflinching; and, in her lofty idea of the dignity of her nature, in her love of truth and in her integrity, she will find support and reward in her various fortunes. What the events are, that have already diversified her existence, cannot now be recounted; and it would require the gift of prophecy to foretell the conclusion. In after times these may be told, and the life of Fanny Derham be presented as a useful lesson, at once to teach what goodness and genius can achieve in palliating the woes of life, and to encourage those, who would in any way imitate her, by an example of calumny refuted by patience, errors rectified by charity, and the passions of our nature purified and ennobled by an undeviating observance of those moral laws on which all human excellence is founded—a love of truth in ourselves, and a sincere sympathy with our fellow-creatures.

Had Mary earlier, in *The Last Man*, converted the story of Fanny Imlay to fiction? Was she the original of Evadne, the Greek girl who loved Raymond and whom Adrian loved, as one of Shelley's biographers believes? The evidence is very slight and uncertain—a mere similarity of dates.[27] In Evadne's history there is no analogue to anything we know or surmise about Fanny's death. Even Godwin's purported theory that she died for love of Shelley will

27. See Peck, *Shelley: His Life and Work*, I, 283. His theory (quoted by White, *op. cit.*, I, 473) that Mary "converted Fanny's pathetic story to the use of fiction" in the misfortunes of Evadne Zaimi is hardly tenable. His quotation of a description of Perdita (*The Last Man*, I, 275) as a description of Evadne raises a doubt at once about the thoroughness of his reading of the novel. Nor is it true that, as he says, the date of Fanny's suicide is the same as that on which Evadne was discovered by Raymond near to death: Fanny died on the ninth of October, not on the nineteenth, which was the date of the inquest. And the circumstances are quite different. Evadne was dying from starvation to which, in her despair, she was yielding willingly; Fanny took poison.

not serve: Evadne loved not Adrian (Shelley) but Raymond (Byron). And there is no good reason for identifying Perdita, Raymond's wife, with Mary. This triangle simply will not coincide with any actual situation.

If the story of Perdita and Raymond has any foundation in reality, it is either a "confused echo" of the separation of Byron and his wife, a possibility which will be considered in a later chapter,[28] or a modified account of Claire's affair with Byron. The modifications of Claire's story are, however, very numerous. Perdita married the Byronic Raymond and lived happily with him in retirement for several years. He deserted Perdita only when he discovered Evadne, whom he had previously loved, living in poverty in London. Even then, although his pride made a reconciliation impossible, he still loved her. And her romantic, enduring love for him drove her to suicide after his death. How different were Byron's casual liaison with Claire, his scorn of her passionate love letters, his unwillingness to see her, his indifference to her pleas for a sight of Allegra, and her final bitter, enduring hatred. Neither the Countess Guiccioli nor any of Byron's other loves can play the part of Evadne. Only the mere fact that Raymond and Perdita had a daughter who reminds one of Allegra links the two stories. Although Edmund Gosse thought Perdita "Claire Clairmont to the life," she does not in her maturity resemble Claire, except for her passionate nature and her "powers of intellect"— powers not specifically defined. By them she was enabled to "assist and guide" Raymond in his official duties as Lord Protector of England; but there is no sign of Claire's wit or of her shrewd observation of life, so apparent in her letters. The younger Perdita was more like Claire in her unequal temper, her unsubdued self-will, her moodiness,

28. See Chapter 5. Cf. Gosse, *Silhouettes*, p. 236.

her tendency to day-dreaming. But her day-dreams did not lead her, as did Claire's, into unconventional behavior.

It is more clearly in Beatrice, the strange *ancilla Dei* in *Valperga*, who turned from her religious calling and offered herself to the Byronic Castruccio, that Mary tried to express her ideas of Claire. She had some of Claire's physical features: her dark hair and eyes, her curved lips, her oval face. Like Claire she sang. She was moody and would sit for hours alone and silent. "I am self-willed," she told Euthanasia, "sullen, and humorous." She had an ardent imagination inflamed by the personal beauty and charm of Castruccio. He deserted her and answered her passion by coldness.

The externals of Claire are certainly here. But Beatrice was Claire seen at a distance in which sharp corners were obliterated and only soft romantic contours and rich colors were visible, the distance of fiction and of the historical past. In real life Mary's affection for Claire was strongest when miles separated them; it was her constant presence in the household that roused irritation and jealousy.

> Heigh, ho, the Claire and the Ma
> Find something to fight about every day,

wrote Claire in her journal, at a time when Byron was being particularly unpleasant to his deserted mistress. But the deserted Beatrice is drawn with sympathy and commended without a trace of the author's irritation or jealousy to the kindness and friendship of Euthanasia—"Shelley in female attire." Whatever the truth about the relationship of Shelley and Claire (and it is far from proved that it was anything but affectionate friendship), whatever may have been Mary's secret doubts and suspicions, she put none of them into this novel. She is not personally involved in the triangle of Beatrice, Euthanasia, and Castruccio. In fact, that triangle represents in real life not the rivalry of two women for the love of one man, but the love of Claire for Byron, his coldness to her, his admiration of Shelley, Shelley's affection for Byron followed by clear-sighted disappointment, and his endeavor to plead Claire's cause with her lover.

Claire does not appear in Mary's fiction after *The Last Man* except to furnish a few details about the life of a governess which Mary used in *Falkner*. Miss Jervis, brought up to be a governess, was the "prim personification" of the proper attendant for a young lady. She was unlike Claire both in character and in appearance, except in the plainness of her clothes. Mary probably drew on Claire's experiences for details about the dress, the salary, the duties, and the anomalous position of a governess, neither servant nor member of the family. It is undoubtedly true that "Hurrying for the horse-tram with dark and rather shabby skirts picked up to avoid the mud, Claire cannot have looked very different from a hundred other governess-gentlewomen." [29] But when her pupils returned from excursions or drives, they would never have found her, as Elizabeth did Miss Jervis, "sitting in the same place away from the window (because, when in London, she had been told that it was not proper to look out of a window) . . . employed on needlework, or the study of some language that might hereafter serve to raise her in the class of governesses." Claire's—and Mary well knew it—was no "drab-coloured mind."

The two remaining members of the Skinner Street household, Charles Clairmont and young William Godwin, are not recognizable as individual figures in Mary's fiction, although the younger improvident Charles may have furnished some hints for her various spendthrifts. His cheer-

29. Grylls, *Claire Clairmont*, p. 204.

ful impecuniousness, his colorful schemes—"wild projects in the Clairmont style"—which he wanted Shelley to finance, such as his plan to marry a Swiss girl and turn farmer, even his soberer experiences in Vienna seem made to order for the novelist. But although Mary could be ironic for a sentence or two (the phrase quoted above is hers), she never tried to sustain satire to the extent of a whole portrait. And the real persons whom she introduced into her fiction—even those whom she had reason to dislike—she romanticized. William, the youngest of the family, had caused some uneasiness as a boy, running away from home, having difficulty in school, making many uncertain starts in business and profession. He was only a little boy when Mary left Skinner Street. In 1822 she asked Jane Williams for her unreserved opinion of him: "having hardly ever seen him during the last eight years, my wishes more than my affections are interested in him and I really wish to know the truth about him." [30] They corresponded briefly in 1823 before Mary returned to England. He married and settled down to a career combining draughtsmanship under Rennie, the architect, and literary work. He served as Parliamentary reporter and wrote a novel and occasional articles and stories, all of which appeared after his death. Several were published in the *Court Magazine* and in *Blackwood's*. His only novel, *Transfusion*, is in the vein of Godwin. In the *English Annual* for 1835 appeared a story, "Dr. Zeb and His Planet," which owes much to *Frankenstein*. His father wrote a prefatory memoir for the novel, and Mary edited it as her service and tribute to her half-brother, the youngest of the Godwins of Skinner Street.

30. From an unpublished letter in Lord Abinger's collection, quoted by his kind permission.

CHAPTER

5

Albé and the Pirate

In spite of a little turn for irony, sporadically directed at her characters or her friends or herself, Mary Shelley was a romantic. In her actions, in her enthusiasms, and especially in her choice and treatment of subject and character in her writings, she showed her preference for those exotic and emotional elements that marked the literary movement of her time. As a novelist, therefore, she naturally appropriated to her own use the two men in her circle of friends who best fitted the romantic pattern, Lord Byron and Edward John Trelawny. Although close acquaintance dulled their glamor, she never forgot the exciting charm of these two *giovanni stravaganti* as she first knew them. Individually or fused into one character they appear in her fiction, rebellious, violent, and moody, fascinating to women, tender toward children, communing with thunderstorm and tempestuous ocean, fighting for the cause of liberty. They made admirable heroes for her romantic stories.

Mary greatly admired Byron's *Cain* ("almost a revelation, from its power and beauty" [1]) and *Don Juan* ("the last Cantos . . . want the deep and passionate feeling of the

[1]. *Letters*, I, 150, to Mrs. Gisborne, November 30, 1821.

first—but they are unequalled in their strictures upon *Life* and flashes of wit" [2]). But it was Childe Harold or Lara or Manfred who furnished the model for what Claire called the modifications "of the beastly character of Lord Byron" in her novels. Disillusioned and weary of life they may be, unfaithful and even dissipated; yet they are seldom bitter or cynical, they question the eternal verities for not more than a moment, and they are, unfortunately, rarely witty. Though hating hypocrisy, they never say, with Byronic italics,

> *What*, after *all*, are *all* things—but a *show?*

They take life seriously, like their creator. They have none of the gay insouciance of Juan as he goes from amorous adventure to amorous adventure. Like Harold and Lara and Manfred, although sometimes they have sighed to many, they love but one. Their pride is an elevated, romantic pride, a sense of their own aristocratic superiority, like that of their prototype, whose intimates, even, must always address him by his title. Like him, too, in what Mr. H. J. Massingham calls his spiritual "rebirth," [3] after dissipation and crime they seek and sometimes fill a soldier's grave, for them the best. Like Manfred they reassert their personal integrity and find it not so difficult to die.

The splendid faults of Byron Mary's heroes embraced; and they justified or redeemed them as Byronic heroes should. His petty faults, venial though she thought them, could not be romanticized and they rarely appear—his parsimony, his selfishness, his unscrupulous inquisitiveness, his almost childish petulance and vanity of which she

2. *Ibid.*, I, 290, to Trelawny, March, 1824.
3. *The Friend of Shelley*, p. 85.

spoke to her friends.[4] She saw clearly enough the complexity of his character. The great charm of Thomas Moore's *Life and Letters of Lord Byron* was to her "that the Lord Byron I find there is our Lord Byron—the fascinating—faulty—childish—philosophical being—daring to the world—docile to a private circle—gloomy and yet more gay than any other."[5] She was able, in a letter to John Murray in 1832, to trace with some acumen the development of his personality as it was reflected in his poems.[6] To depict a complex and changing hero in her novels was a harder task. When she attempted it she was never wholly successful: Castruccio is unconvincing and two-dimensional; Raymond, though by no means a paper doll, is too stereotyped really to bring to life "dear, capricious, fascinating Albé."

It was chiefly from the romantic and attractive Byron of 1816, whom she remembered with affection, that she fashioned her heroes. "Can I forget our evening visits to Diodati?" she wrote on hearing of Byron's death, "our excursions on the lake, when he sang the Tyrolese hymn, and his voice was harmonized with winds and waves?"[7] She used him as model for three leading men, Castruccio, Raymond, and Lodore. He appears momentarily and conventionally in other characters, in the dark and moody young Gerard Neville and in his vain and passionate father, in certain aspects of Falkner himself, in the proud and handsome lovers of some of her short tales—"The Heir of Mon-

---

4. *Letters, passim.* See especially I, 208, 265. There are many comments in the unpublished letters to Jane Williams in Lord Abinger's collection. See also Allsop, *Conversations and Recollections of S. T. Coleridge,* I, 224–225.
5. *Letters,* II, 29.
6. *Ibid.,* II, 61.
7. *Journal,* p. 193.

dolfo," "Ferdinando Eboli," "The Invisible Girl," "The Elder Son," "The Pilgrims," "The Brother and Sister," "A Tale of the Passions." The Middle Ages, the Renaissance, and her own tempestuous times made the right settings for him.

Mary's first Byron was the historical figure of Castruccio, Prince of Lucca, the hero of her second novel *Valperga*. In appearance he is the typical hero, beautiful as a god, with soft yet bright eyes. He is marked by the Byronic pride and arrogance, bold in action, careless of danger, ambitious of glory. Yet he is too fond of pleasure, too unstable to be a wise ruler. He is not as admirable as the later Raymond and Lodore. Although he is softened and romanticized from the tyrant of history, in him can be recognized, as the story develops, the Byron who disappointed and alienated Shelley (Euthanasia) and coldly rejected the claims of Claire (Beatrice). For Beatrice, said one reviewer of the novel, "pity is almost pain . . . it is like a relief to have Castruccio to hate for it." [8] In the same spring when this novel was "in a state of great forwardness," Mary was warning Claire that Byron was "a man reckless of the ill he does others, obstinate to desperation in the pursuance of his plans or his revenge," and she and Shelley were hoping not to be forced to take a house near him.[9] Mary herself may have found relief in setting up a Castruccio for her hate.

By the time she was writing *The Last Man*, Byron was dead in Greece; her memory went back to that earlier, dearer Albé whom she had known at Diodati. Verney's first impressions of Raymond, of whom he had heard much

8. *Literary Gazette and Journal of the Belles Lettres*, No. 319, March 1, 1823, pp. 132–133.

9. *Letters*, I, 140–141. For fuller discussion of the relations of Castruccio, Beatrice, and Euthanasia, see Chapter 4.

that was unfavorable, were without doubt like Mary's of Byron.

> I scanned his physiognomy, which varied as he spoke, yet was beautiful in every change. The usual expression of his eyes was soft, though at times he could make them even glare with ferocity; his complexion was colourless; and every trait spoke predominate self-will; his smile was pleasing, though disdain too often curled his lips—lips which to female eyes were the very throne of beauty and love.

Teresa Guiccioli long remembered of Byron "that noble and exquisitely beautiful countenance! that sublime brow! those eyes so infinitely and intensely soft! those nostrils of the Belvedere Apollo! those lips made for tenderness and disdain!" [10] Raymond's voice, continued Verney,

> usually gentle, often startled you by a sharp discordant note, which showed that his usual low tone was rather the work of study than nature. Thus full of contradictions, . . . gentle yet fierce, tender and again neglectful, he by some strange art found easy entrance to the admiration and affection of women; now caressing and now tyrannizing over them according to his mood, but in every change a despot.

Teresa, like many another woman, had assured Byron that she would be everything he wanted her to be.

> Wit, hilarity, and deep observation were mingled in [Raymond's] talk, rendering every sentence that he uttered as a flash of light. He soon conquered my latent distaste. I endeavoured . . . to keep in mind everything I had heard to his disadvantage. But all appeared so ingenuous, and all was so fascinating, that I forgot everything except the pleasure his society afforded me.[11]

So Mary became reconciled to those waywardnesses of Byron "which annoyed me when he was away, through the

10. Austin K. Gray, *Teresa and Her Demon Lover* (N.Y., Scribner's, 1945), pp. 23–24.
11. These quotations are from *The Last Man*, I, 88–89.

delightful and buoyant tone of his conversation and manners."[12]

The intercourse of the group at Windsor—Raymond, Adrian, Lionel Verney, and Perdita—was like that of Byron, Shelley, Mary, and Claire on the shores of Lake Geneva, although the exigencies of plot required a fifth person in the novel, Verney's wife Idris, who seems to have no prototype.[13] Their days were spent with books and music, talk of the past or dreams of the future, excursions to places of beauty or historical interest, discussions of the affairs of nations and the philosophy of life. It was an idyllic time—the summer days and nights of 1816 seen through the mists of years and loss.

After the first antipathy which Raymond and Adrian had felt for each other, based on their opposite views of life, their relationship became very much like that of Byron and Shelley. "Adrian had the superiority in learning and eloquence; but Raymond possessed a quick penetration, and a practical knowledge of life." The man of action "held in supreme contempt the benevolent visions of the philanthropist." He might well have used the words of Maddalo to Julian, "You talk Utopia." Yet he always recognized the goodness and greatness of Adrian's character; like Byron, he respected and depended on his idealistic friend.[14] Adrian could call out the best in him.

12. *Letters,* II, 29.
13. Mr. Ernest S. Lovell, Jr. ("Byron and the Byronic Hero in the Novels of Mary Shelley," *The University of Texas Studies in English,* Vol. XXX, 1951) identifies her as "Shelley in feminine guise." See p. 167. The identification seems very doubtful to me.
14. Hogg quoted a man named Wright, whom he met in Liverpool, as saying that he had seen at Lord Byron's house "a greater man and a greater poet, whom alone of mankind his lordship manifestly and uniformly revered"—that is, Shelley. See *After Shelley,* p. 79. Thorn-

Raymond, like Byron, was proud, and his pride brooked no opposition, no suspicion. Like Byron he dramatized himself, his egotism preventing him from self-knowledge. When, unfaithful to Perdita, he quarrelled with her, he "personated his assumption of innocence even to self-deception. Have not actors wept, as they pourtrayed imagined passion? A more intense feeling of the reality of fiction possessed Raymond. He spoke with pride; he felt injured." How like the Byron who played the injured husband of an unforgiving wife in what has been called the third act of the Separation-drama! Although Mary had heard only Byron's side of the quarrel, she evidently saw through the play-acting of his "Fare Thee Well." Did she later know or guess at the almost Griselda-like patience of Lady Byron and bestow it on Perdita? Probably not. For there is no other evidence that Mary thought of her as anything but cold and implacable; as will be seen, she so portrayed her ten years later in Lady Lodore. Annabella had to wait many more years for her vindication.[15] Yet the separation of Raymond and Perdita may have recalled to the readers of *The Last Man* the ten-year-old scandal, although the character of Perdita could have had no softening effect on the attacks then being made upon Lady Byron over the burning of Byron's Memoirs. But Mary, who had read the Memoirs in Venice—"There was not much in them," she reported to Trelawny—may have learned from them to read more clearly Byron's "domestic pieces."[16]

ton Hunt also spoke of Byron's respect for Shelley. See "Shelley, by One Who Knew Him," *Atlantic Monthly*, February, 1863.
15. For this interpretation of Byron and Lady Byron, see Ethel C. Mayne, *Life and Letters of Anne Isabella, Lady Noel Byron*.
16. Edmund Gosse suggests that here are "confused echoes of the Lady Byron business of which Mary Shelley probably knew little." See *Silhouettes*, p. 236.

Raymond was always a creature of moods, now gaily singing, as did Byron, the Tyrolese song of liberty, now sinking into gloom. He was ambitious, yet he lacked self-control. "Master yourself, Raymond," cried Adrian, "and the world is subject to you." But Raymond replied moodily, "All this would be very good sense, if addressed to another. . . . I cannot rule myself. My passions are my masters; my smallest impulse my tyrant."

Yet he would have rejoiced to make the world subject to him. His first act, he said, if he became king of England would be to "unite with the Greeks, take Constantinople, and subdue all Asia." He compared himself to Napoleon. "I intend to be a warrior, a conqueror," he told Verney; "Napoleon's name shall vail to mine; and enthusiasts, instead of visiting his rocky grave, and exalting the merits of the fallen, shall adore my majesty, and magnify my illustrious achievements." Byron, when he took the name of Noel Byron on the death of his mother-in-law in 1822, was pleased that his initials were the same as those of Napoleon Bonaparte. The Shelleys substituted for the old affectionate nickname of Albé (from the initials of "Lord Byron") that of Nota Bene, ironically suited to the man of ambitious pride. In his poetry Byron had returned again and again to Napoleon, now praising, now condemning. He analyzed his character in terms that he might well have applied to himself and that Mary echoed in describing Raymond:

> There sunk the greatest, nor the worst of men,
> Whose spirit, antithetically mixt,
> One moment of the mightiest, and again
> On little objects with like firmness fixt;
> Extreme in all things! . . .

> Oh, more or less than man—in high or low,
> Battling with nations, flying from the field;
> Now making monarchs' necks thy footstool, now
> More than thy meanest soldier taught to yield;
> An empire thou couldst crush, command, rebuild,
> But govern not thy pettiest passion, nor,
> However deeply in men's spirits skill'd,
> Look through thine own, nor curb the lust of war,
> Nor learn that tempted Fate will leave the loftiest star.[17]

So Raymond's spirit—and Byron's—was "antithetically mixt." In spite of his ambition, his talents, his gift of leadership, he failed. "He was obstinate, but not firm; benevolent in his first movements, harsh and reckless when provoked. Above all, he was remorseless and unyielding in the pursuit of any object of desire, however lawless."

This Raymond was no longer the genial, fascinating master of Diodati; he was the Byron whose insolent and capricious treatment of Claire, of the Hunts, and of herself Mary well knew. He deserted Perdita for the Greek girl Evadne. He fell into dissipation as had Byron in Venice—a decorous, romanticized dissipation, however, marked by indulgence in wine and song, rather than in women. Even in his cups, Raymond's "natural dignity never forsook him"!

Like Byron, he sought and found his escape, his regeneration, and his death in Greece. Some time earlier he had fought in the Greek wars and had become the hero of the people, the subject of their patriotic songs. Now he determined to abdicate as Lord Protector of England and "to return to Greece, to become again a soldier, perhaps a conqueror." In words much like those which Byron used to

---

17. *Childe Harold*, III, 36 ff.

Trelawny, he urged and persuaded Adrian to accompany him.

There Raymond took an active and leading part in the fighting, commanding the Athenian division of the Greek army. In the battle of Makri, although the Greeks won a decisive victory over the Turks, Raymond was taken prisoner. All Greece and England mourned. Verney and Perdita went to Greece, and by bribery and threats they secured his release. He returned to Athens, welcomed by the populace with manifestations of joy like those that greeted Byron at Missolonghi. Though apparently dying from the rigors of his captivity, he recovered to lead the Greeks to victory at Rodosto, to conduct the siege of Constantinople, and, full of melancholy and of forebodings of his own death, to enter the city. There, when the mines laid by the Turks exploded and the city, already laid waste by the plague, fell in fire and ruins,[18] died Raymond, "ornament of England, deliverer of Greece, 'hero of unwritten story.'" His death cancelled out his faults and crowned his life. "To the end of time it will be remembered, that he devoted himself, a willing victim, to the glory of Greece." He was buried just outside the walls of Athens.

Mutatis mutandis this is the story of Byron in Greece. He went with the presentiment that he would not return and the determination not to survive a failure of the Greek cause. He barely escaped capture by the Turks. The two Englishmen had similar parts in the counsels of the Greeks. The exploits of Raymond were the realization of Byron's hopes and plans. Byron died in his bed at Missolonghi without seeing action. A thunderstorm was the requiem for them both. Stanhope's words were as true of one as of

18. Cf. the concluding lines of Byron's *Siege of Corinth*.

the other: "He sacrificed his comfort, fortune, health and life to the cause of an oppressed nation." And although Byron's body was taken to England for burial, Stanhope added, "Had I the disposal of his ashes, I would place them in the Temple of Theseus or in the Parthenon of Athens." [19]

Lord Raymond was Mary's fullest likeness of Lord Byron. Lord Lodore, who, although he dies in the sixteenth chapter, furnishes the title for her fifth novel, is no soldier, no martyr in the cause of liberty. He is rather the self-exile and wanderer, the reformed libertine, the man of the world, the proud aristocrat, tenacious of his honor, dying in its defense in a duel with pistols by moonlight. For him, as for Raymond, for Byron, and for Napoleon, "quiet to quick bosoms is a hell." Mary uses this line from *Childe Harold* in presenting her Byronic hero isolated in the wilds of "the Illinois." Generous and benevolent but reserved and independent, he lived among the Americans for twelve years, wrapped in the usual cloak of mystery. Any one of his neighbors familiar with Byron's poems should have recognized this stranger at once. "Sadness sat on his brow, and dwelt in his eyes, whose dark large orbs were peculiarly expressive of tenderness and melancholy." Often in company his voice would falter, his countenance would show unspeakable wretchedness, and he would seize the first opportunity to be alone.

> He had been seen, believing himself unseen, making passionate gestures, and heard uttering some wild exclamations. . . . He evidently sought loneliness, there to combat unobserved with the fierce enemy that dwelt within his breast. On such occasions, when intruded upon and disturbed, he was irritated to fury. His resentment was expressed in terms

19. Massingham, *The Friend of Shelley*, p. 104.

ill adapted to republican equality—and no one could doubt that in his own country he had filled a high station in society, and been educated in habits of command, so that he involuntarily looked upon himself as of a distinct and superior race to the human beings that each day crossed his path.

In short, this was Conrad or Lara, with more than a dash of the English milord at Pisa or at Venice.

Lodore had been educated at Eton (like Shelley rather than like Byron), where he was both good-natured and proud, desiring "freedom from all trammels, except those . . . imposed upon him by his passions and pride." At school he formed a deep friendship with the Shelley-like Francis Derham. He went to Oxford (again like Shelley), but he left England without taking a degree and wandered through Europe on a kind of Childe Harold pilgrimage. Recalled to England by the death of his father, he remained for only a month, moody, mysteriously abstracted, restless until he set sail again for Europe. "Sometimes he appeared among the English in the capital towns of the continent, and was always welcomed with delight," especially by the women. To them he was attentive and attractive, but he never succumbed to their charms. For, like Harold, at this time "he loved but one," and mystery and obscurity shrouded her as if she were a Thyrza. She is later discovered to be a Polish countess, his mistress for many years, who managed him, contriving "to make his will her own." Perhaps this jealous and unhappy woman is Augusta Leigh, perhaps Teresa Guiccioli, by whom, according to Mary, Byron was "kept in excellent order, quarreled with and hen-pecked to his heart's content." [20]

When he was thirty-two, Lodore returned to England.

[20]. From an unpublished letter to Jane Williams in Lord Abinger's collection, used by his kind permission.

He failed to make a name for himself in politics. But he became the social lion of the day, sought after and considered intensely romantic by the women, yet apparently cured of love and passionless. "Some spoke of a spent volcano—others of a fertile valley ravaged by storms, and turned into a desert." Resolved not to fall in love again, he still vaguely wished to marry, "and to marry one whom his judgment, rather than his love, should select." Perhaps he again felt, like Byron, the need of someone who would govern him and of the security of a "respectable" marriage.[21]

The hum of the human city of London became torture to him; "he suddenly withdrew himself from the haunts of men, and plunging into solitude, tried to renovate his soul by self-communings, and an intercourse with silent but most eloquent Nature." In the mountains of Wales he sought to mingle with the sky, the peak, to experience

> that feeling infinite, so felt
> In solitude, where we are *least* alone.

His retrospections too were in the vein of Harold, with the metaphors slightly scrambled: "Youth wasted; affections sown on sand, barren of return; wealth and station flung as weeds upon the rocks."

> Alas! our young affections run to waste,
> Or water but the desert; whence arise
> But weeds of dark luxuriance, tares of haste.

"As Lodore was neither a poet nor a student, he began at last to tire of loneliness." With this bit of irony Mary pulls her hero out of *Childe Harold* and plunges him into a marriage whose circumstances appear a fusion of Shelley's marriage to Harriet Westbrook and Byron's to Anna-

21. Mayne, *op. cit.*, p. 117.

bella Milbanke. A convenient thunderstorm throws into his arms a young and beautiful girl, who seems to offer everything to revive his jaded appetite and to give him the security and stability he craves. Cornelia Santerre, Lady Lodore, is no "Princess of Parallelograms." She is frivolous, unintellectual, untaught, at least in her youth. But she is arrogant and uncompromising, and she proves something of an iceberg, a view of Lady Byron natural for one who had obtained all her information from Byron himself. The birth of their child serves only to divide them. Lady Lodore is indifferent and cold to the baby, refusing to nurse her, impatient with her crying. Lady Byron was by no means an adoring parent; she used the neuter pronoun in writing to her mother of little Ada: "I talk of it for your satisfaction, not my own, and shall be very glad when you have it under your eye." [22] Lodore, on the other hand, worships Ethel with all the fervor of Byron's love for Ada and Allegra and with more fidelity and sense of responsibility. When he leaves his wife he takes the child with him. Lady Byron had feared that in the event of a separation Byron would kidnap Ada.

The fundamental reason for the failure of their marriage was the interference between them of Cornelia's mother, Lady Santerre. "A worldly woman and an oily flatterer," she had engineered the marriage. Having secured the future of her child and herself, she settled down in Lodore's house. She convinced Cornelia that her mother was her natural friend, her husband her natural enemy. Cornelia, young and inexperienced, distrusted Lodore's attempt to educate her as tyrannical and cruel. "She retreated from his manly guidance, to the pernicious guardianship of Lady Santerre, and she sheltered herself at her side." Mother

22. *Ibid.*, p. 7.

and daughter were leagued to resist any intrusion or any attempt to separate them. Cornelia "felt only with the feelings implanted by her parent."

The detailed elaboration of this situation bears every evidence of correspondence with reality. "Those who have never experienced a situation of this kind," wrote Mary in the novel, "cannot understand it. . . . But the slightest description will bring it home to those who have known it, and groaned beneath a despotism the more intolerable, as it could be less defined." It has been the generally accepted theory that Lady Santerre represents Eliza Westbrook and that the marriage wrecked by the presence of a third person was that of Shelley and Harriet. This is a possible, even a very probable interpretation.[23] But there were persons whom Byron believed to have interfered with his marriage also: Annabella's mother who, he thought, helped her daughter to entrap him; Mrs. Clermont, Annabella's governess, whom he suspected of spying and of having urged the separation. "I heard afterwards," Medwin reports Byron as saying, "that Mrs. Charlment [Medwin's mistake for Clermont] had been the means of poisoning Lady Noel's mind against me;—that she had employed herself and others in watching me in London." [24] If Byron talked thus to Medwin in Venice, he must have talked thus to the Shelleys. Some of the venom of "The Sketch"—

> Thy name . . .
> . . . festering in the infamy of years—

lingered in his system. For Mary, Lady Noel and Mrs. Clermont—"Mama" and "the Mischief-Maker"—may have

[23]. For discussion of the identification of Lady Santerre as Eliza Westbrook, see Chapter 6.
[24]. Thomas Medwin, *Conversations with Lord Byron* (2nd ed., London, Colburn, 1824), pp. 53, 59.

fused with that other mischief-maker, the maternal elder sister of Harriet Westbrook Shelley, to produce Lady Santerre.

The immediate circumstances of the separation are pure invention on Mary's part: Lady Lodore's flirtation with Casimir, Lodore's unacknowledged illegitimate son; Lodore's attack upon the young man; his refusal to explain or apologize or to accept Casimir's challenge; his departure from England with his honor under a cloud. Pure invention, that is, unless she has turned the circumstances about, unless the potential affair between Lodore's wife and his son was meant to be a faintly scandalous echo of the real scandal—the affair between Byron and his half-sister. The consequences at least touch actuality. Lodore's every attempt at reconciliation failed. Stories were circulated, including the rumor that Lodore was mad. Lady Lodore, like Lady Byron, "was looked upon as an injured and deserted wife, whose propriety of conduct was the more admirable from the difficulties with which she was surrounded." But with the final disappearance of Lodore from her life, she casts off the cloak of her prototype; Lady Byron appears no more.

"I shall be anxious," wrote Claire to Mary while *Falkner* was in progress, "to see if the hero of your new novel will be another beautified Byron." The Byronic hero did show his gloomy face again. Falkner was a wanderer over the continent of Europe; he almost died of a fever when fighting for Greece. He was a passionate man with a mysterious past and a haunting sense of guilt. His attempted abduction of the woman he adored had resulted in her death. Like Manfred, he "loved her and destroy'd her." As he contemplated suicide he thought:

If I could feel secure that memory would cease when my brain lies scattered on the earth, I should again feel joy before I die. Yet that is false. While I live, and memory lives, and the knowledge of my crime still creeps through every particle of my frame, I have a hell around me, even to the last pulsation! For ever and for ever I see her, lost and dead at my feet—I the cause—the murderer!

Echoes of *Manfred* sound on the ear—though without any implication that Falkner's beloved Alithea is Augusta Leigh: [25]

Manfred.   Oblivion, self-oblivion!
    Can ye not wring from out the hidden realms
    Ye offer so profusely what I ask?
Spirit.   It is not in our essence, in our skill;
    But—thou may'st die.
Manfred.   Will death bestow it on me?

          *   *   *

Manfred. The innate tortures of that deep despair,
    Which is remorse without the fear of hell,
    But all in all sufficient to itself
    Would make a hell of heaven.

          *   *   *

Manfred. I loved her, and destroy'd her!
Witch.   With thy hand?
Manfred. Not with my hand, but heart, which broke her heart;
    It gazed on mine and wither'd. I have shed
    Blood, but not hers—and yet her blood was shed;
    I saw—and could not stanch it.

Yet Rupert John Falkner owes more to Edward John Trelawny than to Byron. Trelawny's violent, tormented

25. One of Trelawny's loves, however, was named Alithea or Alethea. See *Letters,* I, 300, and Grylls, *Trelawny,* p. 154.

boyhood, as pictured in *The Adventures of a Younger Son*, was Falkner's too. Although Mary must have known of Byron's tempestuous childhood and adolescence, Trelawny's was fresher in her memory, easier to draw upon. Six years before she wrote *Falkner* Mary saw Trelawny's book through the press. The similarities are close. "Punishment and severity of all kinds," wrote Trelawny, "were the only marks of paternal love that fell to my share." Falkner's father was another of Mary's spendthrifts, not a "prudent man" like the elder Trelawny. He was, however, just as cruel to his children. "His voice," said Falkner, "calling my name, made my blood run cold; his epithets of abuse, so frequently applied, filled me with boiling but ineffectual rage." When Falkner, like Trelawny, "would not be controlled," his father too added blows to abuse. Falkner's blood seethed when his plans were blocked; Trelawny "hated all that thwarted" him.

After his father's death, Falkner was brought up by an uncle. Having shown the temper his father had fostered in him, he was sent to school as a punishment. "I was made over to my new tyrants, even in my own hearing, as a little blackguard, quite irreclaimable, and only to be kept in order by brute force." So Trelawny, for stealing apples, was taken by his father to a school with a door like that of a prison and delivered over to the master with the words: "He is savage, incorrigible! Sir, he will come to the gallows, if you do not scourge the devil out of him." The effect on both boys was the same. Trelawny says, "Every kind and gentle feeling of my naturally affectionate disposition seemed subdued by the harsh and savage treatment of my master; and I was sullen, vindictive, or insensible." And Falkner, "I declared war with my whole soul against the world; I became all I had been painted; I was sullen, vindictive, desperate." Trelawny was expelled after two years for flogging an usher, assaulting the master, and setting fire to his bed. The incident which ended Falkner's school days fused this experience of Trelawny's with his stabbing of the captain's clerk on his first ship, and included an echo of his strangling of his father's raven. Falkner flung out of the window the cat brought in by an usher to kill the boy's pet mice. In the struggle that ensued the usher was cut by his own knife and Falkner followed the cat through the window to freedom.

These two boys grew up to be similar men. Falkner "possessed wild and fierce passions, joined to extreme sensibility, beneficence, and generosity," such as Mary had known in Trelawny. In physical appearance they resembled each other. The description of Falkner when he first appeared at Treby may be annotated by phrases from Mary's journals and letters.

> There was something in the stranger that at once arrested attention—a freedom, and a command of manner—self-possession joined to energy. . . . His figure was active, sinewy, and strong . . . ; he was tall, and, to a certain degree, handsome; his dark grey eyes were piercing as an eagle's, and his forehead high and expansive: . . . his mouth rather too large in its proportions, yet grew into beauty as he smiled. . . . His complexion, naturally of an olive tint, had grown red and adust under the influence of climate—and often flushed from the inroads of violent feeling. You could not doubt at the instant of seeing him, that many singular, perhaps tragical, incidents were attached to his history.

So also Trelawny, six feet tall, with his Moorish face, his dark gray expressive eyes, his "air of extreme good nature which pervades his whole countenance, especially when he smiles," telling "strange stories of himself, horrific ones," that Mary found credible when she saw the man.[26] "A strange yet wonderful being," she thought him in 1832, ". . . destroyed by envy and internal dissatisfaction." Although envy was not in Falkner's nature, he was torn by internal dissatisfaction. He sought death in the Greek wars and, like Trelawny in the cave of Ulysses, he almost found it. At last he found tranquillity through confession and the willingness to make restitution, even to pay with his life, though it was not required of him. Like Manfred, having reasserted his integrity and routed the evil spirits that would have claimed his soul, he found ease in the thought of death.

Trelawny had appeared in an earlier novel, *Perkin Warbeck*, as the Spanish mariner, Hernan de Faro, who espoused Richard's cause and whose caravel effected many a rescue. In the service of the King of Portugal he, like Trelawny, had adventured far. "He was a tower of a man; yet withal one, to whom the timid and endangered would recur for refuge, secure of his generosity and dauntless nature." His skin was dark and made even darker by sunburn and exposure. His hair was black, his eyes dark, not gray like Falkner's and Trelawny's; when he smiled his lowering face grew gentle and kind. He was as tender toward his daughter as Trelawny was to his little Zella. Like Trelawny he was eager to see America, of whose romantic beauties he had heard from Columbus's own lips; and his ship at last disappeared over the western horizon.

Some of the strange tales that Trelawny told to the group in Pisa undoubtedly influenced two of Mary's contributions to the Annuals, "Euphrasia" and "The Evil Eye." There is a Zella—name dear to Trelawny as that of his Arab

26. *Journal*, p. 165. Cf. Fanny Kemble's description (Grylls, *op. cit.*, p. 179).

wife and his Greek daughter—in the latter story. Dmitri, the Klepht with the magic in his eye, and his friend Katusthius have something of the wild look of the Trelawny in Kirkup's portrait, turbaned and black-mustachioed, with knives in his belt and a capote on his shoulder.

So Mary romanticized Byron and Trelawny. After all, they were romantic and they wished to be considered so. Byron had frequently wrapped himself in Harold's mantle. Mary was not sure at first how much of Trelawny's extravagance was natural, how much put on—"but it suits him well." Mr. H. J. Massingham says that Trelawny, "however imperfectly and at times absurdly, lived in and for the romantic tradition," whereas Byron was actually a realist and "the romantic face he put upon the world, both in life and letters, was mainly a costume part." [27] But although Mary knew this to be true of Byron, she knew also that he was still capable, long after Juan had supplanted Harold, of a romantic gesture like that of the splendid helmets he provided for himself and his two friends as they set out for Greece. So it was as *giovanni stravaganti* that she could use them both. Her public, she knew, would take them to its heart. The conventions of contemporary popular fiction required the Byronic hero. Mary gave her readers what they wanted down to the last mustachio.

27. Massingham, *op. cit.*, p. 43.

CHAPTER

6

Friends, Foes, and Family

Except for Shelley, the Godwin family, Byron, and Trelawny, Mary used in her fiction very few of her large circle of friends, foes, acquaintances, and relatives. The reasons for her inclusions and omissions are fairly clear. She could show the world her idealized Shelley; she could bring some relief to her feelings in analyzing Godwin and Claire; she could do justice to Fanny Imlay, now dead; she could create her romantic heroes out of Byron and Trelawny. A few of those she regarded as enemies, she pilloried. But her merely faulty living friends, for whom with all their faults she felt affection, she could not romanticize; nor could she hurt them by realistic or satiric portrayal. Therefore, although the individual is sometimes impaled by a pointed sentence or two in her letters, in her fiction there is no false friend like Jane Williams, no exasperating, helpless, prolific family like the Hunts,[1] no bore like Medwin, no stingy and supercilious Hogg. Many of those whom she loved without reservation had no sharp corners, or so few that even if she was thinking of them as

[1]. The Cecils in *Falkner* resemble the Hunts in no way except in the number of their children and the fact that they were travelling— "a roving horde."

she wrote, they must have flattened out into the paper dolls of her conventional minor characters. It is impossible to recognize the Masons, the Novellos, or the Robinsons, Bryan Procter or John Howard Payne. Her "love of analysis" needed something less smooth to work on.

When her genuine tenderness was engaged, she could draw appealing portraits, as she did of the children whom she knew. Frankenstein's little brother had the name and the blue eyes of her own William. "He is very tall of his age, with sweet laughing blue eyes, dark eyelashes, and curling hair. When he smiles, two little dimples appear on each cheek, which are rosy with health." William also resembles Euthanasia's brother. Percy Florence, left in the care of a widowed mother, may have inspired the pathos of small Elizabeth Raby after her father died; Mary's fears for Percy, as well as the actual deaths of William and Clara, made poignant the stories of Alfred, child of Lionel Verney in *The Last Man,* and of Prince Edward in *Perkin Warbeck.* Allegra is certainly the Louisa Biron who appears briefly in *Frankenstein* as one of William's "little wives"; and she is drawn with sympathy and affection as she might have been if she had grown to girlhood, as Clara, daughter of Raymond and Perdita, in *The Last Man.* The illnesses and the deaths of these fictitious children moved Mary to genuine pathos.

Bitterness also trimmed her quill pen and added a touch of vitriol to her ink. The Harriet who had seemed ripe for Shelley's teaching but had soon found the strenuous intellectual discipline irksome is the real object of the scorn which Mary directed against young Lady Lodore, rebellious against her husband's "tyrannical" efforts to train her mind. And as Harriet had clung to Eliza Westbrook, so Lady Lodore turned to her mother, who, like "that terrible and odious Eliza," had settled down with the newly-married couple to direct their lives in ways to her own liking and profit. Cornelia's child, like Harriet's Ianthe, was "nursed by a stranger" on the advice of Lady Santerre, and Cornelia was cold to the baby, irked and impatient when it cried.

Although Cornelia and Lady Santerre may also parallel Lady Byron and Mrs. Clermont,[2] the full detail with which the elder woman is described is more probably due to Shelley's bitter recoil from Eliza than to Byron's contemptuous hatred of Mrs. Clermont. Lady Santerre was of humble birth, daughter of a country solicitor (a step higher than the former tavern-keeper Westbrook), a clever though uneducated woman, vulgarly ambitious and worldly. Lodore found her disagreeable and forbidding in aspect, though with more than the remains of beauty, suggesting both Hogg's "pasty-faced" Eliza and her great-nephew's "handsome, grand old lady." [3]

Mary Shelley's personal dealings with Sir Timothy Shelley after her husband's death intensified the prejudice which she already felt on Shelley's account. "O when I think of the past," she wrote to Claire in 1845, "and my Percy's childish days—so cramped by my poverty, how I hate the Shelleys." [4] The gist of her first efforts to secure a maintenance for herself and Percy Florence is contained in Mr. Oswi Raby's response to Falkner's appeal that he take and care for Elizabeth, his grandchild: "Edwin himself broke the tie. He was rebellious and apostate. . . . He added imprudence to guilt, by . . . marrying a portion-

2. See Chapter 5.
3. White, *Shelley*, I, 134.
4. *Letters*, II, 246.

less, low-born girl.[5] . . . We were applied to by his widow; but with her we could have nothing to do. She was the partner of his rebellion—nay, we looked upon her as its primal cause. I was willing to take charge of my grandchild, if delivered entirely up to me. She did not even think proper to reply to the letter making this concession." Mary, like Mrs. Raby, had indignantly repudiated such a proposal from Sir Timothy; but she lived, as Mrs. Raby did not, to see some relaxation in the sternness of her father-in-law and to receive limited help in her child's education. It was only after Mr. Raby had become senile that relations were restored between Elizabeth and her family through her aunt, whose actions may have been suggested by the friendliness of Shelley's sister Hellen after their father's death. Although Mr. Raby did not have the tall stature of Sir Timothy or his piercing blue eyes—he was "a diminutive and very white old gentleman" with dim, pale blue eyes—he had the obstinacy and narrow-mindedness which both Shelley and Mary found in Sir Timothy. Indeed, "Oswi Raby looked shrivelled, not so much by age as the narrowness of his mind; to whose dimensions his outward figure had contracted itself." He shared also old Sir Bysshe Shelley's pride in family. Something of the proud violence of Sir Bysshe or the stubborn intolerance of Sir Timothy went into the making of other parents in Mary's stories: the elder Neville, the fathers of Ludovico in "The Heir of Mondolfo" and of Henry in "The Invisible Girl," and perhaps the Countess of Windsor in *The Last Man,* whose unwillingness to accept the marriage of Idris and Verney suggests the attitudes of both Sir Timothy and Godwin.

Another experience in the lives of Shelley and Mary

5. She reminds the reader of both Harriet and Mary.

with a bitter aftertaste was the well-known Emilia Viviani episode, which she used twice.[6] Yet Mary had loved and admired Emilia, and there is remarkably little bitterness in her use of the story. In "The Bride of Modern Italy" there is rather an ironic insistence that Emilia (with her fickle emotions, her tendency to be in love with love, her plans to escape from the convent and an unwanted marriage) was nothing to fear. By emphasizing the youth of Alleyn and the opportunism of Clorinda (any lover will do provided he takes her away) and by keeping the story on the lightest of levels, Mary flicks the back of her hand at the whole incident. Alleyn, holding the wax impression of the key to the convent and hearing again Clorinda's plea that he would take her to England, ruefully recognized that he was being used. "Fear not," were her last words; "my disguise is ready—all will go well." " 'The devil it will!' thought Alleyn . . . carefully placing the waxen impression he had received against a sunny wall—'and the devil take me if I ever go within those walls again! I have sown a pretty crop, but I am not mad enough to reap it.' " There is something akin to bravado in the close correspondence between the real and the fictitious in this tale. Here, Mary seems to say, is the whole story for anyone to read; see how shallow and unimportant were the emotions involved.

Having just reread her journal in preparation for the *Posthumous Poems*, she had the details of Shelley's "Italian Platonics" at the point of her pen and could easily transfer circumstances and character from Emilia to Clorinda.

The general situation of Clorinda Saviani was that of Emilia Viviani. Their ages were the same; they had both

6. For a discussion of the pictures of Shelley in "The Bride of Modern Italy" and in *Lodore*, see Chapter 3.

been immured in a convent for five years [7] watched over by a Sister named Eusta; they were both expecting the same fate, marriage with men whom they had never seen. To each of them was introduced a young Englishman, whose interest and compassion and love were soon aroused and whose aid in escaping the convent was sought. The real Conservatorio di Santa Anna in Pisa and the imaginary Convent of St. S—— in Rome are similar in general character—the high walls, the desolate and limited garden, the bare rooms, "the bitter cold, which was unalleviated by anything except fire-pots" in Rome, while the poor Pisan pensionnaires were "allowed nothing to warm them but a few ashes, which they carry about in an earthen vase." [8] But other convents, especially that at Bagnacavallo where Allegra died, may have contributed to the picture of St. S——.

In character Clorinda is a more frivolous, empty-headed Emilia. Her Catholic upbringing and convent life were the reasons "why with a tender heart and much native talent, there was neither constancy in Clorinda's love nor dignity in her conduct." The two girls were equally handsome, however, equally talented, and equally—to use Medwin's words—"made for love." Clorinda, whose "fine features expressed the *bisogna d'amare* which ruled her heart," might well have written Emilia's prose rhapsody, "Il Vero Amore": "*Oh amore! Io non sono che amore. Io non posso esistere senza amare.*" They were equally fickle and marked their changes of heart in the same way, as their women friends bear witness. "Teresa smiled: 'I remember,'

7. So Shelley and Mary thought about Emilia. Actually she had been there only three years. See Enrica Viviani, *Vita di una donna*, p. 62 and note 2.
8. Thomas Medwin, *Revised Life of Shelley* (ed. by Forman, Oxford, 1913), p. 278.

she said, 'that at Christmas you fulfilled such a vow to San Francesco,—was not that for the sake of Cieco Magni? for you change your saint as your lover changes name;—tell me, sweet Clorinda, how many saints have benefited by your piety?'" And Claire Clairmont recorded in her journal for July 23, 1821: "Emilia says that she prays always to a Saint, and every time she changes her lover, she changes her Saint, adopting the one of her lover." [9] Finally they wrote the same letters, Clorinda's being mere translations of Emilia's rhapsodic laments and appeals.

The bride of modern Italy is more frivolous and empty-headed not only than Emilia herself but also, and in even greater degree, than the Clorinda of Mary's novel, *Lodore*. This later Clorinda, while owing much to Emilia, takes on a life of her own. As the plot of the novel is richer and more complex than that of the short tale, so is the characterization. The events of the earlier part of the episode are similarly close to the facts: Horatio Saville's introduction to Clorinda, daughter of the Principe Villamarina, "a Neapolitan nobleman of the highest rank"; his visits to her in the convent where she was shut up (like Emilia) by a jealous mother; her appeal for sympathy and help. But this Clorinda was not fickle and shallow. She fell deeply and passionately in love with her potential rescuer, something which could not be said of Clorinda Saviani or even of Emilia.[10] She had the power to win Saville to pity, admiration, and tenderness which, coupled with a desire to rescue her and make her happy, were strong enough to lead him into marriage. She was "full of genius and sensibility, a creature of fire and power," "eloquent and beautiful, and full of enthusiasm and feeling." As

9. Grylls, *Claire Clairmont*, p. 128.
10. See White, *Shelley*, II, 256.

Shelley's conception of Emilia's talents had augmented every day, so Saville's admiration of Clorinda's "talents, her imagination, her ardent comprehensive mind, increased on every interview. They talked of literature—the poets —the arts; Clorinda sang to him, and her fine voice, cultivated by the nicest art, was a source of deep pleasure and pain to her suitor." Thus she was endowed not only with Emilia's talents and temperament, somewhat heightened, but also with Claire Clairmont's voice. Mary's words are a sober, flat version of Shelley's lines in "To Constantia Singing":

> My brain is wild, my breath comes quick—
> The blood is listening in my frame,
> And thronging shadows, fast and thick,
> Fall on my overflowing eyes;
> My heart is quivering like a flame;
> As morning dew, that in the sunbeam dies,
> I am dissolved in these consuming ecstasies.

The intensity and the singleness of Clorinda's love for Saville, joined to the romantic richness of her personality and her unfortunate situation, serve for Mary to justify Shelley's long-past attraction to Emilia. Mary will not deny it nor make light of it; in this novel she will even heighten it. But she will not allow it to be love. Shelley-Saville must be freed to return to his one true love, freed by something more dramatic than disillusionment and more complimentary to his own judgment. After their marriage Clorinda is revealed as passionately jealous, almost to the point of madness. She can not bear any reminder of Lady Lodore, whom she knows that Saville still loves. It is a reference to her that brings on the paroxysm which results in Clorinda's death.

The fact that Mary used the Emilia Viviani episode

twice in fiction, once playing it down and once playing it up, indicates that it had burnt more deeply into her emotions than her ironic dismissal of it in her letters would suggest.[11] Yet neither Clorinda is drawn in bitterness. Nor is either probably Mary's real estimate of Emilia. Each is fitted to the circumstances of the plot, to the stand-in for Shelley who plays opposite to her, and to the mood in which Mary wrote. In *Lodore* Mary needed the marriage for her plot. She needed a Clorinda who could attract and, in spite of her faults, could hold at least by the bonds of loyalty a mature man with much of Shelley's nature. The earlier Clorinda had only to fascinate for a moment a boy of seventeen. In 1824 Mary was nearer to the difficult year in Pisa, more intensely conscious of what she must have felt as a loss of weeks of companionship so near to the time of her final loss. Eight years later, when she was writing *Lodore*, she was living over again in the story of Villiers and Ethel her own early happiness with Shelley. She could view the Pisan Platonics with more detachment, could be more generous to her memory of Emilia Viviani.

11. E. g., *Letters*, I, 160–161: "Emilia married Biondi—we hear that she leads him & his mother (to use a vulgarism) *a devil of a life*— The conclusion of our friendship *a la Italiana* puts me in mind of a nursery rhyme which runs thus—

>As I was going down Cranbourne lane,
>Cranbourne lane was dirty,
>And there I met a pretty maid,
>Who dropt to me a curtsey;
>I gave her cakes, I gave her wine,
>I gave her sugar candy,
>But oh! the little naughty girl!
>She asked me for some brandy.

Now turn Cranbourne lane into Pisan acquaintances, . . . & brandy into that wherewithal to buy brandy (& that no small sum *però*) & you have the whole story of Shelley's Italian platonics."

Shelley was introduced to Emilia by Professor Francesco Pacchiani, Alleyn to his Clorinda by her lover, Saville to his by an Englishwoman. Although Pacchiani played no part in the fictional versions of the Emilia story, he had already appeared, drawn, said Medwin, "to the life," [12] as Benedetto Pepe in *Valperga*. Pepe might, in fact, have sat for the portrait of Pacchiani reproduced in Enrica Viviani della Robbia's *Vita di una donna* and for her verbal picture of him.[13] Pepe, like Pacchiani, had a thin, dry, wrinkled face; black, sparkling eyes; lips which were like a line in his face, uncurved and unmarked save by deep creases at the corners; eyebrows "elevated as in vanity"; a high flat forehead that denoted understanding. He was a vivacious and energetic speaker, with a gift of wit and eloquence like that which made Shelley think that Pacchiani might equal Coleridge as a conversationalist.[14] This Pepe, regarded by Castruccio as half buffoon, half madman, is Pacchiani as Mary saw him after some of the enthusiasm of their first meeting had worn off. She had early described him to Marianne Hunt as "really the only Italian who has a heart and soul. He is very high spirited, has a profound mind and an eloquence which enraptures." [15] As their acquaintance grew, the original eccentric showed himself rather as the "inquisitive and indelicate" buffoon.[16]

One other member of the Pisan circle, Prince Mavrocordato, appears momentarily in *Valperga*. Young and handsome, he came every morning to give Mary lessons in the Greek language and stayed to talk about freedom for the Greek people. So Euthanasia learned to love liberty

12. Thomas Medwin, *Life of Shelley* (London, 1847), II, 60.
13. *Vita di una donna*, pp. 44, 45.
14. White, *Shelley*, II, 242.
15. *Letters*, I, 117.
16. White, *op. cit.*, II, 243.

from a young and comely Greek. Nameless and shadowy, he owes nothing but his existence to his prototype; he is like some other vague reflections of reality in Mary's fiction. Tita, Byron's bearded servant, may have given Mary a few hints for the bandits in "The Evil Eye." Hogg or Peacock may have been in her mind when she created Frankenstein's friend Clerval. But these identifications are more than doubtful; and we look in vain for the rest of her friends and associates, with one possible exception.

One of Mary's closest friends from the time the Shelleys met her in Leghorn in 1818 was Maria Gisborne, the charming and clever wife of a rather dull husband. Her earlier acquaintance with Godwin and Mary Wollstonecraft and the fact that she might, had she so chosen, have been Mary's stepmother made her at once an object of interest. With only one rift, their friendship endured until Mrs. Gisborne's death in 1836.[17] Mary wrote her long and numerous letters, filled with warm affection; she made her the confidante of her joys and her sorrows. In her notes for the biography of Godwin, she included an interesting account of the earlier life of her friend, ending with her refusal of Godwin's proposal of marriage after the death of her first husband.

Maria's girlhood experiences in the Near East, where, having been virtually kidnapped from her mother, she was brought up by her father, may have given Mary some suggestions for the stories of the kidnapped Ethel in *Lodore* and of Elizabeth in *Falkner*. "Many accomplishments were taught her," she wrote of young Maria, "and on one of the

---

17. Mary's last letter to her, on the occasion of Mr. Gisborne's death, is dated March 4th, 1836. Miss Grylls (*Mary Shelley*, p. 231) mistakenly says that they both died in 1835, Mrs. Gisborne first.

first side-saddles which appeared in the East, she accompanied her father in his rides in the environs of Constantinople." So Ethel rode with Lodore in the Illinois and Elizabeth with Falkner at Constantinople and at Baden. All three girls combined childlike and womanly traits, and Elizabeth and Maria "entered into the society of European merchants and diplomatists." All three (until Miss Jervis took charge of Elizabeth) had "no proper chaperon." But Mary could not allow either of her heroines, destined as they were to appeal to well-brought-up ladies of the 1830's, "to run wild as she might" like Maria. Although Ethel's innocence was threatened by her drawing master (Maria also showed artistic talent), neither she nor Elizabeth could be said "at a very early age" to have "gone through the romance of life." Yet Maria and Ethel (and Mary herself) married young and happily though they suffered poverty, strict economy, and self-denial.

Of the young Mrs. Reveley, Mary draws a charming picture: "She was very young and very beautiful, and possessed a peculiar charm of character in her deep sensibility, and an ingenuous modesty that knew no guile: this was added to ardour in the pursuit of knowledge, a liberal and unquenchable curiosity." To Godwin at that time she appeared "a favorite pupil, a charming friend, a woman whose conversation and society were fascinating and delightful." [18] But this promising young woman does not grow in Mary's fiction into any recognizable portrait of the undeniably attractive mature Mrs. Gisborne whom Mary knew well and loved sincerely. Mary did not even attempt her character in her notes or in her letters and journals.

* * *

18. Paul, *William Godwin*, I, 81–83.

These, then—from Shelley to Maria Gisborne, poets, adventurers, philosophers, eccentrics, companions, loved and hated, respected and despised—these were the members of Mary Shelley's circle as Mary Shelley saw them. Perhaps they were not the real people: perhaps she looked through rose-colored or yellow, jaundiced spectacles, not through the clear, undistorting glass of dispassionate, disinterested observation. Yet, that point granted, her view of the great and the small who surrounded her is the view of a woman who, though much smaller than the giants who were her husband, her parents, and some of her friends, yet knew the giants well. Of certain of Bryan Procter's comments on Byron she said that they "made me smile, knowing what is behind the curtain as well as I do." Sometimes she lifts a corner of the curtain and throws a little new light on her companions or introduces us to a person whom we might not otherwise have met. At the very least, her novels and tales are *romans à clef* which furnish the fun of identity-spotting. At best they present characters that take on something of the actuality of the real persons who were their models. They use plots and episodes whose firm basis in real events compensates for the decline of invention in her later works and makes them not wholly unworthy of the familiar ascription: "By the Author of *Frankenstein*."

CHAPTER

7

The Author: Eager Aspirant

"In our family," said Claire, "if you cannot write an epic poem or novel, that by its originality knocks all other novels on the head, you are a despicable creature, not worth acknowledging." It was indeed a writing family: Mary Wollstonecraft, Godwin, Mary, Claire, young William all had the itch; only the second Mrs. Godwin and her elder son were without it. It is not surprising that Mary, brought up in such an atmosphere and marrying into a circle of poets, became an author.

When things were going well and her imagination was active, Mary enjoyed writing. She also enjoyed it when she could use it as a vehicle for her own emotions. She thought of herself then as an author, linked by her art to human experience. In Lionel Verney's romantic attitude toward his writing she has expressed her own:

> As my authorship increased, I acquired new sympathies and pleasures. I found another and a valuable link to enchain me to my fellow-creatures; my point of sight was extended, and the inclinations and capacities of all human beings became deeply interesting to me. Kings have been called the fathers of their people. Suddenly I became as it were the father of all mankind. Posterity became my heirs.

My thoughts were gems to enrich the treasure house of man's intellectual possessions; each sentiment was a precious gift I bestowed on them. Let not these aspirations be attributed to vanity. They were not expressed in words, nor even reduced to form in my own mind; but they filled my soul, exalting my thoughts, raising a glow of enthusiasm, and led me out of the obscure path in which I before walked, into the bright moon-enlightened highway of mankind, making me, citizen of the world, a candidate for immortal honors, an eager aspirant to the praise and sympathy of my fellow men.

Mary's theories of the function of the writer fitted admirably into the didactic tendencies of much of the minor fiction of her day. Even in *Frankenstein* she was concerned to avoid "the enervating effects of the novels of the present day" and to exhibit "the amiableness of domestic affection, and the excellence of universal virtue." In her own deep sorrow she would be "happy if anything I ever produce may exalt and soften sorrow." An author should, she believed, "teach always that adversity and prosperity are both lessons in wisdom." These lessons are explicit in her short stories and in her later novels, especially *Lodore* and *Falkner*; in her earlier and better work they are only implicit.

The long history of Mary's authorship begins early. In the 1831 preface to *Frankenstein* she tells of her earliest compositions, some of them written down "in a most commonplace style," some of them—"my true compositions" —apparently spun in her imagination only. "I did not make myself the heroine of my tales. Life appeared to me too common-place an affair as regarded myself. I could not figure to myself that romantic woes or wonderful events would ever be my lot; but I was not confined to my own identity, and I could people the hours with creations far more interesting to me at that age than my own sensations."

What she did write down of these products of a lonely child's day-dreams she took with her in her box when she eloped with Shelley. In Paris she looked them over and promised Shelley that he might read and study them. "I shall claim this promise," he vowed, "at Uri."[1] But there is no record of his reading them, nor any sign that they have survived. Nor is there any sign of her story "Hate" (a strange subject to attract her on her "honeymoon") begun at Marsluys, giving Shelley "the greater pleasure," and apparently abandoned at once, or of the life of Louvet which she embarked on after they had returned to London.

Her first appearance between boards was in a little book compiled out of her and Shelley's journal of their experiences on the continent when they ran away from Skinner Street, two of Shelley's letters from Geneva to Peacock and two of her own, unaddressed and perhaps written for the book, and Shelley's "Mont Blanc." The thin volume was issued anonymously in 1817 with the title, *History of a Six Weeks' Tour through a Part of France, Switzerland, Germany, and Holland: with Letters Descriptive of a Sail round the Lake of Geneva, and of the Glaciers of Chamouni*—a cumbersome title which does not match the simplicity and charm of most of the contents. Mary reprinted it in her edition of Shelley's prose in 1840. Shelley spoke of it to Thomas Moore as "our book." It made a pleasant little stir in the literary world, especially among their friends.

Mary had appeared in print earlier in the same year when Hunt included in a footnote to the leading article in the *Examiner* for October 5 a paragraph on Cobbett from her letter to Shelley of the week before. "I must say," she wrote on the seventh, "that the paragraph from my

1. *Journal*, p. 5 and note 3. This box was evidently left in Paris and never recovered. See *Letters*, II, 264.

letter which Hunt has done me the honour to quote—cuts a very foolish figure—it is so femininely expressed that all men of letters will on reading it acquit me of having a *masculine* understanding. If Hunt had told me he meant to put anything of mine in I think I could have worded it with more print-worthy dignity." [2]

What she had written the year before was hailed on publication by many of the reviewers as the work not merely of a masculine understanding but of a man. *Frankenstein, or the Modern Prometheus*, published in March, 1818, was so considered by the *Quarterly*, the *Edinburgh*, and *Blackwood's*. Even in 1824 *Knight's Quarterly Magazine*, comparing it with *Valperga*, speculates that the difference between the two novels shows that the earlier one may have been by Shelley.

Novels of "the marvellous and the terrible" had, of course, been written in the past by women: Mrs. Radcliffe and Charlotte Dacre were familiar names to readers like Jane Austen's Catherine Morland. But Shelley and Monk Lewis and Godwin probably had a greater share in the inception of *Frankenstein* than any of Mary's feminine predecessors. Godwin's *St. Leon* both followed and set a fashion; the elements of the Gothic novel persisted and were blended with revolutionary doctrines. Shelley had experimented with the supernatural as a boy and had written *Zastrozzi* and *St. Irvyne* under the influence of Charlotte Dacre's *Zofloya*, Lewis's *The Monk* and *The Bravo of Venice*, and *St. Leon* itself. Later he and Claire Clairmont sat up all night experiencing "the horrors," scaring each

---

2. *Letters*, I, 41. The paragraph is printed as it stood in the letter to Shelley (*ibid.*, I, 37). Hunt had said that it was by "a lady of what is called a masculine understanding, that is to say, of great natural abilities not obstructed by a *bad* education."

other with looks of mysterious sadness and talk of ghosts and of pillows and chimney-boards that moved about with no human aid. Peacock laughed at them, and Mary remarked drily in her journal, "I go to bed soon; but Shelley and Jane sit up, and, for a wonder, do not frighten themselves." [3] Yet she too listened eagerly to the German ghost stories read and the tales told by Monk Lewis and the Chevalier de Mengaldo at Diodati. There Shelley had his vision of the woman with eyes in her breasts. There the whole company began to write their "ghost stories": Byron, *The Vampyre*, Shelley, one based on his own life, Claire, one that is nameless, and Mary, after many days without inspiration, her *Frankenstein*.

Frankenstein was an immediate sensation. Peacock wrote to Shelley in August, "I went to the Egham races. I met on the course a great number of my old acquaintance, by the reading portion of whom I was asked a multitude of questions concerning 'Frankenstein' and its author. It seems to be universally known and read." [4]

The book was reviewed with considerable enthusiasm, tempered by some fear of its impiety and some shudders at the general theme. The *Quarterly* called it a tissue of horrible and disgusting absurdity but admitted that there was something "highly terrific" and tremendous in the language. *Blackwood's* gave it first place in the March issue with an eight-page article. Except for a doubt, admitted to be perhaps captious, about the improbability of the Monster's self-education and about his ability to elude capture and even detection, the review is highly favorable. It praises the author ("said to be . . . Mr. Percy Bysshe Shelley, who, if we are rightly informed, is son-in-law of

3. *Journal*, pp. 18–19, 21.
4. *Shelley and Mary*, II, 327.

Mr. Godwin") for vigor, clarity, plainness, and force of expression and for the truth, freshness, precision, and beauty of the descriptions of nature. "Upon the whole," it concludes, "the work impresses us with a high idea of the author's original genius and happy power of expression. We shall be delighted to hear that he has aspired to the *paullo majora;* and in the meantime congratulate our readers upon a novel which excites new reflections and untried sources of emotion." Its "uncommon powers of poetic imagination" were able to shake the nerves of the reviewer.

Other sensations dulled the excitement over *Frankenstein* until, five years later, Richard Brinsley Peake realized that it could shake the nerves of theater-goers as well as of reviewers. A dramatic version entitled *Presumption, or the Fate of Frankenstein* was produced at the English Opera House on July 28, 1823, with Wallack playing the title role and T. P. Cooke stealing the show as the Monster. Mary had news of it in Paris from Horace Smith, who told her that they "vivified the monster in such a manner as caused the ladies to faint away & a hubbub to ensue—however they diminished the horrors in the sequel, & it is having a run." [5] The news about the ladies proved an invention. But when she reached London in September, *Presumption* was still playing. The story, she thought, was not well managed, but Wallack was satisfactory and Cooke played the Monster's part with skill and imagination. "I was much amused, and it appeared to excite a breathless eagerness in the audience." [6]

So popular was it that in the same autumn two other romantic adaptations and three burlesques were produced at as many theaters in London. Peake's and Milner's ver-

5. *Letters,* I, 251.
6. *Ibid.,* I, 259.

sions were revived year after year, sometimes with changes; between 1826 and 1933 five new serious dramas were produced, two of them in Paris. There were six burlesques in all, one of them French. And the series of moving pictures with Boris Karloff and his successors "looking ghastly" as the Monster seems destined never to end.[7]

On the strength of the success of *Presumption*, a new edition of *Frankenstein* was published in 1823. It was included in Bentley's "Standard Novels" in 1831, with a new preface explaining the circumstances of its composition. Other editions have followed, some of them attracting the pencils of famous illustrators. It has been translated into several modern languages. It was imitated in English and in French.[8] Although most of those who know the name of Frankenstein through the cinema or through the numerous allusions of journalists and statesmen to Frankenstein monsters have never read the book, it has never died.

The reasons for its long life must be sought in the book itself. The twentieth century is inclined to turn it off with a glance at the screen, a shiver, and a shrug. But anyone who takes the trouble to return to the book is soon caught by its power. It is, to be sure, an amazing achievement for a girl of nineteen. But it is far more than that. It is no immature spinning of a "ghost story." The structure of the plot is remarkable in its symmetrical intricacy. The characters, showing sharp contrasts with each other and in themselves, are convincing in their combination of strangeness and reality. The descriptions of natural scenery have a power not greatly inferior to that of the poets who were

7. See Appendix IV. Even Abbott and Costello have met Frankenstein and his Monster!
8. See Chapter 2, note 14.

Mary's contemporaries. The novel is interesting too, as has already been pointed out, for its reflection of contemporary thought in the fields of science and education, and most of all for its understanding of the tragedy of the creature who is "born with a different face," who can find no secure place in society.[9]

Frankenstein, although the best known and the best, is by no means the only novel by Mary Shelley. Except for the two years immediately following Shelley's death, she always had a novel or a novelette in preparation from the time of the inception of *Frankenstein* in 1816 to that of the publication of *Falkner* in 1837. Her name did not appear on the title pages of the first editions: each novel was "by the Author of *Frankenstein*." This fact was due to Sir Timothy's injunction that the name of Shelley was not to be brought before the public, but it was effective advertising. Frankenstein's Monster carried on his powerful and ungainly shoulders five very different beings.

The first of them was the fourteenth-century Florentine tyrant, Castruccio, Prince of Lucca, who furnishes the subtitle for the novel *Valperga*. The work was one of long gestation and of slow and difficult birth. Mary conceived the idea of it at Marlow in 1817, read and studied for it in Naples in 1818, and began it in 1820 in a period of contentment and peace of mind. Her wish expressed in the last entry in her journal for 1819 had been fulfilled: the new year had proved to be happier than "the last unhappy one," when her two children had died. Percy Florence had been born and was, except for the usual ailments of children, a healthy baby. Her normal relations with Shelley had been restored. Writing in her journal in the autumn of 1827, she said, "*Quanto bene mi rammento sette anni*

[9]. See Chapters 1 and 9.

fa, in questa medesima stagione i pensieri, i sentimenti del mio cuore! Allora cominciai Valperga. Allora sola col mio Bene fui felice." [10] She worked over it for about two years, with Shelley constantly urging her on. It was completed in the spring of 1822. They endeavored to make arrangements with Ollier, Shelley's bookseller, for its publication. But he delayed so long in answering and was so unwilling to make any advance payment, that Mary refused his offer. Meanwhile Godwin's debts became so pressing that early in 1822 Mary sent *Valperga* to him to dispose of for his own benefit. But he postponed offering it to any bookseller, fearing that his distressed state might cheapen it.

Finally in November he wrote, "I have a plan upon the house of Longman respecting 'Castruccio'; but that depends upon coincidences, and I must have patience." With praise for the characters of Euthanasia and Beatrice and for some "parts of high genius," he told Mary that it was far too long. On February 14, 1823, he reported that the novel was now fully printed by Whittaker and ready for publication. "I have taken great liberties with it," he continued, "and I fear your *amour propre* will be proportionately shocked." [11] Although she was eager to see it, even with its curtailments, the glow of its composition was a little dulled by the long delays—so long that Shelley was not there to see it too. "After all," she said to Hunt, "Valperga is merely a book of promise, another landing place in the staircase I am climbing." It "never had fair play," she wrote Ollier in 1839, suggesting that it be offered to Bentley for his Standard Novels, "never being properly published." [12]

10. *Journal*, p. 199.
11. *Shelley and Mary*, III, 904B–904C; IV, 915.
12. *Letters*, I, 243; II, 144.

It deserved fair play, her friends thought. Much work had gone into it—it was "raked out of fifty old books," Shelley told Peacock. Yet he considered it "wholly original," "a living and moving picture of an age almost forgotten. The author visited in person the scenery which she describes; and one or two of the inferior characters are drawn from her own observation of the Italians." [13] The periodicals in general praised the book, inevitably comparing it with *Frankenstein*. *Blackwood's* again gave Mary ten pages of favorable publicity; the *Literary Chronicle*, which had been highly critical of Shelley's morals, of the *Liberal*, and of Mary's "Tale of the Passions," expressed ardent admiration and prophesied long life for *Valperga*. There was general agreement that Euthanasia and Beatrice outshone the nominal hero of the book.

In her next novel Mary turned from history to prophecy. She had been temporarily attracted by the subject of Alfred of Triamond and had asked Hunt, who had suggested it, what books she should read. But in October, 1823, when she had been examining the journals and other manuscripts in preparation for Shelley's *Posthumous Poems*, she wrote, "I am now busy writing an article for the London—after which I shall begin a novel—not Alfred—more wild & I think more in my way. Novello will help it greatly—as I listen to music (especially instrumental) new ideas rise & develope themselves, with greater energy & truth [than] at any other time." [14] This novel was *The Last Man*, published by Colburn in 1826, interesting for its expression of

---

13. Shelley, *Letters*, X, 223, 327. See Chapter 6.
14. *Letters*, I, 272. Vincent Novello was an organist, composer, editor, and arranger. He founded the publishing house of Novello and Company. His brother was also an organist; his daughter Clara, a singer.

THE AUTHOR: EAGER ASPIRANT 151

Mary's liberal social and political views, for its biographical significance, especially in the portrait of Shelley as Adrian, and for the vivid and often poetic descriptions of the ravages of the plague which wiped out all but one member of the human race.[15]

It was not a success.[16] Hogg, recognizing the character of Adrian as "most happy and just," read it "with an intense interest and not without tears."[17] But Trelawny could hardly get through it, "nothing but words jangling against each other—but never in tune or in their places."[18] The reviewers agreed with him: they were almost to a man contemptuous or abusive. *Blackwood's,* so enthusiastic about *Frankenstein* and *Valperga,* spoke of Mrs. Shelley's "stupid cruelties." The *London Magazine* called it "an elaborate piece of gloomy folly—bad enough to read—horrible to write." Although recognizing some powers of composition, the *Monthly Review* considered it the product of a diseased imagination and a polluted taste, which described the ravages of the plague in such minute detail that the result was not a picture but a lecture in anatomy. The *St. James Royal Magazine* asked why this unhappy, unfortunate gentleman should ever have been created, why the fair authoress did not write about the *Last Woman*—"her wanderings in search of a *helpmate*—her dismay at finding no one *to talk to.*" The *Wasp* announced among forthcoming publications "The Last Woman; by Mrs. Shelley"; and the *Literary Chronicle,* "The Last Pigtail—Mrs. Shelley." Even an apparent defender, Mrs. Carey, writing an

15. See Chapters 1, 2, 3, 4, 5, and 9.
16. Grylls (*Mary Shelley,* p. 190) says that it was, but I can find no evidence therefor.
17. *Shelley and Mary,* IV, 1077.
18. Trelawny, *Letters,* p. 127.

"Impromptu, On hearing some ill-natured remarks on Mrs. Shelley's Last Man," could do nothing but joke:

> The ladies will read, since there's not one of them
> But must wish to behold the *Last Man*.

The free use of Mary's name in unfavorable reviews so annoyed Sir Timothy Shelley that he threatened once more to withhold her allowance.[19] He had made no objection when *Valperga* was being praised.

Perhaps the public had had a surfeit of Last Men. Thomas Campbell had been writing to the papers that his poem by that name was not an imitation of Byron's "Darkness," but that in fact he had suggested the subject to Byron fifteen or more years before and wrote his own poem only when he learned that an acquaintance (probably Beddoes) intended to write a long poem with that title. Thomas Hood included in his *Whims and Oddities* a "Last Man" which *Blackwood's* considered "worth fifty of Byron's 'darkness' (a mere daub) a hundred and fifty of Campbell's Last Man, and five hundred of Mrs. Shelly's [sic] abortion." And they had all been antedated by a novel, *The Last Man, or Omegarus and Syderia*, "a romance in futurity," published in 1806. In 1823 Beddoes was working on a play with the same title as Mary's novel. And many Last Men were to follow: beside Hood's burlesque, there were poems by E. J. Ousley and Edward Wallace, a sketch in *Blackwood's*, and a play by George Dibdin Pitt, which the playbill of 1842 evidently thought would be helped by the statement (completely unjustified) that it was "partly founded on Mrs. Shelley's thrilling novel." A number of

---

19. See letter from Peacock to Mary, March 9, 1826. *Shelley and Mary*, IV, 1076.

twentieth-century novels have dealt with the extermination or threatened extermination of the human race by war, by plague, or by lethal or sterilizing gases.[20]

There is no record of how Mary took her unfavorable press; she is silent on the subject in letters and journal. It must have hurt her, however, for she had put into the story of Adrian and Lionel Verney much of Shelley and herself. It was the closest she ever came to biography and autobiography; except for her poems it was the freest and fullest expression of her own experience outside the envelopes of her letters or the covers of her journal. It was, in this writer's opinion, her best work after *Frankenstein*, especially in the parts which tell of the devastation caused by the plague and in the final picture of the cities and fields of Italy, devoid, except for the Last Man, of human life. Overwritten at times, tedious in its opening volume, the novel has toward its close an intensity of incident, scene, and feeling which is often exciting and impressive. It was the last novel in which she allowed her imagination to play freely with the wonderful and the strange. Thenceforward she took the advice of the *Ladies Monthly Museum*, which had urged her to write on subjects not "too extravagant for common conception." She recognized its worldly wisdom. Save for two short stories her subsequent narrative writing avoided the unnatural.

The Last Man was also the last novel which she wrote with full enthusiasm and concentration, the last into which she poured her emotions. In *Lodore*, nearly ten years later, she was to return nostalgically to the early years of her life with Shelley and describe them with sentiment. But the

20. See Bailey, *Pilgrims through Space and Time*, pp. 84, 89–90, 174–175. Cf. Aldous Huxley, *Ape and Essence*; Pat Frank, *Mr. Adam*.

passion had gone, and the novel was trimmed to suit the prevailing taste for romance. Though the best of her potboilers, it obviously was written mainly for money, not for love. The real urge was over.

Her three published novels by no means occupied all her time during what may be called her creative period, from 1817 to 1826. While Shelley took his notebook and pencil to the woods or the hills of Italy, Mary was driving her quill pen at her desk. When Shelley was away, he sent her letters urging her to write, to have something to show him when he returned: "Remember Charles the First." She was constantly making plans for writing, scribbling tentative beginnings and rough drafts of stories, some of which she completed, translating Aeschylus and Alfieri and Apuleius. After Shelley's death she still sat with copybook open or paper spread on her desk, starting a biography of Shelley, writing verses about her grief, sketching out scenes of a play, sorting manuscripts for the *Posthumous Poems*, writing a reminiscent article or two, and finally linking biography, narrative, and lyric in *The Last Man*, her novel of loss and loneliness. Her journals, letters, notebooks, and stray manuscript pages bear witness to her literary activity. Some of the unpublished material cannot be dated; some of it probably represents her later efforts to write stories and books that would sell. Much of it, however, and the best of it, was written either because Shelley urged her to produce or because some inner need for expression impelled her pen.

This last was certainly true of the novelette *Mathilda*, written in 1819, earliest and most important of the unpublished stories. As has already been shown, the tale has interesting biographical significance: into it Mary wrote her grief over her broken relationships with Shelley and with

THE AUTHOR: EAGER ASPIRANT

her father.[21] And it gave her some relief.[22] Yet she did not write only for herself; she wanted to publish it. She read it aloud to Edward and Jane Williams. She sent it to England by the Gisbornes, who showed it to Godwin. If any of them recognized characters or situations, they apparently gave no sign. Godwin and the Gisbornes all admired it greatly, although Godwin took exception to portions of it and felt that the subject—that of attempted incest—was disgusting and detestable.[23] He kept the manuscript without, apparently, doing anything about publication, and Mary was evidently unable as long as she was in Italy to get it back or to have a copy made.

In the more serene years that followed, Mary completed a tale for little Laurette Mason,[24] an unnamed story which she sent to Hunt for the *Indicator* and which arrived in 1821 after the *Indicator* had expired,[25] and one which was a byproduct of *Valperga*, "A Tale of the Passions." The child's story may have been "Maurice," about which Godwin wrote to Mary on October 10, 1821:

> I received your tale of 'Maurice' about a month ago, but I did not see the Gisbornes; they sent it to me with a note. . . .
> Your tale I think very pretty, but it would not make more than a shilling book, and this, I suppose, neither you nor I would approve of. If you were disposed to add more—

21. See Chapters 1, 3, and 4 and Appendix III.
22. An unpublished entry in the journal for October 27, 1822, reads: "Before when I wrote Mathilda, miserable as I was, the inspiration was sufficient to quell my wretchedness temporarily."
23. Mrs. Gisborne's journal for August 8, 1820. See *Maria Gisborne & Edward E. Williams, Shelley's Friends, Their Journals and Letters* (ed. by F. L. Jones, Norman, University of Oklahoma Press [c. 1951]), pp. 43–44.
24. *Journal*, p. 136.
25. *Shelley and Mary*, III, 652.

enough to make up a volume—I should be very happy to publish it; but I would not have you give yourself trouble about it; such books do not make ready money.[26]

As this letter indicates, Mary evidently thought that her father might issue it himself with the imprint of M. J. Godwin & Co., publishers of children's books. The contribution to the *Indicator* may have been *The Heir of Mondolfo*, a novelette of about 6,500 words, which was found among the papers of Leigh Hunt and published in *Appleton's Journal* for January, 1877.[27] This is a romantic tale of a King Cophetua love affair spiced by paternal disapproval. Although there is no sure method of dating it, it seems hardly of the same vintage as *Mathilda* or *Valperga*; it belongs rather to the type of story that Mary was writing later for the *Keepsake*. "A Tale of the Passions," however, a story of the conflict between the Guelphs and the Ghibellines, was apparently written while Shelley was alive,[28] and it might well have been sent to Hunt in England in 1821 and brought by him to Italy. It was published in the *Liberal* in 1822.

Most of Mary's pleasure and virtually all her popular success as a creative writer lay in her fiction. Yet she had other ambitions. It was almost inevitable that she should write verse. Most women writers of the time attempted it. Then too it was Shelley's medium; she must have felt some compulsion to write about her poet in poetry. Whether she found a market for her verses or not, it was a comfort to

26. *Ibid.*, III, 698C-698D.
27. A manuscript of this was loaned to the Keats Museum in Hampstead by Mr. Kenneth A. Brooks. Its many corrections show that it is not a fair copy. But it was from Mr. Brooks's collection of Hunt papers.
28. The MS bears an endorsement by Shelley.

set down her emotions in meter and rhyme.[29] Most of her poems are on the theme of her personal loss. Four of them appeared in *The Keepsake*. In other Annuals and periodicals there are a few that tantalize with the signatures Mary S——, M. S., Σζ (the initials used for her article "On Ghosts" in the *London Magazine*), and even M. W. S. But there is no assurance that any of these is by Mary, not even internal evidence except some echoes of Shelley in Mary S's "A Night Scene":

> I see yon brilliant star and waving tree,
> Through which its beams rain down inconstantly.
> I see ten thousand of those radiant flowers
> Which shed light on us in dim silver showers,
> High in the glorious heavens.

One surprising contribution, if it is hers, quite out of her ordinary line, is a humorous and satiric poem "Fame" quoted and commented on in *Fraser's* review of *The Drawing-Room Scrap-Book* for 1835 as from "the pen of Mrs. S., a female friend of Edward Lytton Bulwer, Esq." [30]

In considering the total of Mary's acknowledged or possible poems one must admit that as a poet she is negligible or worse. *Proserpine* and *Midas* contain some competent and pleasant blank verse, but they are distinguished only by the lyrics that Shelley wrote for them. "The Choice" is occasionally touched by vivid phrasing, but it is important only as autobiography. She wrote to Mrs. Gisborne that "A Dirge" was the best thing she ever wrote: "Poor dear Lord

29. See Appendix V.
30. *Fraser's*, X, 618. Mary was a friend of Bulwer. These verses must have been included only in advance review copies of the *Scrap-Book*, for they do not appear in any copy that I have seen. Mrs. S.'s poem and several others mentioned by the reviewer, which were in a different tone from the rest of the contents of this issue, were apparently omitted when the Annual was bound for the holiday trade.

Dillon spoke of it as you do of the rest; but 'one swallow does not make a summer.' I can never write verses except under the influence of a strong sentiment, and seldom even then." [31]

She could, she thought, have written plays. "As to a tragedy," she continued in the same letter, "Shelley used to urge me—which produced his own. When I returned first to England and saw Kean, I was in a fit of enthusiasm—and wished much to write for the stage—but my father very earnestly dissuaded me—I think that he was in the wrong—I think myself that I could have written a good tragedy—but not now." Shelley had suggested that she write on the subjects which he used himself in *The Cenci* and the unfinished *Charles the First*, and that she translate Alfieri's *Myrrha*. Her two little classical verse dramas, *Proserpine* and *Midas*, were written under Shelley's guidance and with his help: he supplied the lyrics "Arethusa" and "Invocation to Ceres" for the one, and the "Hymn to Pan" for the other. *Proserpine* was published in *The Winter's Wreath* for 1832, Alaric A. Watts having refused it for *The Literary Souvenir* in 1826. *Midas* was also offered to him or to Mrs. Watts for *The Juvenile Souvenir* in 1832, but it apparently remained unpublished until Mr. Koszul printed both plays in 1922.[32] The reviewers of his book, who included J. Middleton Murry writing for the *Nation and Athenaeum*, found them distinctly Shelleyan, but one of them saw "Mary tiptoeing so gently with her husband's wings."

The dramatic effort which Kean inspired was a verse tragedy to be called *Manfred*—not Byron's Manfred but

---

31. *Letters*, II, 98.
32. See Sylva Norman, "Mary Shelley: Novelist and Dramatist," in *On Shelley*, pp. 89–99, and *Letters*, I, 350 and n; II, 59 n.

THE AUTHOR: EAGER ASPIRANT 159

the Ghibelline King of Naples whom she had used in "A Tale of the Passions." She had thought about the subject before she left Italy and had consulted her father, who replied, " 'Manfred' is a subject that nobody interests himself about." She persisted, however, and wrote several scenes. She showed them to Procter and possibly to Kelsall,[33] and she sent them to Godwin. It was his unfavorable criticism that shattered her "dream of the buskined muse": "Your personages are mere abstractions—the lines and points of a mathematical diagram—and not men and women. If A crosses B, and C falls upon D, who can weep for that?" [34] Since she threw her manuscript into the fire, there is no way of judging whether or not Godwin was right.

Eager as Mary was to be known as novelist, poet, and dramatist, she found certain kinds of nonfictional prose absorbing and rewarding. She had basked in the approval of her first book, *A Six Weeks' Tour*, and in spite of her fatigue and the drive to make money, she felt some pleasure in writing her last work, another successful book of travel, *Rambles in Germany and Italy*. The delight of investigating the "fifty old books" which she had used for *Valperga* was renewed as she undertook in 1834 an ambitious project in biographical research.

She was commissioned to write a series of biographies for Lardner's *Cabinet Cyclopedia*. She furnished all but four of the Italian "Lives" in the three volumes of *Eminent Literary and Scientific Men of Italy, Spain, and Portugal* and all those in the two similar volumes on Frenchmen.[35]

33. Beddoes' *Works*, pp. 586, 747.
34. *Shelley and Mary*, IV, 1016B.
35. See Appendix II. Grylls (*Mary Shelley*, p. 323) gives incomplete dating for the five volumes. Jones (*Letters*, II, 99 n. 2) says er-

The work kept her busy for several years and gave her pleasure. It was no small or unimportant task to collect the material for biographical sketches of nearly fifty distinguished Europeans. She could use the material gathered and perhaps the contacts made ten years before when she offered to write for Murray on Madame de Staël. But her other research took her to many books and frequently to individuals who could help her. Through Gabriele Rossetti she sought information about Alfieri. Dr. (later Sir John) Bowring was particularly kind about lending her Spanish books which were difficult to obtain. She was especially interested in the Spanish "Lives" and especially challenged by the problems they posed. "The best is," she wrote to Bowring, "that the very thing which occasions the difficulty makes it interesting—namely—the treading in unknown paths & dragging out unknown things—I wish I could go to Spain." [36] She enjoyed the kind of study demanded by such writing. Once she had quoted with approval her father's words that "to read one book without others beside you to which you refer is mere child's work." [37] In writing she could use her critical powers and her vigorous style uncontaminated by the emotional extravagance of autobiographical fiction. Trying to be objective and accurate, she yet found scope for the analysis of social conditions and of character and achievement that made her sketches individual and creative.

The volumes caught little public attention. *Fraser's* lamented the distaste of the reading public for rational works

---

roneously that there was only one volume of French lives and fails to mention the fact that Mary wrote the Portuguese as well as the Spanish lives.
36. *Letters*, II, 104.
37. *Ibid.*, I, 91.

like "the still-born *chefs-d'oeuvres* . . . that are monthly brought forth by the *Cabinet Cyclopedia;* and which are duly buried, after having been properly christened by the Rev. Dionysius Lardner." Mary herself thought them good. In 1843, when Moxon approached her about writing, she said, "Is it a novel or a romance you want?—I should prefer quieter work, to be gathered from other works—such as my lives for the Cyclopedia—& which I think I do *much* better than romancing." [38]

She had scarcely finished the last of the "Lives" before all her interest and energy and power were engaged by a delightful yet nerve-wracking task which had been close to her heart ever since Shelley's death. Stopped from her early plan to write his biography partly by Sir Timothy's prohibitions and even more by her own inhibitions, she yet wished to find some way to enable others to see Shelley as she saw him—not as Hunt or Trelawny saw him. It could be done through letting them read his poetry. So she gathered and edited and printed his *Posthumous Poems* in 1824. But Sir Timothy spoke, and the edition was recalled. Sir Tim soon would die, however; until then she could wait and write of Shelley under various disguises, as Adrian, as Villiers, as Saville. Sir Tim lived on. But finally his opposition began to relax. So when in 1835 Edward Moxon offered her £600 for an edition of Shelley's poems with life and notes, she began to think about it seriously, asking Mrs. Gisborne and other friends for Shelley's letters, although she knew then and later that "the *life* is out of the question." Requesting a copy of *Queen Mab* from Hogg in 1838, she wrote, "Sir Timothy forbids Biography, under a threat of stopping the supplies. What could I do then? How could I live? And my poor boy! But I mean to write a few Notes appertain-

38. *Ibid.*, II, 200.

ing to the history of the Poems." [39] In this way she achieved her purpose without violating either Sir Timothy's wishes or her own privacy. With the exception of some strictures on the handling of *Queen Mab*, the reviews praised the edition. They recognized at last the quality and importance of Shelley's poetry. They expressed gratitude for Mary's notes, with some regret that they were not fuller and more informative.

The problem of what to do with *Queen Mab* had been from the first a vexing and a pressing one. Moxon had urged her to leave out the sixth part as "too atheistical." Unable to decide, she had consulted her friends: "I don't like Atheism—nor does he *now*," she wrote to Hunt. "Yet I hate mutilation—what do you say?" And when Hunt, like Hogg and Peacock, had replied that she must do as she thought best, "I have not yet made up my mind. Except that I do not like the idea of a mutilated edition, I have no scruple of conscience in leaving out the expressions which Shelley would never have printed in after life. I have a great love for *Queen Mab*—he was proud of it when I first knew him—& it is associated with the bright young days of both of us." [40]

The four volumes of the *Poetical Works* came out successively in the early months of 1839, with parts of *Queen Mab* omitted, one of them the Dedication to Harriet. Mary had yielded to Moxon's insistence because he feared for his copyright. On March 4 Mary wrote to him, "I have heard much praise of the mode the book is got up—but regrets *from all parties* on account of the omissions in Q. M. I trust you will not think it injurious to the copyright to in-

39. *Ibid.*, II, 126.
40. *Ibid.*, II, 127.

sert them in the next edition. I think it would improve the sale." The reviewers in the liberal journals criticized Mary severely for this fault; Hogg wrote her an insulting letter because of the omission of the Dedication; Trelawny sent back the first volume in a rage. In the next edition, in one volume, late in 1839, Mary got her way and the omitted portions were restored. A year and a half later Moxon was brought to trial for blasphemous libel, indicted by a radical bookseller who was concerned, not to injure Moxon or Shelley, but to make this a test case to establish the right to free publication of religious opinions. Moxon, though eloquently defended by T. N. Talfourd, was found guilty; but judgment was waived. The prosecution had achieved its purpose in forcing a trial, under the same law that had been used against radicals, of "a gentleman and a reputable publisher whom it would embarrass the government to prosecute." [41] But the 1841 edition was forced to omit *Queen Mab*.

Shelley's prose works, also edited by Mary, were published in 1839 [42] in two volumes entitled *Essays, Letters from Abroad, Translations, and Fragments*. They included his "Defense of Poetry" and other essays, the translation of Plato's *Symposium*, and their joint "History of a Six Weeks' Tour." Mary had some doubts about the "Essay on Devils" as *"too shocking"* for some readers "who else might snatch at the book—for so many of the religious particularly like Shelley." [43] It was put into type but not included in the volumes. So generally favorable had the reception of the *Poetical Works* been that Mary was encouraged to think

41. See White, *Shelley*, II, 408.
42. But dated 1840.
43. *Letters*, II, 139.

of a second edition of the prose even before the first was out. It appeared in 1841, with some additional letters.[44]

"I desire," Mary wrote in her journal on February 12, 1839, "to do Shelley honour in the notes to the best of my knowledge and ability; for the rest, they are or are not well written; it little matters to me which." The last clauses were dictated by the sufferings of an approaching illness and of the memories by which she was "torn." But she need not have doubted. The notes were indeed well written and, as the reviewers and readers found, full of intense interest. Her desire was fulfilled. Shelley was at last finding a place of honor in the world of letters, and she had contributed to that end.

44. Mary had secured these from a number of Shelley's friends. Ollier, however, refused to let her use Shelley's letters to him, because "no money was offered." (*Letters*, II, 144)

CHAPTER

8

The Author: No Idle Acclivity

Godwin once assured Mary that it was laziness that made her feel that she could succeed more quickly with a play than with a novel. "But as there is no royal road to geometry, so there is no idle and self-indulgent acclivity that leads to literary eminence." [1] Idle and self-indulgent Mary never was. Struggling with poor health and low spirits after her return to England, she kept doggedly at her writing, sometimes with enjoyment but oftener, as time went on, with a sense of necessity and pressure. As she wrote to Trelawny, she knew "too well that that excitement [of writing] is the parent of pain rather than pleasure." [2] And soon the pain lost its creative thrill and subsided into the dull ache of a burden to be borne, a driving task to be accomplished. "I am sorry," wrote Mrs. Mason to her in 1836, "that you are *obliged* to write, for nothing can render that sort of occupation agreeable, except its being voluntary." [3] It was one

1. *Shelley and Mary*, IV, 1016A–1016C.
2. *Letters*, II, 18.
3. *Shelley and Mary*, IV, 1079.

thing while Shelley was alive to believe in her powers and to criticize and encourage her, and to take it for granted that they would both write—"I could get [other lodgings] something cheaper . . . ; but if we would write it is requisite to have space."[4] But it was quite another matter after his death and after she had written out her loneliness in *The Last Man*.[5] Then she must write to support herself and Percy and to meet some of the increasing demands of Godwin. Eliza Rennie, finding her in those later years "almost morbidly averse to the least allusion to herself as an authoress," believed that it was only the compulsion of the need for hard cash which kept her at her desk. Indeed, she pointed out, after Percy succeeded to his title and his inheritance, Mary brought out no more work.[6]

Fiction long and short was her main occupation; Godwin had encouraged her in 1822 to believe that she contained within herself the means of her subsistence and that her talents were "turned for the writing of fictitious adventures." But she wrote much nonfiction also. She had ambitious plans for far more writing than she ever accomplished: she mentioned in her letters many possible topics for articles or even books. In 1829 and 1830, for example, in order to liquidate a debt of £100, she was offering to write for John Murray on any of the following subjects: the lives of the Empress Josephine, of Mme. de Stael (she wrote the

4. Shelley, *Letters*, X, 195.
5. See *Journal*, p. 195, for Sept. 3, 1824: "I write, at times that pleases me; though double sorrow comes when I feel that Shelley no longer reads and approves of what I write; besides, I have no great faith in my success. Composition is delightful, but if you do not expect the sympathy of your fellow creatures in what you write, the pleasure of writing is of short duration."
6. *Traits of Character*, I, 113–114.

latter for Lardner's *Cyclopedia*), and of Mahomet; the conquests of Mexico and Peru as forming in some sort a continuation to a life of Columbus; a history of the manners and literature of England from Pope to Horace Walpole and a corresponding volume on continental manners and literature; lives of the English philosophers (endorsed by Murray, "capital, if Mrs. S. be capable of undertaking it"); an account of the Earth in prehistoric times (a subject of great interest to her but possibly difficult to write without entrenching on orthodoxy); lives of celebrated women; a history of woman; a history of chivalry.[7] But to her regret and chagrin Murray accepted none of these suggestions.

In addition to her own writing she was frequently involved in literary services for her friends: marketing and seeing through the press Trelawny's *Adventures of a Younger Son*; "making an article" for the *Examiner* at his request out of his account of his experiences with Odysseus;[8] trying to place articles for Claire or Gatteschi and a play for Mrs. Williams; editing young William Godwin's posthumous novel; endeavoring to enlist Murray's interest in her father's *Lives of the Necromancers* and Colburn's in a new book by David Lyndsay; furnishing comments and notes for Moore's *Life of Byron*.

The failure of *The Last Man* had had its effect on her relations with publishers. Henry Colburn took *The Fortunes*

7. *Letters*, II, 20, 31, 32, 33, 34, 35. See also her suggestions to Colburn that she translate Thierry's *History of the Norman Conquest* and abridge Lastri's *L'Osservatore Fiorentino* (*Letters*, I, 353).

8. With considerable editing and revision, Trelawny's "Description of the Cavern Fortress of Mount Parnassus," which he sent to Mary in 1824 (see *Shelley and Mary*, IV, 1027–1031), was printed in the *Examiner* for November 14, 1825, incorporated in a long article on "Greek Affairs."

of *Perkin Warbeck*, her next novel, after Murray had refused it. Yet she could not make as good a bargain as Godwin had for *Valperga*, which he sold for £400: she had to be content with "the sale of Poor Perkin Warbeck for £150." Even this was preferable to Colburn's other proposition, that they share the profits, although he was so slow in paying that her desire to get money to meet immediate needs was not satisfied. He finally paid her with a bill— "As if I could do anything with a Bill! . . . Before he paid me in a gentlemanly way with a cheque." Colburn "neglected" the book but finally brought it out in March of 1830.[9]

The Fortunes of Perkin Warbeck appeared at almost the same time as a three-volume historical romance by Alexander Campbell, *Perkin Warbeck; or, the Court of James the Fourth of Scotland*. Foreknowledge of this competitor may have contributed to Colburn's hesitancy. Yet he did not need to fear for Mary's book. The reviewers, though not so numerous or so distinguished as those who approved her first two novels, returned to adjectives of praise for her powerful mind and her vigorous descriptive style and judged Mary's novel far superior to Campbell's. One reviewer questioned her historical accuracy in some small points. She had tried to make it accurate, drawing on Godwin for information and on John Murray for reference books. She had put into it more careful study than into *The Last Man* and less personal feeling than into *Valperga*. "An historical subject of former times," she wrote Murray, "must be treated in a way that affords no scope for *opinions*." [10] The novel attained a mild success but it remains one of the least alive and least interesting of her works,

9. *Letters*, II, 27, 29, 31.
10. *Ibid.*, II, 37.

"talented," as one reviewer said, "but a little tedious and heavy."

In *Lodore*, published by Bentley in 1835, Mary turned for the first time to writing a novel about English people of her own day. She hoped, with reason, that a romance about contemporary lords and ladies, younger sons and fatherless daughters would please the reading public. And she wrote the book, it is clear, with more interest and pleasure than she found in *Perkin Warbeck*. It roused wistful memories of her own happy days with Shelley and brought her a mournful satisfaction in the retelling of them. The public welcomed her Ethel as an appealing heroine. The frequent emphasis in the reviews on the characters of Cornelia and Ethel must have pleased her. In spite of the title, this is a book without a hero, and she so intended it. "I do not know," she wrote Ollier on sending him the first volume as a sample, "how briefly to give you an idea of the whole tale— A Mother & Daughter are the heroines— The Mother who after sacrificing *all* to the world at first —afterwards makes sacrifices not less entire, for her child —finding all to be vanity, except the genuine affections of the heart. In the Daughter I have tried to portray in its simplicity, & all the beauty I could muster, the *devotion* of a young wife for the husband of her choice—the disasters she goes through being described—& their result in awakening her Mother's affection, bringing about the conclusion of the tale." [11]

That these women and their men fitted into the pattern of contemporary romantic fiction made the book an immediate success. It was, said one reviewer, "exquisite ro-

11. See Elizabeth Nitchie, "Eight Mary Shelley Letters," in *Keats-Shelley Memorial Bulletin, Rome*, No. III (ed. by Dorothy Hewlett, London, the Saint Catherine Press, 1950), pp. 28–29.

mance . . . the romance of *sentiment,* not of *incident."* Most of the critics spoke of the sentimental bias of the story, which lacked anything of the sordid and dispensed entirely with a villain. Yet, although they were unaware of how firm a basis the story of Villiers and Ethel had in reality, they recognized the personal and subjective quality of the characterization. "Mrs. Shelley's actors are creatures like herself, compounded of sentiment and feeling." [12] Instead of introducing " 'fashionables' notorious for good or evil" as many lady novelists had done, she had drawn from her own experience.[13]

And they were more right than they knew. The scenes were chiefly those with which Mary was familiar—Italian palaces and convents or London lodging houses. Of the forests of the New World she had heard from Frances Wright and Trelawny. Real people move through this story, as has already been shown: Byron and Lady Byron, Shelley and Mary, Eliza and Harriet Westbrook, Emilia Viviani and Fanny Imlay.[14] Yet only the reviewer of *Fraser's,* who may possibly have been Bryan Procter, recognized Byron in Lodore and Shelley in Horatio Saville. And even he thought the love story of Ethel and Villiers like that of "Trelawny's hero and his Arab bride" as told in *The Adventures of a Younger Son.*

Trelawny would have hooted at this identification. Mary rightly believed that he would not like her later novels. "You will not approve," she wrote him in connection with *Falkner,* "of much of what I deem natural feeling because it is not founded on the New Light." [15] Indeed the

12. *New Monthly Magazine,* XLIV, 236–237.
13. *Fraser's,* IX, 600–605.
14. See Chapters 3, 4, 5, and 6.
15. *Letters,* II, 120.

story of Ethel and Villiers in *Lodore*, though following that of Mary and Shelley, is the story not of the unsanctioned elopement of two young radicals but of the marriage of two respectable young people. The breaking up of Lodore's marriage, though similar to that of Byron's or Shelley's in its circumstances, was not accompanied or followed by irregular conduct. The story of Saville and Clorinda had no unconventional suggestions: Saville was a bachelor when he met Clorinda and, although he still loved Cornelia, after his marriage he "never permitted himself to think" of her and attached himself "truly and affectionately to his wife." Thus all the events on which the hard New Light had shone were softly illuminated by the shaded lamps of Respectability. There was "nothing in these volumes which a lady might not have known, and felt, and written,"—and read. Consequently (for the rules governing best sellers were different a century ago), although Mary was not sure whether *Lodore* would succeed ("There is no writhing interest—nothing wonderful, nor tragic— Will it be dull?"),[16] it sold so well that Ollier and Bentley urged her to write another novel.

A serious illness and occupation with her writing for Lardner's *Cabinet Cyclopedia* prevented her from beginning it immediately. But in February of 1836 she told Mrs. Gisborne, "I am busy writing another novel—but the exertion, though necessary to my purse—and not difficult, since my story writes itself—yet is not beneficial to my languid irritable state." [17] *Falkner*, which was published by Saunders and Otley in 1837, was another novel of contemporary

16. *Ibid.*, II, 73, to Mrs. Gisborne, January 16, 1833.
17. *Ibid.*, II, 110. In an unpublished entry in the journal for June 7, 1836, Mary wrote, "I am now writing a novel 'Falkner.' My best it will be—I believe."

English life, less dependent than *Lodore* upon actual events and real persons, yet glancing occasionally at Shelley and Mary, Sir Timothy, Claire, and Byron, and especially Trelawny.[18] The story, however, though with overtones of *Manfred*, was Mary's own invention. It was, she said, devoted to the celebration of fidelity. But the reviewers chiefly saw it as an elevating and impressive study of remorse; and indeed its value lies in its analysis of Falkner's sin and regeneration. The novel may have written itself; it would have benefited from direction of the plot by its author. It is complex and improbable. The style that still impressed the critics as energetic and eloquent seems to the modern reader languid and verbose. The novel is the work of a tired woman at the end of twenty-one years of fiction writing, almost fifteen of them one continuous effort to keep her purse from getting empty. It was her last published novel.

In what year she wrote a novel the heroine of which was named Inez de Medina, it is impossible to say. She never referred to it in journal or letters, and only two chapters, the eighth and ninth, have survived in manuscript. But it does not matter. Those chapters are hopelessly bad, more melodramatic and sentimental than *The Heir of Mondolfo* or anything that she wrote for the Annuals. Except for some mournful passages on death and the loss of love, they do not have even autobiographical interest.[19]

After Mary returned to England she had found a profitable market in the "splendid Annuals." Put out at the end of the year as gift books to lie on parlor tables, printed on heavy paper with pages sometimes tinted and bordered,

18. See Chapters 3, 4, 5, and 6.
19. This MS was found in Lord Abinger's collection by Mrs. Lucia Moholy, who was examining the papers for me.

illustrated by engravings, often bound in sumptuous silk or leather, the Annuals were popular in both England and America. Hundreds of them sprang up—sometimes twenty-five in a single year—appeared for a season or two or three, and died. But a few lived for ten, twenty, or even more than thirty years. *Forget-me-not*, the pioneer, ran from 1823 to 1847, *Friendship's Offering* from 1824 to 1844, *The Regent* from 1831 to 1854, *Fisher's Drawing-Room Scrap-Book* from 1832 to 1854, *Heath's Book of Beauty* from 1833 to 1847, and—longest-lived of all—*The Keepsake* from 1828 to 1861. Each issue included original, unpublished stories, poems, and sketches and sometimes excerpts from published works. A few were made up wholly from material printed elsewhere. The list of names in the tables of contents of the better Annuals was distinguished: poems by Byron and Shelley appeared; Wordsworth and Scott and, later, Thackeray and Mrs. Browning were represented; many of the fashionable and titled authors of the day contributed verse and prose. The *Athenaeum's* review of *The Keepsake* for 1829 spoke of the high quality of the writers represented: in the first class, Coleridge, Scott, Southey, Shelley, and Wordsworth; in the second, Banim, Lockhart, Mackintosh, Moore, and Mrs. Shelley, "who, *vix et ne vix quidem*, escaped being placed with those we have just mentioned." Two years before the first Annual appeared, the *Literary Chronicle* had noted the increasing love of desultory reading ministered to by various books of selections. The time was ripe for the Annuals. They were profitable for their editors and they paid their contributors fairly well.

At least seventeen short stories by Mary were published during a period of ten years from 1829 to 1839,[20] most of

20. See Appendix II. "The Pole," which appeared in the *Court*

them in *The Keepsake*. While Frederick Mansel Reynolds was its editor, Mary was a frequent contributor of both stories and poems: there was something in each issue from 1829 to 1839 except in that for 1836. This was edited by Mrs. Norton, who, in spite of their friendship, had not, Mary said, invited her to contribute. "The Elder Son" appeared in *The Book of Beauty* for 1835, and *Proserpine*, one of her two verse dramas, in *Winter's Wreath* for 1832.

Some of Mary's tales were reprinted in collections, such as *The Casquet of Literature*, or in the *Keepsake Français*. At least one was dramatized. "The Sisters of Albano" appeared in *The Keepsake* for 1829; on October 21 of the same year the Lord Chamberlain's Office licensed a play, *The Italian Sisters; or the Brigands of Albano*, and on November 19 it began a short run at the Adelphi Theatre. It follows Mary's story very closely, but it has a happy ending. It may have been by J. B. Buckstone. More simple in plot and less like the story in dialogue, the "opera" *The Sisters of Charity*, submitted by R. B. Peake,[21] who had dramatized *Frankenstein*, had also been licensed earlier in 1829. It had a good summer run at the English Opera House and was later revived. The author of *Demetri the Outcast; or The Klepht of the Evil Eye*, "an entirely new melodrama" on

Magazine for 1832 under Mary's name, was probably by Claire, though Mary revised it, almost certainly writing the conclusion. It is possible that other stories by Mary than those listed in Appendix II appeared in various annuals and periodicals, without ascription to her. "The Pilgrims," which was unsigned, is included in Garnett's *The Tales of Mary Shelley*. Other stories, some unsigned, some with the initials M. S., might with equal ease be assigned to her on the basis of theme and style; for example, "The Silver Lady" (*Keepsake* for 1838) and "The Ghost of Private Theatricals" (*Keepsake* for 1844), except that the latter is rather late.

21. But apparently written by Mr. Banim, author of *The O'Hara Tales*.

the bill of the Royal Theatre in November, 1835, may have been rummaging through the *Keepsake* for 1830. Since the melodrama was evidently not licensed, no manuscript of it survives for comparison with Mary's "The Evil Eye," the story of an outcast Klepht named Dmetri. One fact is fairly sure: Mary did not profit financially from reprints or dramatizations. But her tales were popular with readers and audiences. They were often singled out for favorable mention by reviewers of the Annuals.

Ranging from the simple retelling of an old story through semi-historical narratives and romantic episodes of love running now rough, now smooth, to tales of alchemy and magic, occasionally making use of personal themes and situations, they rolled quickly from her pen. She found that she could with relative ease turn out several romantic tales each year between novels and even when she was occupied with her books or her nonfictional writing. The chief problem she had to solve was that of brevity. She wrote to Mrs. Gisborne, who had asked for advice about publishing a story by Mr. Gisborne, that it was four times too long for the Annuals. "When I write for them, I am worried to death to make my things shorter and shorter, till I fancy people think ideas can be conveyed by intuition, and that it is a superstition to consider words necessary for their expression." [22]

Mary's work for the periodicals was less copious and probably less lucrative than her fiction. It also apparently pleased her less, except as it sometimes carried her back into her happier past. Beginning with an article on Villani for the *Liberal* of 1823, she wrote for various magazines: *La Belle Assemblée, The Spirit and Manners of the Age,* the *London Magazine,* the *Examiner,* and the *Westminster*

22. *Letters,* II, 97.

Review. She drew the material for those articles published in 1823 and 1824 from the journals and letters which she was examining for the edition of Shelley's *Posthumous Poems*. Her contributions to the *Westminster Review* beginning in 1829 were literary reviews. To the *Examiner* she sent a defense of the Italian male soprano, Velluti. None of these articles is signed, except "Recollections of the Lake of Geneva" in *The Spirit and Manners of the Age* for December, 1829, which is followed by the initials M. W. S. They can be attributed to Mary either because of her own references to them in her letters or by internal evidence: close correspondence with the text of letters and journals or use of identifiable ideas, incidents, and hitherto unpublished passages by Shelley.[23] Most of this writing was task work for Mary: "I write bad articles which help to make me miserable—but I am going to plunge into a novel, and hope that its clear waters will wash off the mud of the magazines." [24]

Mary's last literary work, her *Rambles in Germany and Italy, in 1840, 1842, and 1843*, was undertaken with mixed feelings. "It is true," she told Claire, "I am writing—there were certain things I could not manage without it. . . . It does not hurt my health—yet I am sorry so to do—I earnestly wished never again to publish—but one must fulfil ones fate— However I dont work hard—& by twelve my task is always over." [25] The chief "certain thing" was financial assistance for Gatteschi, the young Italian political exile whose poverty had won her quick and unrestrained sympathies. "I own myself I am sorry I am writing—but I feel that I shall save poor G from starvation—from des-

23. See Appendix II for a list of her published articles.
24. *Letters*, I, 287.
25. *Ibid.*, II, 209.

peration & the lowest depths of misery—I know this—& write when otherwise I never would." [26] Gatteschi, as is well known, repaid her ill.[27]

She wrote this book in response to a suggestion from Moxon, the publisher of her editions of Shelley's works, that she submit something to him. On the basis of "a few words" that he "let fall," she told him that she thought a journal of her recent tour on the continent with Percy and his friends might be interesting and useful to other travellers. Reminding him of the public approval of her *Six Weeks' Tour*, she expressed her confidence that she could make her later travels pleasing also: "I mean therefore to make my present work as light—as personal to myself—& as amusing as I can. I think you will like it as a reader —as a publisher I hope it will meet your approbation." [28]

About two weeks later, having had no reply, she pressed her query, excusing herself by confessing that she wanted money sadly. She was willing even to write another novel or, preferably, a book "gathered from other works." But Moxon accepted her first suggestion, and in 1844 he published the *Rambles* in two neat, attractive volumes.

"A poor affair," Mary herself thought it. But it is an eminently readable and often amusing record of her experiences. Rewards came to her from the reviewers. A book by a real traveler, they called it, a traveler by feeling as well as by experience, vigorous, independent, sagacious in its comments, charming, repaying perusal by both the most intellectual and the most idle of readers. The author herself had many claims to consideration: "The daughter of William Godwin, the friend of Byron, the creator of

26. *Ibid.*, II, 206–207.
27. For Gatteschi see *ibid.*, II, 193–194, especially note 1.
28. *Ibid.*, II, 195–196.

Frankenstein, the relict of one of our most adventurous poets." [29]

So at the end of Mary Shelley's career critics were recognizing the importance of her relation to Shelley as well as her own abilities. They were still speaking of her masculine mind. She was, one of them wrote, "a woman who thinks for herself on all subjects, and who dares to say what she thinks; a woman, moreover, whose masculine and original mind has been strengthened in its habits of thought and reflection, not only by the acquisition of high and varied accomplishments but by a daily association for many years with several of the very highest and finest intellects of an age which has been unrivalled for its intellectual wealth." [30] Mary could not have asked for a more gratifying valediction.

29. *New Edinburgh Review,* Quarterly Part I, 1844, pp. 33–38.
30. *New Monthly Magazine,* LXXII, 284–286.

CHAPTER

9

The Keepsake of Mary Shelley

With the publication of the *Rambles in Germany and Italy* in 1844, Mary Shelley's writing life was over. It had been an arduous discipline, successful in that it had made for her and Percy a living, limited and sometimes precarious as it was. Yet she left only two works that have survived as wholes on their own merits: the notes to Shelley's works largely because of their subject matter, *Frankenstein* because of the strange, imaginative conception and compelling writing. It is easy to dispose of her as the unworthy companion of a great poet, the progressively worsening author of sentimental fiction. Such a judgment, however, neglects the strength of her nonfiction and the positive merits of her novels and tales.

To her contemporaries, not only her friends but also her reviewers, she was among the first of the *"stellae minores"* in current literature. In 1837 Crabb Robinson named her as one of "the only three writers of note" who had not signed the petition in regard to the American copyright for English authors.[1] Ten years later George Gilfillan spoke of

1. *Correspondence of Henry Crabb Robinson with the Words-*

her inferiority yet similarity to Shelley in her true and positive genius.[2] When *Shelley Memorials* was published eight years after her death, the *Saturday Review* commented, "Her writings have long ago established her literary reputation, but these new documents will confirm and add to it."[3] Even in the twentieth century a journalist could speak of her literary gifts and of her "brilliant biographical sketches."[4] Her best recent biographer singles out for commendation the subtle psychology "in the monster's *apologia* for his malignity" and the imaginative powers displayed in *The Last Man*.[5] The editor of her letters and journals speaks of the unfulfilled promise of *Valperga*, the richness of its imaginative style, the creative force and the thorough scholarship which in his opinion make it far superior to *Frankenstein*.[6]

Mary's writing has many faults, most of which were obvious even to her contemporary admirers: lack of humor, monotony, verbosity, overwriting, sentimentality of plot and character, fondness for beautiful, blameless heroines, reliance on analysis of character at the expense of dramatic action and dialogue. With all these faults there are still positive merits that even a modern critic must allow. The charges against her as a writer can be, not refuted, perhaps, but modified, some of them considerably, some of them at

---

worth Circle (2 vols., Oxford, Clarendon Press, 1927), I, 348. His reason for mentioning her was that *Lodore* had been published in America.

2. In *Tait's Edinburgh Magazine*, December, 1847; reprinted in *A Second Gallery of Literary Portraits* (Edinburgh, 1850), pp. 283–296.
3. *The Saturday Review*, July 30, 1859.
4. "Shelley's Mother-in-law," by "Mimnermus," *The Freethinker*, August 13, 1922.
5. Grylls, *Mary Shelley*, pp. 320–321.
6. Jones, *The Letters of Mary W. Shelley*, I, xxx.

least by the exception that proves the rule. The charge of impiety brought against *Frankenstein* obviously need not be considered. And that of wild imagination in *Frankenstein* and *The Last Man* seems rather absurd in an age of robots, of air-borne travel, and of a socialized Britain—and of Aldous Huxley and George Orwell. But other—and serious—literary sins must be examined.

Except for *Frankenstein* Mary's fiction reveals little originality and invention in plotting. She depended too much either on actual events or on stereotyped situations. She repeated devices, such as the riding accident which she used many times in her novels and tales in order to throw a character where she wanted him, frequently at the feet of the heroine. The endings of her stories, though not always conventionally happy and sometimes even tragic,[7] are usually contrived and foreseeable. *Falkner*, said the *Examiner*, failed in the fifth act. She included too much in her plots, too many incidents that were merely incidental. Godwin cut *Valperga* drastically, and yet the reviewers thought it still burdened by episodes and minor characters. She had difficulty in sustaining a long, involved plot; her use of the flash-back too often results in confusion and diffusion rather than in clarity and conciseness; occasionally, as in one hastily written short story, she herself loses track of her plot.[8]

Yet she had a sense of dramatic structure. Even in *Falkner* the basic irony of the situation, though marred by overemphasis and repetition, is striking. Gerard Neville, having vowed to seek out and punish his mother's destroyer, falls in love with Elizabeth, not knowing that her foster-

---

7. Her story "The Sisters of Albano," which ended tragically, was given a conventionally happy ending in the dramatic version, *The Italian Sisters*.

8. "Euphrasia," in the *Keepsake* for 1839.

father Falkner is the man he seeks. He even helps Elizabeth to nurse Falkner back to life after a severe illness. The plot of *Frankenstein* is tightly knit, with contrasts creating dramatic tensions. Two main ideas, loneliness and scientific curiosity with its hopes and fears and pains, are foreshadowed in the introductory letters of Walton to his sister and developed throughout the novel.

This entire story is set in strangeness: Walton and Frankenstein meet in the mysterious white world of the ice-bound Arctic—Coleridge's "land of mist and snow." Consciously or unconsciously, Mary owed much to *The Rime of the Ancient Mariner*. In Walton's letters to his sister there are several references to the poem. Indeed he attributes his passionate enthusiasm for "the dangerous mysteries of the ocean, to that production of the most imaginative of modern poets." And the loneliness of the Mariner appealed to the lonely creator of the lonely Monster.

And as was said of Coleridge,[9] it is not in the invention of wonders that Mary excelled—striking as her central invention is—but in the extraordinary skill with which she "paints the passions they excite." Frankenstein's exaltation and terror, his doubt and dread and remorse, his wild grief and his passion for revenge are the chief means by which we are impressed with the frightfulness of his unhallowed creation. Just as in *The Ancient Mariner* we see and feel the horrors first with the Mariner and second with the Wedding Guest, so in *Frankenstein* the wonder is twice removed from the reality. Frankenstein's horror is told in his own words, like the Mariner's story, to Walton, a man who has no personal connection with the supernatural events but who "cannot choose but hear." And there is another layer

9. C. H. Herford, *The Age of Wordsworth* (London, G. Bell & Sons, Ltd., 1914), p. 180.

of narrative: the Monster tells his story to Frankenstein, who tells it to Walton. Yet at the end, with Frankenstein's death, the middle layer disappears and reality meets wonder—Walton comes face to face with the Monster.

There are bright fragments of reality within the inner layers: Clerval's normalcy, the idyllic home of Felix (yet broken in upon by the strange girl from the East), Elizabeth's first letter with news of their happy family life. They serve only to thicken the strange darkness that surrounds and engulfs them. The words *strange* and *unnatural* become key words, appearing and reappearing on page after page.

Thus the structure of the novel is an ingenious, strangely wrought nest of boxes, reality on the outside and horror at the core. The chief persons in this story too are both real and strange. Walton combines practical, painstaking industry with "a love for the marvellous, a belief in the marvellous" which hurries him away from normal living to exploration of the "wild sea and unvisited regions." Frankenstein goes away to the university like any other young man but is caught by the magic of modern science until he is driven into experiments unhallowed and presumptuous in their invasion of the power of the Creator. The Monster himself is non-human in his origin, his physical frame and appearance, but human in his longings and desires and even in that passion for revenge which leads him to commit inhuman crimes.

In *The Last Man* there are dramatic foreshadowings and contrasts. Raymond, foreseeing his death, looks upon the earth as a tomb, each man he meets as a corpse; thus, as the story progresses, Verney and the reader come to look upon mankind. The beauty of nature and the gaicty or the idyllic happiness of man are broken in upon by word of the progress of the plague. Adrian's dream of a paradise on earth, Merrival's prediction of eternal spring to come a hundred thousand years in the future, little Alfred's birthday party, a service at Westminster Abbey are interrupted by news of fresh victims or the actual presence of Pestilence. A sense of dramatic fitness animates the account of a performance of *Macbeth* at Drury Lane Theatre in plague-stricken London:

> A shudder like the swift passing of an electric shock ran through the house, when Rosse exclaimed, in answer to "Stands Scotland where it did?"
>
>> Alas, poor country;
>> Almost afraid to know itself! It cannot
>> Be called our mother, but our grave: where nothing,
>> But who knows nothing, is once seen to smile;
>> Where sighs, and groans, and shrieks that rent the air,
>> Are made, not marked; where violent sorrow seems
>> A modern extasy: the dead man's knell
>> Is there scarce asked, for who; and good men's lives
>> Expire before the flowers in their caps,
>> Dying, or ere they sicken.
>
> Each word struck the scene, as our life's passing bell; we feared to look at each other, but bent our gaze on the stage, as if our eyes could fall innocuous on that alone. The person who played the part of Rosse, suddenly became aware of the dangerous ground he trod. He was an inferior actor, but truth now made him excellent; as he went on to announce to Macduff the slaughter of his family, he was afraid to speak, trembling from apprehension of a burst of grief from the audience, not from his fellow-mime. Each word was drawn out with difficulty; real anguish painted his features; his eyes were now lifted in sudden horror, now fixed in dread upon the ground. This show of terror increased ours, we gasped with him, each neck was stretched out, each face changed with the actor's changes—at length while Macduff, who, attending to his part, was unobservant of the high wrought sympathy of the house, cried with well acted passion:

> All my pretty ones?
> Did you say all?—O hell kite! All?
> What! all my pretty chickens, and their dam,
> At one fell swoop!

A pang of tameless grief wrenched every heart, a burst of despair was echoed from every lip.—I had entered into the universal feeling—I had been absorbed by the terrors of Rosse—I reechoed the cry of Macduff, and then rushed out as from an hell of torture, to find calm in the free air and silent street.
Free the air was not, or the street silent.

These moments of dramatic tension, however, do not save most of Mary's stories from prolixity and confusion.

As she had difficulty in sustaining an involved plot, so she could rarely sustain the drawing of an important character. Her heroes and heroines are usually two-dimensional, cut out like paper dolls from a pattern of Byronic gentleman or beautiful and virtuous maiden. She lacked skill in presenting the mingling of good and bad—although she had known it well in her friends. The faults in the fundamentally noble persons are of the grand sort, due to strong passions or to bad bringing up. The villains are either idle, profligate spendthrifts or tyrannical and prejudiced old men, cold of heart. It is in minor characters seen comparatively briefly or in flashes of insight into personality that Mary is successful and impressive. Mrs. Elizabeth Fitzhenry, good-natured, simple, stupid, adoring but not understanding her brother Lodore, doing her duty by Ethel in the great city of London but never dreaming that a love affair is going on under her nose, retiring with thankfulness to her quiet country life after Ethel's marriage—here is a real "character," drawn, as far as anyone knows, from Mary's own imagination. Miss Jervis, Elizabeth Falkner's governess, in her crispness and primness, her intellectual limitations and her professional conscientiousness, is a real person. Merrival, the astronomer in *The Last Man*, absorbed in the writing of his learned treatise while the plague advances, is interesting and original. So is Monna Gegia, the sharp-tongued, warm-hearted old Guelph woman of "A Tale of the Passions," with her "Ghibelline leg" which kept her from walking out to join the celebration of her party's triumph.

Not all of the principal characters are flat. Adrian in *The Last Man*, though shadowy when compared with his living model, is drawn with delicate sympathy and with the rounded knowledge which his creator had of his original. Beatrice, the strange, dark, passionate girl in *Valperga*, deserves the praise she received from Shelley, Godwin, and the reviewers. Euthanasia, except for her typical extreme beauty, is an interesting woman because of the conflict within her between her love for Castruccio and her love for her own people. Her gradual disenchantment is convincing in its clarity and logic.

Mary Shelley frequently used characters confused by mixed emotions and motives. The most interesting person in *Lodore* is Cornelia, whose pride is always at war with her affections and keeps her for a long time from both her daughter and her lover. In *Falkner* most of the characters are thoroughly wound up in mixed motives: Falkner in his wish for death and his love and sense of responsibility for Elizabeth; Neville in his honorable desire to vindicate his mother and his love for Elizabeth to whom such vindication would bring sorrow; Elizabeth in her own involved loyalties to Neville and to Falkner. Even when Falkner has been acquitted, he and Neville are still hampered by conflicting delicacies of feeling that delay the conclusion. Part of the drama and the tragedy of *Frankenstein* lies in the conflicts in the young scientist's own soul: his glory and his horror at his scientific achievement; his pity and his hatred of the Monster.

The Monster himself, that earliest creation of Mary's, is probably her best, most subtle, most perceptive characterization. It has already been shown that in his loneliness he is a projection of Mary herself. It is that which makes him human, which is responsible for the changes in his character, which makes him tragic. Improbable as are the circumstances of his creation—why, asked one reviewer, did Frankenstein make him so huge and so hideous —and of his self-education, he becomes a real and convincing person, viewed in the round, whose motives are clear and valid. He runs through an arc of experience and of feeling for others, from love through fear and hatred to a final compassion for mankind and even for his creator. To the last he justifies his crimes by the fact that he is alone and that every man's hand has been against him. "Robbed of its romantic form," said Bertrand Russell, "there is nothing unreal in this psychology. . . . To an English visitor, the ex-Kaiser, at Doorn, lamented that the English no longer loved him. Dr. Burtt, in his book on the juvenile delinquent, mentions a boy of seven who drowned another boy in the Regent Canal; his reason was that neither his family nor his contemporaries showed him affection. Dr. Burtt was kind to him, and he became a respectable citizen; but no Dr. Burtt undertook the reformation of Frankenstein's monster." [10]

Vague and diffuse as Mary's characterizations sometimes are, she often presents an attitude, a characteristic, or a whole character in a concise and telling comment that

10. "Byron and the Modern World," *Journal of the History of Ideas* (January, 1940), I, 33.

shows her observant and ironic eye. "She satisfied her conscience . . . by cherishing a little quiet stock of family hate." "My aunt . . . was as a plant beneath a thick covering of ice; my hands would have been frozen in any attempt to get at it." Castruccio, the man of war, was accustomed "to count men as the numerals of a military arithmetic." And with a turn of phrase that gives fresh meaning to a cliché Mary sums up the character of Miss Jervis: "She has a heart of gold, though it does not shine."

Her letters too are punctuated by the lively, revealing sentence that characterizes, sometimes with what she called "a little knife," the people she knew intimately as well as those whom she met briefly. There is "the menagerie," Peacock and Hogg: Peacock who "dines here every day to drink his bottle," and Hogg, who "wraps himself up in a triple veil," "queer, stingy, and supercilious" in his later years when "to have his dinner and not be bored is all his object in life." Medwin is "Common Place personified," "as silent as a fireskreen but not half so useful, except that he sometimes mends a pen." Taaffe, that "wise little gentleman," butt of Lord Byron's quizzing and poet laureate of Pisa, "translates Dante and rides fine horses who perpetually throw him." Mrs. Gaskell is "the Beau ideal of a County Blue grafted on a sort of Lady Bountiful." Henry Reveley is "the pattern of good boys." Everina Wollstonecraft died without pain "of natural decay aided by her determination to do nothing she was told." Hunt is "a person whom all must love and regret." [11]

She often records an extended description or analysis of a person she has met. Her first impressions of Trelawny

11. *Letters*, I, 24, 30, 66, 307; II, 162; I, 130, 131, 165, 161, 310; II, 107; I, 77; II, 181, 42.

and of Sgricci the improvisatore are skillful miniatures.[12] She sent to Mrs. Gisborne a lively sketch of the Ricci family, their landlords in Leghorn, the daughters Appolonia and Carlotta who sighed for the beaux yeux of Henry Reveley, and the baby, "ugly and black as a walnut table." Mme. Merveilleux, with her temper like wildfire and her head like a sieve, had not even the brains of a goose. And Mary's well-bred eyebrows rose in astonished amusement at the Falstaffian Colonel Finch who at a conversazione gave "an account of his warlike feats and how at Lisbon he had put to flight thirty well armed & well mounted robbers (he on foot) with two pistols that never missed their aim." [13]

Sometimes it is human nature in general that draws her fire. And she began young. Commenting on Godwin's concern over Sir Bysshe Shelley's will, she says in her journal with an air of experience that sits oddly on her seventeen-year-old shoulders, "All this is very odd and inconsistent, but I never quarrel with inconsistency; folks must change their minds." [14] Writing to Hunt of a festival held before a little chapel on the barren top of a high, steep Italian mountain, she observes, "Now this pleases me—this is something like—one can conceive of animals, dogs and cows, going to pleasant places to enjoy themselves—but it belongs to that queer animal man alone, to toil up steep & perilous crags, to arrive at a bare peak, to sleep ill & fare worse, & then the next day to descend & call this a feast." [15]

12. *Journal*, p. 165; *Letters*, I, 122–124.
13. *Letters*, I, 108–109, 92, 68–69. For "Colonel" Finch see Elizabeth Nitchie, *The Reverend Colonel Finch* (N.Y., Columbia University Press, 1940).
14. *Journal*, p. 37, entry for February 5, 1815.
15. *Letters*, I, 239.

Her comments on the morality of society or the vanity of human wishes, her wistful reflections on life and death, on youth and age may not be original in thought. But often she finds for them a turn of phrase that stamps them with interest and individuality. "We never do what we wish when we wish it, and when we desire a thing earnestly, and it does arrive, that or we are changed, so that we slide from the summit of our wishes and find ourselves where we were." [16] "What a mart this world is! Feelings, sentiments . . . are the coin, and what is bought? Contempt, discontent and disappointment. . . . And what say the worldly to this? Use Spartan coin, pay away iron and lead alone, and store up your precious metal. But alas! from nothing, nothing comes, or, as all things seem to degenerate, give lead and you will receive clay." [17]

Mary's descriptive style, generalized and elaborate as much of it seems today, was considered vigorous, clear, and nervous by her contemporaries. Individual words are often precise and expressive: "the light waves coursed one another," "dusky manuscripts," "the snowdrift, whirring past the lattice." Figures of speech are often fresh and vivid. Verney speaks of "the inch and barley-corn growth of my life." Of the small remnant of English waiting on the Dover cliffs to cross to the hoped-for safety of the continent, he says, "Death had hunted us through the course of many months, even to the narrow strip of time on which we now stood." "I believe that I am aware," wrote Mary in Germany, "of the moment when the [church] clock strikes; on comes the sound, louder and louder, till my room is filled as with thunder. . . . You can form no idea what it is *to have twelve o'clock thus walk up bodily*

16. *Ibid.*, I, 262.
17. *Journal*, p. 169.

to your pillow, in the otherwise deep silence of the night." [18]

In longer passages of description, although they are often colored and weakened by romantic diction, Mary can sustain a mood and create a distinct picture. She can describe scenery, especially that which she had known herself: the landscape of Tuscany through which she passed on her return to England and of which she wrote to Hunt; the streets and houses of Geneva; the country around Albano; the peaks and valleys and glaciers of the Alps. In *Frankenstein* Walton's "land of mist and snow," which she had never seen, owes much to her reading of Coleridge. But the journey of Frankenstein and Clerval down the Rhine is lively and full of detail like that in Mary's own *History of a Six Weeks' Tour*. And her vivid pictures of the grand scenes among which she began to write *Frankenstein*—the thunderstorm in the Alps, the valleys of Servox and Chamounix, the glacier and the precipitous sides of Montanvert, and the smoke of rushing avalanches, the "tremendous dome" of Mont Blanc—are not shamed by comparison with the poems written in the same months and on the same ground, Byron's third canto of *Childe Harold* and Shelley's "Mont Blanc."

> I spent the following day roaming through the valley. I stood beside the sources of the Arveiron, which take their rise in a glacier, that with slow pace is advancing down from the summit of the hills, to barricade the valley. The abrupt sides of vast mountains were before me; the icy wall of the glacier overhung me; a few shattered pines were scattered around; and the solemn silence of this glorious presence-chamber of imperial Nature was broken by the brawling waves, or the fall of some vast fragment, the thunder sound of the avalanche, or the cracking reverberation along the mountains of the accumulated ice, which, through the si-

18. *Rambles in Germany and Italy*, I, 249–250. Italics mine.

lent working of immutable laws, was ever and anon rent and torn, as if it had been but a plaything in their hands.

In *The Last Man* she marks the progress of the remnant of the English upward to the barren solitude of the highest Alps:

> We left the fair margin of the beauteous lake of Geneva, and entered the Alpine ravines; tracing to its source the brawling Arve, through the rock-bound valley of Servox, beside the mighty waterfalls, and under the shadow of the inaccessible mountains, we travelled on; while the luxuriant walnut-tree gave place to the dark pine, whose musical branches swung in the wind, and whose upright forms had braved a thousand storms—till the verdant sod, the flowery dell, and shrubbery hill were exchanged for the sky-piercing, untrodden, seedless rock.

She can catch the spirit of a human scene and reproduce the details of movement and costume: a *festa* at Cadenabbia, a wedding dance in Bavaria, Euthanasia's court, the description of which recalled Boccaccio to the mind of one reviewer of *Valperga*. There is the feeling of hysteria in the movements and sounds of the crowd gathered to see Beatrice invoke the Judgment of God by walking barefoot over flaming plowshares:

> The square presented a busy, but awful scene; the houses, the windows of the monastery, the walls of the convent, were covered by people; some clinging to the posts, and to the walls; fixing their feet upon small protuberances of stone, they hung there, as if they stood on air. . . . [Their] fury of hope and fear approached madness: their voices it is true were still, . . . but their bodies and muscles were in perpetual motion; some foamed at the mouth, and others gazed with outstretched necks, and eyes starting from their sockets.
> . . . the crowd spoke not as she appeared, but a sound, as of the hollow north-wind among the mighty trees of a

sea-like forest, rose from among them; an awful, deep and nameless breath, a sigh of many hearts.

Other darkly dramatic moments stand out against the flatter narrative in her novels: the Monster's drawing back of the curtains on Frankenstein's bed; the collapse of the bridge of Carraia at the Spectacle of Hell in Florence; the exhumation of the body of Falkner's Alithea; Lodore's fatal duel with the American, their figures silhouetted against a moonlit sky; the discovery of Raymond's body in the ruins of Constantinople guarded by his dying dog; the climax of Mathilda's search for her father; the portentous setting for doomed humanity in *The Last Man:*

> The sky was stripped bare of clouds by the increasing gale, while the tide at its ebb seceded entirely from the town. The change of wind rather increased the fury of the sea, but it altered its late dusky hue to a bright green; and in spite of its unmitigated clamour, its more cheerful appearance instilled hope and pleasure. All day we watched the raging of the mountainous waves, and towards sunset a desire to decypher the promise for the morrow at its setting, made us all gather with one accord on the edge of the cliff. When the mighty luminary approached within a few degrees of the tempest-tossed horizon, suddenly, a wonder! three other suns, alike burning and brilliant, rushed from various quarters of the heavens towards the great orb; they whirled round it. The glare of light was intense to our dazzled eyes; the sun itself seemed to join in the dance, while the sea burned like a furnace, like all Vesuvius a-light, with flowing lava beneath. . . . The time occupied by the apparition of these meteors was comparatively short; suddenly the three mock suns united in one, and plunged into the sea. A few seconds afterwards, a deafening watery sound came up with awful peal from the spot where they had disappeared.
>
> Meanwhile, the sun, disencumbered from his strange satellites, passed with its accustomed majesty towards its western home. When—we dared not trust our eyes late dazzled,

but it seemed that—the sea rose to meet it—it mounted higher and higher, till the fiery globe was obscured, and the wall of water still ascended the horizon; it appeared as if suddenly the motion of earth was revealed to us—as if no longer we were ruled by ancient laws, but were turned adrift in an unknown region of space.

Mary's style had considerable range. It is at its most elaborate in *The Last Man*. Here she uses the romantic poetic devices of alliteration and assonance, echo and repetition, question and apostrophe to heighten the mood. "Who was there indeed to save? What troop had we brought fit to stand at bay, and combat with the conqueror? We were a failing remnant, tamed to mere submission to the coming blow. A train half dead, through fear of death. . . . Like a few furrows of unreaped corn. . . . Like a few straggling swallows. . . . Like a stray sheep. . . . Like a cloud. . . . Such were we." The threnody of coming destruction and solitude mounts as the novel draws to its emotional close: "Thus around the shores of deserted earth, while the sun is high, and the moon waxes or wanes, angels, the spirits of the dead, and the ever-open eye of the Supreme, will behold the tiny bark, freighted with Verney—the LAST MAN."

Mary could also write simply and directly.

> Early, therefore, on Monday, August 8th, Sxxx and Cxxx went to the ass market, and purchased an ass, and the rest of the day, until four in the afternoon, was spent in preparations for our departure. . . . Packing up a few necessaries, leaving the rest to go by diligence, we departed in a fiacre from the door of the hotel, our little ass following.
>
> We dismissed the coach at the barrier. It was dusk, and the ass seemed totally unable to bear one of us, appearing to sink under the portmanteau, although it was small and light. We were, however, merry enough, and thought the leagues short. We arrived at Charenton about ten.

Finding our ass useless, we sold it before we proceeded on our journey, and bought a mule, for ten Napoleons. About nine o'clock we departed. We were clad in black silk. I rode on the mule, which also carried our portmanteau; Sxxx and Cxxx followed, bringing a small basket of provisions. At about one we arrived at Gros Bois, where, under the shade of trees, we ate our bread and fruit, and drank our wine, thinking of Don Quixote and Sancho.

This account, "unpresuming," as Mary calls it in her preface, gives a bright, clear picture of the "six weeks' tour" of the three light-hearted young runaways. It can be matched by direct and simple writing in the narrative of her travels with her son and his friends nearly thirty years later.

In her biographical studies is some of her most concise and intellectual writing, effective for narrative, characterization, or criticism.

In her life of Petrarch she tells of the year of Laura's death:

The fatal year now began which cast mourning and gloom over the rest of his life. It was a year fatal to the whole world. The plague, which had been extending its ravages over Asia, entered Europe. As if for an omen of the greater calamity, a disastrous earthquake occurred on the 25th of January. Petrarch was timid: he feared thunder—he dreaded the sea; and the alarming concussion of nature that shook Italy filled him with terror. The plague then extended its inroads to increase his alarm. It spread its mortal ravages far and wide: nearly one half of the population of the world became its prey. Petrarch saw thousands die around him, and he trembled for his friends: he heard that it was at Avignon, and his friend Sennucio del Bene had fallen its victim. A thousand sad presentiments haunted his mind. He recollected the altered countenance of Laura when he last saw her; he dreamed of her as dead; her pale image hovered near his couch, bidding him never expect to see her more. At last, the fatal truth reached him: he received intelligence of her death on the 19th of May.

A similarity to her own nature made Mary write sympathetically of Madame de Staël in exile:

> She was, with all her vivacity, naturally melancholy. . . . Death and solitude were, in her mind, closely allied. Take away the animation of conversation; the intercommunication of ideas among the many; the struggle, the applause, the stirring interest in events; the busy crowd that gave variety to every impression; and the rest of life was, in her eyes, a fearful vigil near the grave.

Mary never pretends to original critical powers. But she can say what everyone knows without boring us:

> From the publication of these [early] works to "Don Quixote," what a gap! He would seem to have lived as an unlighted candle—suddenly, a spark touches the wick, and it burst into a flame. "Don Quixote" is perfect in all its parts. The first conception is admirable. The idea of the crazed old gentleman who nourished himself in the perusal of romances till he wanted to be the hero of one, is true to the very bare truth of nature, and how has he followed it out? Don Quixote is as courageous, noble, princely, and virtuous as the greatest of the men whom he imitates: had he attempted the career of knight errantry, and afterwards shrunk from the subsequent hardships, he had been a crazy man, and no more; but meeting all with courage and equanimity, he really becomes the hero he desired to be.

Like many authors, Mary Shelley revised her writing, often drastically, from rough draft to finished work and sometimes even beyond the printed book. The manuscripts that have survived show that she wrote hastily and carelessly at first, the dash almost her only mark of punctuation, and then polished carefully. Usually the revision brought improvement. Sometimes it resulted in an elaboration that diluted and diffused her meaning.

Most interesting to study are the changes which she suggested and which she actually made in *Frankenstein*. Before the book was sent to a publisher Mary had polished her manuscript. Day after day she entered in her journal, "Correct Frankenstein." But she was not content with the printed book. In a copy which she gave to Mrs. Thomas in 1823 she made numerous notes and suggestions for a possible second edition.[19] At the end of Chapter II of the first volume she wrote: "If there were ever to be another edition of this book, I should re-write these first two chapters. The incidents are tame and ill-arranged—the language sometimes childish. They are unworthy of the rest of the narration." She noted also that Elizabeth's letter to her foster-brother ought to be rewritten. Sometimes the specific correction is in the interest of accuracy, as when she altered "the sun in the Arctic is for ever visible" to "the sun is constantly visible for more than half the year." Sometimes she increased the sense of strangeness. "Are we then near the land," asks Walton, after he and his crew, with "greatest attention," have watched the Monster passing on his dog-sled, "and is this unknown waste inhabited by giants?" She intensified the Monster's bitterness by an added passage describing his furtive actions as he ventured out of his hovel only by night:

> Nay if by moonlight I saw a human form, with a beating heart I squatted down amid the bushes fearful of discovery. And think you that it was with no bitterness of heart that I did this? It was in intercourse with man alone that I could hope for any pleasurable sensations and I was obliged to avoid it— Oh truly, I am grateful to thee my Creator for the gift of life, which was but pain, and to thy tender mercy

19. This copy is in the J. Pierpont Morgan Library. The quotations from the MS annotations are made with the kind permission of the Trustees.

which deserted me on life's threshold to suffer—all that man can inflict.

These changes were not incorporated in the second edition, that of 1823, which Godwin hurried through the press on the strength of the success of *Presumption*. It followed the text of 1818. When in 1831 *Frankenstein* was issued in the series of Standard Novels, changes were made, but they were not the changes of these marginal notes. Since Mrs. Thomas had not continued her acquaintance with Mary Shelley, the author probably never saw her annotated copy again, and she began the process of revision anew. She did rewrite to some extent the first two chapters. Her third thoughts on a passage were often the best. The long paragraph describing the childhood of Victor and Elizabeth, full of irrelevant detail, was marked *bad* in Mrs. Thomas's copy and a brief passage was substituted:

> With what delight do I even now remember the details of our domestic circle, and the happy years of my childhood. Joy attended on my steps—and the ardent affection that attached me to my excellent parents, my beloved Elizabeth, and Henry, the brother of my soul, has given almost a religious and sacred feeling to the recollections of a period passed beneath their eyes, and in their society.

It is vague and ineffective. In the 1831 edition three paragraphs analyzing the characters of the three children take the place of the condemned passage and a flat statement about Henry. Then by a few changes in phrasing in the next paragraph these pleasing recollections are no longer recorded for their own pleasing sake: they are closely tied in with the theme of the novel:

> I feel exquisite pleasure in dwelling on the recollections of childhood, before misfortune had tainted my mind, and changed its bright visions of extensive usefulness into

> gloomy and narrow reflections upon self. Besides, in drawing the picture of my early days, I also record [the first edition reads, "But, in drawing the picture of my early days, I must not omit to record"—a clumsy transitional device] those events which led, by insensible steps, to my after tale of misery: for when I could account to myself for the birth of that passion, which afterwards ruled my destiny, I find it arise, like a mountain river, from ignoble and almost forgotten sources; but, swelling as it proceeded, it became the torrent which, in its course, has swept away all my hopes and joys.

And Frankenstein proceeds with an account of his introduction to Cornelius Agrippa and of his father's cursory glance at the book and careless protest.

There is little reward for a reader of Mary Shelley's poems. As Sylva Norman has said, "It is not to be wondered at that her 'poetical works' are few; those who live in permanent close contact with a poet (as Mary did mentally, even after Shelley's death) must be conceited or hard of hearing if they insist on adding their small tinkle to the sonorous note. Mary had sense and judgment enough to leave the poetry in Shelley's hands, and to concentrate on fiction, which financial returns and a genuine if unexalted gift both served to justify." [20] Her "tinkle" was not unmusical—she had a sense of rhythm and harmony. But except for an occasional phrase or line—

> The bride of Time no more, I wed Eternity—
>
> She is immortal—yet unusual fear
> Runs through my veins—

the diction is obvious, commonplace, imitative and sentimental.

Against her work as a whole so harsh a charge cannot

20. "Mary Shelley, Novelist and Dramatist," in *On Shelley*, p. 99.

be brought. Although the general reader would hardly care to peruse Mary Shelley's works, yet there is reward for so doing. There are familiar people to be met again, disguised and perhaps distorted, but always seen, however myopically, through the eyes of Shelley's wife. There are lesser persons, new and interesting, flashing momentarily from the pages. There are tales of power and scenes of horror to take permanent hold on the imagination. There are landscapes of beauty and of association to remain in the memory. There is writing to be admired—lucid and moving. These discoveries might well be enclosed within rose-colored silken covers, as in a Keepsake of Mary Shelley. There is the woman herself, to be seen in a fuller, truer light than that cast upon her by the words of worshippers or detractors or even by her own letters and journals. It is a woman neither angel nor devil, full of faults, full of merits: brave in spite of her self-pity, liberal in her views in spite of her compromises with society, endowed with intellectual powers that command respect in spite of their limitations and with imagination capable of creative achievement in spite of her later taming of it to meet the taste of the reading public. There is in all her work, however dulled and diluted, the young author of *Frankenstein*.

Appendix

APPENDIX I
Outline of Mary Shelley's Life
(A chronological list of the chief events relevant to her writings)

1797 Birth, August 30
 Death of mother, September 10
1807 Removal to Skinner Street
1812 First meeting with Shelley and Harriet, November 11
1812–14 Residence with Baxters in Dundee
1814 Meeting with Shelley, May 5
 Elopement with Shelley, July 28
 Return to England, September 14
 Poverty in London and threat of Shelley's arrest, October–November
1815 Birth of daughter, February 22
 Death of daughter, March 6
 Residence at Bishopsgate, August, 1815–May, 1816
1816 Birth of son, William, January 24
 Residence in Switzerland, May–August
 Return to England, August 29
 Suicide of Fanny Imlay, October 9
 Harriet Shelley found drowned, December 10
 Marriage, December 29
1817 Birth of Allegra, daughter of Claire Clairmont and Byron, January 12
 Residence in Marlow, March, 1817–March, 1818
 Lord Eldon's judgment against Shelley, March 27
 Publication of *History of a Six Weeks' Tour*
 Birth of daughter, Clara Everina, September 2
1818 Christening of William, Clara, and Allegra, March 9
 Publication of *Frankenstein*, March 11
 Departure for Italy, March 11
 Residence in Bagni di Lucca, June–August
 Death of Clara at Venice, September 24
1819 Residence in Rome, March–June
 Death of William at Rome, June 7

Residence in Leghorn, June
Birth of son, Percy Florence, at Florence, November 12
1820 Residence in Pisa, January–June
Residence in Leghorn and Baths of San Giuliano, June–October
Residence in Pisa, October, 1820–May 1, 1822, except for summer of 1821 at the Baths
Introductions to Mavrocordato, Pacchiani, Emilia Viviani, October–November
1821 Arrival of Edward and Jane Williams, January 16
Arrival of Byron, November 1
1822 Arrival of Trelawny, January 14
Death of Allegra, April 19
Removal to Casa Magni at Lerici, April 30
Miscarriage, June 16
Arrival of Hunts in Leghorn, June
Drowning of Shelley and Williams, July 8
Removal to Genoa, September
1823 Refusal of Sir Timothy's offer to take Percy Florence, January
Publication of *Valperga*
Return to England, August 25
1824 Publication of Shelley's *Posthumous Poems*
Death of Byron, April 19
1826 Publication of *The Last Man*
Death of Harriet's son, Charles Bysshe, making Percy Florence heir to the title, September 14
1828 Visit to Paris and attack of smallpox
1830 Publication of *Perkin Warbeck*
1833 Residence in Harrow
1835 Publication of *Lodore*
1836 Death of Godwin, April 7
1837 Publication of *Falkner*
1839 Publication of Shelley's *Poetical Works*
Publication of Shelley's *Essays, Letters from Abroad, Translations and Fragments* (dated 1840)
1840 First trip on continent with Percy and his friends
1842–43 Second trip on continent with Percy and his friends
1844 Publication of *Rambles in Germany and Italy*

APPENDIX

Death of Sir Timothy Shelley, April 23, and succession of Percy Florence to title and estate
1848 Marriage of Sir Percy, June 22
1851 Death of Mary Shelley at Chester Square, London, February 1

APPENDIX II

List of Mary Shelley's Works

NOVELS

(including the principal editions and reprints)

Hate (begun in 1814, unfinished, and lost)

Frankenstein
    Frankenstein; or, The Modern Prometheus, 3 vols., London, Lackington, 1818
    Frankenstein; ou le Prométhée Moderne, par Mme. Shelley, 3 vols., traduit par J. S.———, Paris, Corréard, 1821
    Frankenstein; or The Modern Prometheus, by Mary Wollstonecraft Shelley, 2 vols., a new edition, London, Whittaker, 1823
    Frankenstein; or The Modern Prometheus, revised, with an introduction by the author, Bentley's Standard Novels, No. 9, London, Colburn, 1831 (reissued, 1849)

    Note: This novel has been reprinted many times, often in inexpensive editions (Everyman's Library, Lovell's Library, The Gem Classics, Readers' Library, Sixpenny Library, etc.), also in expensive editions illustrated by Nino Carbe (N.Y., Illustrated Editions Co., [c. 1932]), Lynd Ward (N.Y., Harrison Smith and Robert Haas, 1934), Everett Henry (N.Y., Limited Editions Club, 1934). There was also an edition illustrated with "stills" from the moving picture (N.Y., Grosset and Dunlap [n.d.]). There have been recent translations into French, German, and Spanish.

Valperga
    Valperga: or, the Life and Adventures of Castruccio, Prince of Lucca, by the Author of Frankenstein, 3 vols., Whittaker, 1823

The Last Man
    The Last Man, by the Author of Frankenstein, 3 vols., London, Colburn, 1826
    The Last Man, by the Author of Frankenstein, 3 vols., Paris, Galignani, 1826

Perkin Warbeck
    The Fortunes of Perkin Warbeck, by the Author of 'Frankenstein,' 3 vols., London, Colburn and Bentley, 1830
    Perkin Warbeck, new edition, London, Routledge, 1857

Lodore
    Lodore, by the Author of 'Frankenstein,' 3 vols., London, Bentley, 1835
    Lodore, by the Author of 'Frankenstein,' Paris, Galignani, 1835
    Lodore, by the Author of 'Frankenstein,' Franklin Library Edition, N.Y., Wallis and Newell, 1835 (reissued, 1846)
    The Beautiful Widow, by Mrs. Percy B. Shelley, Widow of Percy B. Shelley, the Poet; and Author of 'Frankenstein,' Philadelphia, Peterson [n.d.]

Falkner
    Falkner: a Novel by the Author of 'Frankenstein'; 'The Last Man,' etc., 3 vols., London, Saunders and Otley, 1837
    Falkner: a Novel by the Author of 'Frankenstein,' 'The Last Man,' etc., Complete in one volume, N.Y., Harper, 1837

?   An unpublished novel, two chapters of which (Chapter VIII: "Again Don Juan" and Chapter IX: "A Step Backward") are among the MSS in the collection of Lord Abinger

APPENDIX

NOVELETTES OR LONG SHORT STORIES

Mathilda (unpublished), 1819. The MS is in the collection of Lord Abinger. Part of the rough draft is also there, part in the Bodleian Library, under the title of *The Fields of Fancy* (MS. Shelley d. 1). There are fragments also among the Shelley-Rolls papers (MS. Shelley adds. c. 5) in the Bodleian.

The Heir of Mondolfo, posthumously published in *Appleton's Journal: a Monthly Miscellany of Popular Literature*, New Series, Vol. II, pp. 12–23, January, 1877. A MS in rough form is in the Keats Museum in Hampstead.

SHORT STORIES

A "story for Laurette" Mason (probably *Maurice*, lost), 1820
A "story for the Indicator" (unnamed and lost—unless it is *Mondolfo*), 1821
"A Tale of the Passions," in the *Liberal*, No. II, 1823 (reprinted in *The Romancist and Novelist's Library*, London, 1839)
"The Bride of Modern Italy," in the *London Magazine*, April, 1824
"The Sisters of Albano," in the *Keepsake*, 1829
"Ferdinando Eboli," in the *Keepsake*, 1829
"The Evil Eye," in the *Keepsake*, 1830
"The Mourner," in the *Keepsake*, 1830
"The False Rhyme," in the *Keepsake*, 1830
"The Swiss Peasant," in the *Keepsake*, 1831
"Transformation," in the *Keepsake*, 1831
"The Dream," in the *Keepsake*, 1832
"The Invisible Girl," in the *Keepsake*, 1833
"The Brother and Sister," in the *Keepsake*, 1833 (translated into French and printed in *Le Salmigondis, Contes de Toutes les Couleurs*, Paris, 1832, Vol. III, pp. 159–219)
"The Mortal Immortal," in the *Keepsake*, 1834 (reprinted in *The Casquet of Literature*, Vol. III, pp. 369–375)
"The Elder Son," in the *Book of Beauty*, 1835
"The Trial of Love," in the *Keepsake*, 1835

"The Parvenue," in the *Keepsake*, 1837
"The Pilgrims," in the *Keepsake*, 1838
"Euphrasia," in the *Keepsake*, 1839
Story about Valerius, an ancient Roman brought back to life in modern Italy (untitled, unfinished, unpublished), in Lord Abinger's collection
Story set in 18th century England (untitled, merely begun, unpublished), in Lord Abinger's collection

BIOGRAPHICAL WORKS

Life of Louvet (unfinished and lost), 1814
Lives of the Most Eminent Literary and Scientific Men of Italy, Spain, and Portugal, 3 vols., Nos. 63, 71, and 96 of Lardner's *Cabinet Cyclopedia*, London, 1835–1837
Lives of the Most Eminent Literary and Scientific Men of France, 2 vols., Nos. 105 and 117 of Lardner's *Cabinet Cyclopedia*, London, 1838–1839
Life of Godwin (unfinished and unpublished except for passages used in Kegan Paul's *William Godwin: His Friends and Contemporaries*)
Life of Shelley (eleven manuscript pages in the Shelley-Rolls papers in the Bodleian Library; unpublished except as incorporated in T. J. Hogg's *Life of Shelley*)

ARTICLES

"Giovanni Villani," in the *Liberal*, No. II, 1823
"Narrative of a Tour Round the Lake of Geneva, and of an Excursion through the Valley of Chamouni," in *La Belle Assemblée*, July, 1823
"Recollections of Italy," in the *London Magazine*, January, 1824
"On Ghosts," signed Σζ, in the *London Magazine*, March, 1824
Article on Byron (unpublished, lost), 1824
Defense of Velluti I, in the *Examiner*, June 11, 1826: a letter signed Anglo-Italicus
Defense of Velluti II, printed in *Letters of Mary W. Shelley*, ed. F. L. Jones, Appendix III, Vol. II, pp. 354–356
"The English in Italy," in the *Westminster Review*, October,

APPENDIX

1826: a review of *The English in Italy*, by Lord Normanby, *Continental Adventures*, and *Diary of an Ennuyée*

Review of Prosper Mérimée's *La Guzla* and *La Jaquerie*, in the *Westminster Review*, October, 1829

"Modern Italy," in the *Westminster Review*, July, 1829: a review of *Italy As It Is* and Simond's *A Tour in Sicily and Italy*

Review of *The Loves of the Poets*, in the *Westminster Review*, October, 1829

"Recollections of the Lake of Geneva," signed M. W. S., in *The Spirit and Manners of the Age*, December, 1829

Review of Moore's *Life of Lord Edward Fitzgerald*, in the *Westminster Review*, January, 1832

BOOKS OF TRAVEL

History of a Six Weeks' Tour through a part of France, Switzerland, Germany, and Holland, London, Hookham, Ollier, 1817

Rambles in Germany and Italy, in 1840, 1842, and 1843, by Mrs. Shelley, 2 vols., London, Moxon, 1844

EDITORIAL WORK

The Posthumous Poems of Percy Bysshe Shelley, London, J. Hunt, 1824

Adventures of a Younger Son [by E. J. Trelawny], London, Colburn and Bentley, 1831

"The Pole" [by Claire Clairmont, but attributed to the Author of 'Frankenstein'], in the *Court Magazine and Belle Assemblée*, August and September, 1832

Transfusion, by William Godwin, Jr., London, Macrone, 1835

The Poetical Works of P. B. Shelley, 4 vols., London, Moxon, 1839

Essays, Letters from Abroad, Translations and Fragments, by P. B. Shelley, London, Moxon, 1840

William Godwin's Works (projected but never carried out)

POETIC DRAMAS

Manfred (unpublished and lost), 1824

Proserpine, a Mythological Drama (written, with Midas, in 1820), in the *Winter's Wreath*, 1832

Midas, posthumously published, with Proserpine, in *Proserpine and Midas, Two unpublished Mythological Dramas*, by Mary Shelley, edited by A. Koszul, London, Humphrey Milford, 1922. The MSS are in the Bodleian Library (MS. Shelley d. 2)

POEMS

"The Choice," 1822(?), posthumously published by H. Buxton Forman, 1876

"On Reading Wordsworth's Lines on Peel [sic] Castle," 1825, posthumously published in R. Glynn Grylls, *Mary Shelley* (1938), pp. 302–303

Fragment "to Jane with the Last Man," 1826(?), posthumously published, *ibid.*, p. 303

"Absence," in the *Keepsake*, 1831

"A Dirge," in the *Keepsake*, 1831 (reprinted by Mary with revisions at the head of her notes to the poems of 1822 in her edition of Shelley's *Poetical Works*, 1839)

? "A Night Scene," by Mary S., in the *Keepsake*, 1831

"Alas I weep my life away," 1831 (unpublished, in journal in Lord Abinger's collection)

"Struggle no more," 1831 (unpublished, in journal in Lord Abinger's collection)

"Sadly borne across the waves," 1833 (unpublished, in the Shelley-Rolls collection in the Bodleian Library)

? "Ode to Ignorance," by M. W. S., in the *Metropolitan*, 1834

"The tide of Time was at my feet," 1834 (unpublished, in the Shelley-Rolls collection in the Bodleian Library)

? "Fame," by Mrs. S., in advance copies of the *Drawing-Room Scrap-Book*, 1835

"O Listen while I sing to thee," set to music and published by Henry Hugh Pearson (London [n.d.]), and printed by F. L. Jones, *The Letters of Mary Shelley*, II, 159 n. The MS, with some different readings, in the Shelley-Rolls collection, is dated March 12, 1838.

"Stanzas: O, come to me in dreams," in the *Keepsake*, 1839

"Stanzas: How like a star," in the *Keepsake*, 1839

APPENDIX III

Mary Shelley's *Mathilda*

An Unpublished Story and Its Biographical Significance [1]

One of the most interesting passages in Professor White's *Shelley* is his analysis of the estrangement between Mary and Shelley after the death of Clara, of the basis for it and the effects of it on his poetry, notably on "Julian and Maddalo." [2] Briefly put, his theory is as follows: Mary, in the unreasoning agony of her grief, blamed Shelley for her child's death and for a time felt toward him an extreme physical antagonism which subsided into apathy and spiritual alienation. Shelley, himself stricken with grief and deeply wounded by this spiritual desertion, fell into a mood of dejection the extent of which he concealed from Mary and from the world. Never acknowledging openly his belief that Mary had ceased to love him, he expressed it in veiled terms through the Madman in "Julian and Maddalo" [3] and in certain lyrics of 1818—"all my saddest poems"—poems which he did not show to Mary. Professor White, acknowledging the subjective nature of his interpretation and conclusions, says, "Neither Mary's journal nor Shelley's letters give any hint of the abnormal emotional situation which both concealed from their friends, but which nevertheless dominated most of Shelley's poetry at the time." [4] He

1. Part of an article published in *Studies in Philology*, XL, 447–462, July, 1943. Some changes have been made in the footnotes as the result of further research. Other portions of the article have been incorporated in the book.
2. White, *Shelley*, II, 40–56.
3. But Carlos Baker believes that the story of the Madman is not autobiographical but a semi-fictional account of Tasso's imprisonment as a madman. See his "Shelley's Ferrarese Maniac," *English Institute Essays*, 1946.
4. White, *op. cit.*, II, 56.

finds Mary's only recognition of it in the remorseful lines of her poem, "The Choice," written after Shelley's death, and in her editorial notes on Shelley's poems of 1818.[5]

But if Shelley's poems are the obverse of this coin, it has also a reverse which Mr. White apparently has not seen. This reverse is an unpublished story by Mary Shelley entitled *Mathilda*, written in 1819 after the death of William, which renewed Mary's grief and despair but not her antagonism to Shelley, and before the birth of Percy Florence, which restored her to something like her normal mood. Into this story Mary poured the suffering and the loneliness, the bitterness and the self-recrimination of the past twelve months. As will be shown below, she was beginning to write it in August, 1819, at the time when she resumed her journal with the entry of August 4:

> I begin my journal on Shelley's birthday. We have now lived five years together; and if all the events of the five years were blotted out, I might be happy; but to have won, and then cruelly to have lost, the association of four years is not an accident to which the human mind can bend without much suffering.[6]

In support of Professor White's theory, *Mathilda* expresses a sense of estrangement from, even of physical repulsion toward, one whom she had deeply loved, a realization of her own selfish, petulant, and unreasoning absorption in her grief, and an acknowledgment that the man she loved, concealing or at least setting aside his own trouble, was unfailingly unselfish and kind—although, she felt, he did not love her. It contains other matters of interest too: references to her own birth and childhood, evidence of the attraction in the theme of incest for Mary as well as for Shelley, an expression of her feeling that she had "lost" her father by reason of his lack of sympathy toward her, and a portrait of Shelley comparable to those she was to draw of him again and again in her later fiction.

The evidence for the dating of this story comes partly from the manuscript, partly from Mary Shelley's journal. The manuscript is contained in three notebooks, two in the possession of

5. *Ibid.*, II, 46, 55.
6. *Journal*, p. 122.

Lord Abinger, the third in the Bodleian Library.[7] Of the former, one contains the apparently final copy of the tale (226 pages), entitled *Mathilda*, the other, a portion of the first draft (116 pages), entitled *The Fields of Fancy*. The Bodleian notebook[8] contains the concluding portion (54 pages) of *The Fields of Fancy*, followed by a part of the opening (32 pages). Of these thirty-two pages, three and a half are scored out, and the last four comprise a different introduction to the story. On the remaining pages of the notebook are some of Shelley's manuscript drafts of prose and verse.[9] Since the Shelley selections all belong to 1819, 1820, or 1821, the probability is that Mary was finishing her rough draft some time in 1819 and that when she had copied her tale Shelley took over the notebook and filled it up. Chapter I of *Mathilda*, the revised form of the story in one of the notebooks in Lord Abinger's possession, is headed, "Florence Nov 9th. 1819." As the whole of Mathilda's story takes place in England and Scotland, the date must be that of the completed manuscript. Mary was in Florence at that time.

Mary's journal indicates that she probably began the story in August, while they were living in the Villa Valsovano, midway between Leghorn and Monte Nero. On August 4, 1819, after a gap of two months from the time of William Shelley's death, she resumed her diary. Almost every day thereafter for a month she recorded, "Write," and by September 4 she was saying, "Copy." On September 12 she wrote, "Finish copying

7. There are also 25 pages of fragments of a rough draft of *Mathilda* among the Shelley-Rolls papers now in the Bodleian Library (MSS. Shelley adds. c.5).

8. MSS. Shelley d.1. I am grateful to the Curators of the Bodleian Library for permission to quote [in my article] from this manuscript in the reserved Shelley collection. The quotations in the text of this book are from the final draft of the story in Lord Abinger's collection, and are used by his permission and that of the Duke University Library.

9. Notably the "Ode to Naples" and "The Witch of Atlas," both written from the other end of the book; some prose fragments, parts of *Prometheus Unbound* in Italian, fragments of *Epipsychidion* in Italian and of its preface in English, and extended portions of *The Defense of Poetry*, all following Mary's tale.

my Tale." The next entry to indicate literary activity (unless the occasional word "work" indicates literary work) is the one word "write," on November 8. On the 12th Percy Florence was born, and Mary did no more writing until March, when she was working on *Valperga*. *Mathilda*, therefore, was probably written and copied between August 4 and September 12, 1819, although Mary may have done some revision on November 8 and finally dated the completed manuscript November 9.

The subsequent history of the manuscript is recorded in letters and journals. When the Gisbornes left for England on May 2, 1820, they took *Mathilda* with them to show it to Godwin and to get his advice about publishing it.[10] Although Medwin heard about the story when he was with the Shelleys in 1820,[11] and Mary read it to Edward Williams on August 6, 1821, and to Jane on September 4,[12] this manuscript of it apparently stayed in Godwin's hands. There is, however, no

10. Mr. Gisborne comments enthusiastically on it in his journal entry of May 8, concluding, "I am well persuaded that the author will one day become the admiration of the world." (See *Maria Gisborne & Edward E. Williams . . . Their Journals and Letters*, p. 27. Mr. Jones reads *be* instead of *become*. All the entries in Mrs. Gisborne's journal through that for May 11 are in Mr. Gisborne's hand. Whether he is the author or amanuensis makes here no material difference.) Godwin's approval was somewhat qualified. Mrs. Gisborne wrote on August 8: "Mr. G. . . . thinks very highly of some of the parts: he does not approve of the fathers letter, . . . The pursuit however (and *I add* the catastrofe [sic] which closes it) he thinks the finest part of the whole novel. The subject he says is disgusting and detestable; and there ought to be, at least if [it] is ever published, a preface to prepare the minds of the readers, and to prevent them from being tormented by the apprehension from moment to moment of the fall of the heroine; it is true (he says) that this difficulty is in some measure obviated, by Mathildas protestation at the beginning of the book, that she has not to reproach herself with any guilt; but, yet, in proceeding one is apt to lose sight of that protestation; besides (he added with animation) one cannot exactly trust to what an author of the modern school may deem guilt." *Ibid.*, pp. 43–44.

11. Medwin, *Revised Life of Shelley*, p. 252.

12. *Journal*, pp. 159, 160.

record of his making any attempt to publish it. From February through April, 1822, Mary was repeatedly asking Mrs. Gisborne to try to get *Mathilda* from her father and have it copied for her, and Mrs. Gisborne invariably answered that she had been unable to do so. The last references to the story are in two of Mary's letters to Mrs. Gisborne after Shelley's death. On August 15, 1822, in describing the journey of herself and Jane to Pisa and Leghorn to seek news of Shelley, she wrote, "It must have been fearful to see us—two poor, wild, aghast creatures—driving (like Mathilda), towards the sea, to learn if we were to be for ever doomed to misery." [13] And on May 6, 1823, after speaking of the prophetic character of the catastrophe of *Valperga*, she continued: "But it seems to me that in what I have hitherto written I have done nothing but prophecy what has arrived to. [Sic] Mathilda foretells even many small circumstances most truly—and the whole of it is a monument of what now is." [14]

* * *

The story is told in the first person. The narrator is a young woman of twenty-two, the Mathilda [15] of the title. Her father was a proud, passionate, distinguished, and at first conventional man. Her mother, beautiful, intelligent, and adored, died a few days after Mathilda's birth. The father, crushed by grief, left the baby in the care of his stern elder sister, who lived in Scotland, and went abroad. Mathilda had a lonely childhood. When she was sixteen her father returned from India. She lavished her affection on him; but after a few months of happiness [16] she discovered that he loved her not as a daughter, but incestuously, putting her in the place of her dead mother. In the period of horror and agony which followed her discovery, she was visited by a nightmare in which

13. *Letters*, I, 182.
14. *Ibid.*, I, 224.
15. The name probably came from Dante. Mary's journal shows that she was reading the *Purgatorio* in August, 1819. There are in her story several references to and quotations from the *Purgatorio*, notably one from the description of Mathilda gathering flowers in Canto 28.
16. Do these few months correspond to the four years in Mary's journal entry for August 4? See above.

she pursued her father, dressed in a white robe, to the summit of a high rock. One morning early her father departed secretly, leaving a long letter for her. Mathilda and an old steward took post horses and pursued him, first toward London and then toward the sea. Finally they reached a cottage on a cliff—a rock like that in her dream—where they found her father's corpse covered with a white sheet lying on the bed. Unable to bear human society, Mathilda decided to disappear as if she too had died.

She went back to Scotland and lived alone in a little cottage on the heath, waited on by an attendant from the village two miles distant, feeding the wild animals and brooding on her sorrows, feeling that she was branded like Cain as a result of her father's guilty love for her. After two years of solitude there came to her neighborhood a young poet named Lovel or Woodville,[17] seeking to be alone with his grief over the recent death of his betrothed. At first she shunned him. But one day his horse threw him and she went to his aid. Soon they became friends; he told her his sad story, but she, though constantly lamenting her misfortune, kept her secret. She fell in love with him but, selfish and exacting in her temper, still convinced that life held nothing for her, she prepared two glasses of laudanum and tried to persuade him to die with her that they might both rejoin their loved ones, she her father, he his Elinor.[18] He dissuaded her in an eloquent speech, saying that he did not dare to die so long as he, though unhappy, could make even one other person happy. Calmed for a while, she gave up her purpose, but she could not put aside her grief. When Lovel was called away by the illness of his mother, she walked part of the way toward town with him. On her return she was overtaken on the heath by darkness and lost her sense of direction. She slept on the ground, caught a fever which turned into a rapid consumption, and died peacefully

17. The name Lovel is used in *The Fields of Fancy*; in *Mathilda* it is changed first to Herbert, then to Woodville.

18. Cf. Shelley's suggestion to Mary that they both commit suicide in the agonizing days before their elopement. Shelley offered her a bottle of laudanum and vowed that he would use a pistol on himself. See White, *op. cit.*, I, 343–344.

in a few months, leaving behind her for Lovel a letter and the manuscript of her story.

To make the heroine's description of her own death plausible, Mary experimented with an opening section and a closing paragraph which set Mathilda's tale as the narrative of a soul in the Elysian Fields waiting to be purged of her selfishness before she was permitted to rejoin the soul of her father.[19] In Lord Abinger's notebook containing *The Fields of Fancy* the first sentence is: "It was in Rome, the Queen of the World, that I suffered a misfortune that reduced me to misery and despair." The "I" of this sentence, which was evidently the original opening of the story, is not Mathilda but another soul who listens to Mathilda's story.[20] The cancelled passage in the Bodleian notebook, which begins: "My visits to these fields of Elysium had now become regular," was intended as the end of the introductory framework. Mary discarded this opening, however, and wrote another (the last four pages in the Bodleian notebook) in which the heroine, knowing that she is about to die, is sitting at four o'clock on a winter day in her cottage on the heath beginning to write out her tragic history for the benefit of her friend.

19. Mary may have been influenced here not only by Dante but also by Mary Wollstonecraft's unfinished tale, *The Cave of Fancy*, in which one of the souls confined in the center of the earth to purify themselves from the dross of their earthly existence tells to Sagesta the story of her ill-fated love for a man whom she hopes to rejoin after her purgation is completed. See *Posthumous Works of the Author of a Vindication of the Rights of Women* (4 vols., London, 1798), IV, 97–155. The similarity in titles is worth noting. Mary had read and reread her mother's writings many times.

20. This "I" is perhaps Mary herself, who had lost little William in Rome. In a long introductory framework of thirty-seven pages, she is conveyed by Fantasia to the Elysian Fields. There she listens to a philosophical discourse by Diotima and meets various souls who have suffered greatly in life, among them Mathilda. On page 38, Mathilda begins her story.

APPENDIX IV

The Stage History of *Frankenstein* [1]

Theatrical history, as well as that of empires, sometimes repeats itself. The last few years have witnessed on the screen a double bill—"We double dare you to see this double scare show of the century"—of *Dracula* and *Frankenstein*. On the London stage of 1823 *Presumption; or the Fate of Frankenstein* trod on the heels of *The Vampyre* and was crowded off the boards in its turn by *Der Freischütz*. "Terrific! Mysterious!" shouted the playbills of the 1820's. "Fearsome! Ferocious! Frightful!" scream the advertisements of the 1940's.

Mary Wollstonecraft Shelley, the creator of Frankenstein and his Monster, could hardly have anticipated the numerous dramatic versions of her novel. Interested in the theater from her childhood, so that the prospect of seeing a play was a pleasure exquisite enough to take away her appetite for dinner, she wanted to write for the stage. No manuscript of hers in dramatic form has apparently survived, however, except those of *Proserpine* and *Midas*; none was printed except *Poserpine*, which appeared in one of the annuals; no play by her found its way to the stage.

But if her desire had been only to see the creatures of her imagination in action, it would have been amply satisfied from the time that she returned to England in 1823 until the time of her death, and the ghost of that "sedate-faced young lady" whom Hunt described might have come back many times to sit in her box and watch Frankenstein and his Monster. Whether she would always have retained that sedateness, as she seems to have done in the face of some dramatic incidents in her life, it is hard to say. What she thought of some of the burlesques of her novel or even some of the serious melodra-

---

1. Reprinted from the *South Atlantic Quarterly*, Vol. XLI, Number 4 (October, 1942), pp. 384-398.

matic versions, we shall never know. Although she may have commented on those produced in her lifetime in letters now lost or in conversation, we have only the record of her response to the performance by Wallack and T. P. Cooke in Peake's *Presumption* in 1823. On September 9 she wrote to Leigh Hunt:

> But lo and behold! I found myself famous. "Frankenstein" had prodigious success as a drama, and was about to be repeated, for the twenty-third night, at the English Opera House. The playbill amused me extremely, for, in the list of *dramatis personae*, came "————, by Mr. T. Cooke;" this nameless mode of naming the unnameable is rather good. On Friday, August 29th, Jane, my Father, William, and I went to the theatre to see it. Wallack looked very well as Frankenstein. He is at the beginning full of hope and expectation. At the end of the first act the stage represents a room with a staircase leading to Frankenstein's workshop; he goes to it, and you see his light at a small window, through which a frightened servant peeps, who runs off in terror when Frankenstein exclaims, "It lives." Presently Frankenstein himself rushes in horror and trepidation from the room, and, while still expressing his agony and terror, ("————") throws down the door of the laboratory, leaps the staircase, and presents his unearthly and monstrous person on the stage. The story is not well managed, but Cooke played ————'s part extremely well; his seeking, as it were, for support; his trying to grasp at the sounds he heard; all, indeed, he does was well imagined and executed. I was much amused, and it appeared to excite a breathless eagerness in the audience. It was a third piece, a scanty pit filled at half price, and all stayed till it was over. They continue to play it even now. . . . On the strength of the drama, my Father had published, for *my benefit,* a new edition of "Frankenstein." . . .[2]

Had she wished, Mrs. Shelley might have gone, that same year, to see two other serious melodramatic versions of the story at the Coburg and the Royalty and three burlesques at the Surrey, the Adelphi, and Davis's Royal Amphitheatre. In 1824 she might have seen *Presumption* revived at the English Opera House and at Covent Garden and witnessed a fourth burlesque at the Olympic. In 1826 she might have seen at the

2. *Letters,* I, 259.

Porte St. Martin in Paris a melodrama in which T. P. Cooke played the Monster for part of the run, and a burlesque at the Gaieté. In London a translation of the French piece was produced at the West London Theatre, a sixth romantic melodrama at the Coburg, and a revival of *Presumption* at the English Opera House, after Cooke's return from Paris, with an entirely new last scene. Through the years that followed there was scarcely a season which did not include the revival of one or other of the melodramas, at Covent Garden, the Adelphi, the Surrey, the Victoria, Sadler's Wells, and the provincial theaters. On Boxing Day in 1849 the Brothers Brough staged a sixth burlesque at the Adelphi; on Christmas Eve in 1887 a burlesque by "Richard Henry" was produced at the Gaiety; and within the last fifteen years there have been two serious dramas in England and four American-made films.

* * *

With no legal hindrance in the form of copyright, and with every encouragement in the immense success of Peake's play, it is no wonder that hack dramatists and stage managers made capital out of one of the most original mystery melodramas of the day. The decades between 1820 and 1850 were years of great popularity for the melodrama. They were years, too, when the love of the supernatural and of the macabre and the horrible was very strong, as attested by the popularity of such plays and operas as *The Vampyre* and *Der Freischütz*. Edward Fitzball asserted that his *Flying Dutchman* was by no means behind *Frankenstein* or *Der Freischütz* in horrors and blue fire. In the *Opera Glass* for October 9, 1826, appeared a poem of ten stanzas on "The Devil Among the Players"—*Faustus, Frankenstein,* and *The Vampyre.* Once Peake had shown the way, therefore, other writers, named and unnamed, naturally followed. It is surprising only that *Frankenstein* had not been adapted for the stage before 1823. Possibly the attitude toward Shelley was in part the cause of the delay. The morality of a story which, as everyone soon knew, was the work of Shelley's wife, might have been questioned even more generally had it been presented to the English public in visible form before Shelley's death. As it was, there were protests, even to the extent of a placard which, according to the *London Magazine*, "was stuck about the streets, professing to come from a knot of 'friends of humanity,' and calling on the fathers of families, &c, to set their faces against the piece." And this happened even though S. J. Arnold, the producer, had put upon the playbill for the opening performance not only a quotation from the Preface to the novel but also the statement: "The striking moral exhibited in this story, is the fatal consequence of that presumption which attempts to penetrate, beyond prescribed depths, into the mysteries of nature." The very title—*Presumption: or the Fate of Frankenstein*—underlined and pointed up the moral.

That such placards had no harmful effect upon the success of the play—indeed one periodical surmised, with reason, that they might stimulate curiosity—is abundantly clear. Mary Shelley says that when she saw it on August 29 it was a third piece and was played to a scanty pit filled at half price. But that was its twenty-third performance and it had led the bill until Mathews began his annual "monopologues" on August 18. Throughout the month the playbills had been bristling with such phrases as "thunders of applause," "breathless interest," "crowded and elegant audiences," "immense overflow," with emphasis on the unimpeachable MORAL as well as the new and striking EFFECTS. On August 14 the bill announced: "Presumption: or the Fate of Frankenstein notwithstanding the abortive attempts which have been made to prejudice the Publick, being fully established, will be acted until further notice." It ran until October 4, the end of the season, having been produced thirty-seven times. It was revived at the English Opera House and at Covent Garden the next two years, though the novelty, *Der Freischütz*, finally crowded it out, and in 1826 it had another fairly long run, being played thirteen times at the English Opera House, a record which was not surpassed and was equaled only by Mathews's immensely popular *Jonathan in England*. Meanwhile it had crossed the Atlantic to New York in 1825 and it had gone out to the provincial theaters in England and Scotland.

Pleased and amused as Mary was by *Presumption*, she was dissatisfied, it will be remembered, with the management of the story. And well she might be, if she expected to see upon the stage any adequate representation of the breadth and depth of the novel. The exigencies of the theater left no room for the character of Walton, whose scientific curiosity and loneliness reinforce the two major themes of the novel, and no time for the gradual development of the Monster's acquaintance with the world, the sequence of his abortive attempts to serve the men and women whom he was so ready to love, and the repeated experiences which turned that love into hatred and a desire to injure and even to destroy his creator. There was no time either for the moral struggle of Frankenstein over the creation of a mate for the being whom he had doomed to loneliness, or for his long, relentless pursuit of the Monster after the death of Elizabeth. The dramatist must concentrate on the horror of Frankenstein's presumptuous experiment. He must condense and knit together the scattered episodes of the novel and devise an ending to replace the dramatically impossible death of Frankenstein from exhaustion and exposure on Walton's ship and the departure of the Monster over the ice fields to the North Pole, there to make of his sledge his own funeral pyre. He must, in conformity to the conventions of the melodrama, introduce songs and incidental music and produce some comic relief. Richard Brinsley Peake, it must be admitted, succeeded fairly well in accomplishing these ends, although the critic for *The Drama* insisted that the theme of Frankenstein was too bold a task for him, "a magic circle where he must not tread," and would have preferred George Soane with his "Germanic temperament." He threw the whole weight of horror upon the Monster himself, partly by the use of effective spectacle and partly by the reduction of his killings to two; and he solved some of the most difficult problems in presenting such a character by listing him among the dramatis personae as "(———)" and by never allowing him to speak. He secured a kind of unity by making Elizabeth Frankenstein's blood sister and the betrothed of his friend Clerval instead of his foster sister and his own bride, and by uniting in the character of Agatha de Lacey the girl whom the Monster saved from drowning and the fiancée of Frankenstein. He devised as denouement the death of the Monster and his creator in an avalanche loosened by Frankenstein's pistol shot, a conclusion which most of the dramatic critics approved, in spite of its suddenness, for, as *The Drama* said, "it is natural to suppose that the end of such an abortive creation could only be brought about by some terrible convulsion of nature." [3] About the music and about the comic relief in the persons of the servant Fritz and his wife, the dramatic critics differed, although most modern readers would probably agree with *The Drama's* estimate of them as "those nonsensical frivolities, which are so unsparingly interlarded, . . . and which greatly detract from the interest of the piece." Yet when it was revived at the Adelphi in 1833, compressed into two acts (a fairly common fate of popular stock pieces to make them more useful in filling up a program), it was preceded by Winter's *Grand Overture to Calypso* and enriched by several additional "introduced" songs—partly for the benefit, perhaps, of Clara Novello, who played the part of Madame Ninon.

The secret of *Presumption's* success was partly its novelty, partly the spectacle, and largely the superior acting of Wallack and Cooke. Of the novelty, it is unnecessary to do more than speak. Here was a new and better Vampire, here was a fit predecessor to Zamiel and all his brood that were to follow. Although one dramatic critic, speaking contemptuously of the novel and the play, could flout the originality of the idea, referring to "a factitious man made by chemistry in one of D'Israeli's fictions," no one had ever seen such a creature with his own eyes. And the Monster was the chief element in the spectacle. The playbill of Covent Garden of July 9, 1824, announced, in capitals of mounting size: "Among the many striking effects of this Piece, the following will be displayed: Mysterious and terrific appearance of the Demon from the Laboratory of Frankenstein. DESTRUCTION of a COTTAGE by FIRE. And the FALL of an AVALANCHE." But the Demon,

---

3. Yet in 1826 this ending was changed and *Presumption* was produced "*with an entirely new last scene,* conformably to the termination in the original story, *representing a schooner in a violent storm!* In which *Frankenstein* and *the Monster* are destroyed." (Playbill of the E. O. H. for September 20, 1826.)

as contemporary accounts would indicate, must have been the most mysterious and terrific. From one magazine we get a vivid description of him: his green and yellow visage, his watery and lack-lustre eye, his long-matted, straggling black locks, the blue, livid hue of his arms and legs, his shriveled complexion, his straight black lips, his horrible ghastly grin. One daily critic compared him to a wax representation of a victim of the plague in a Florentine museum. It is doubtful whether Mr. Boris Karloff, with all the aids which cinematic technique can give him, looks any ghastlier or frightens any more people into fits than did T. P. Cooke.

Cooke's acting, however, made of this creature something more than a wax image of decay and horror; it stirred in some at least of the spectators and critics human interest and even a trace of the sympathy which Mary Shelley herself intended her novel to produce. Wallack, as Frankenstein, also was highly successful. He headed the bill and was obviously intended to be the chief actor. But T. P. Cooke stole the show. Although both are praised by the critics, Cooke's performance is called "unparalleled," and, with only a breath or two of unfavorable comment, he is commended for his remarkable portrayal of the Monster's awakening to sense impressions and of his fluctuating emotions—all, of course, in pantomime. "With the art of a Fuseli," said *The Drama,* "he powerfully embodied the horrible, bordering on the sublime and the awful." When Wallack withdrew to keep other engagements, the play went on with undiminished success; and until Cooke finally abandoned the part for his famous nautical roles, his name and the title *Frankenstein (Presumption* was often so referred to) were almost synonymous. Frankensteins might come and go—Wallack, Rowbotham, Bennett, Baker, Perkins, Diddear—but the Monster was forever Cooke, "the very *beau idéal* of that speechless and enormous excrescence of nature." It almost seems as if he might have been responsible for the common confusion that transformed "the Frankenstein monster" into "the monster Frankenstein." He took the role with him: *Presumption* was presented for the first time in Covent Garden at the benefit of Mr. Cooke and Mr. Connor, "by permission of S. J. Arnold, Esq.," manager of the English

Opera House; it formed part of his repertory when he toured the provinces; he was invited to go to Paris in the summer of 1826 "to look ghastly" for the benefit of the French. Mr. O. Smith filled the role acceptably after Cooke had exchanged his blue paint for the blue of a sailor's costume and was dancing hornpipes instead of leaping the laboratory staircase; but he apparently never equaled the creator of the part.[4]

The various versions of the story which followed *Presumption* had, of course, much in common with it. The basic idea and the main characters remained fixed. There were certain matters of setting, costuming, and stage business which became traditions rarely to be broken by dramatist, producer, or actor. The laboratory at the top of a staircase leading from the back of the stage, with a door for the Monster to break down and a window for the frightened servant to peer through, was part of the setting for each play. There was almost invariably a cottage to be burnt. The Monster always leaped the railing of the staircase; he always seized and snapped Frankenstein's sword; he always experienced wonder at sounds and was charmed by music. He was always nameless. He was always painted blue. These things were accepted as conventions and passed into the realm of casual allusion.

But there were also many differences. The Monster seemingly had as many lives as a cat, and each necessitated a different end. In 1823 at the English Opera House he perished in an avalanche, at the Coburg in a burning church. In 1826 he was killed by a thunderbolt in Paris and at the West London Theatre, he leapt into the crater of Mount Aetna at the Coburg, he died in an Arctic storm at the English Opera House. In the twentieth century, on the stage he committed suicide by a leap from a crag in 1927 and was shot to death in 1933; on the screen he apparently was consumed in a burning mill in the first Frankenstein film and in an explosion in the second, only to be revived and perish once more in a pool of boiling sulphur, and finally—one hopes—he returned as a ghost. Other melodramatic changes and additions were made. Mil-

---

4. The contemporary engraving of Smith as the Monster does not represent him as very terrifying.

ner's 1826 version (he was responsible also for *The Daemon of Switzerland* at the Coburg in 1823) transplanted Frankenstein to Sicily to the court of the Prince of Piombino—one of Irving's early roles—brought Frankenstein's deserted wife and child and her aged father on foot from Germany to Sicily in search of him, exposed two boys, the sons of Frankenstein and of the Prince, to the violence of the Monster, and ended in a series of scenes picturing the wild pursuit up Mount Aetna, with no dialogue but with a sufficiency of violent action, confused shouts, and agonized shrieks. The Paris version left not one person alive at the final curtain, and, as *Le Journal de Paris* reported, it would have been difficult to do more unless one killed also the prompter and the musicians in the orchestra. The last two films double the horrors by adding a criminal cut down for dead from the gallows who uses the Monster for his own nefarious purposes.

Some of the versions softened the horror by sentimentalization of character and incident. Milner's 1823 version, according to the playbill, took every care to avoid any possible objection in Principle and Morality and instead of being offensive to the Fastidious, conveyed an Instructive Lesson. The Daemon, in the opinion of the reviewer for *The Drama*, "was so heavily laden with speeches, tinged with moral maxims, that he appeared lost in a mist," and "so much endowed with the milk of human kindness" that he preserved his creator twice from destruction. In 1861 Ferdinand Dugué rewrote Merle and Antony's 1826 success, *Le Monstre et le Magicien*, adding to the characters the Phantom of the first wife of Zametti (the Parisian Frankenstein), who vainly tries to turn him from his purpose, rises to protect her child from the Monster, and at the end of the play, when the Monster only has been killed, tells Zametti to reconcile himself with God, blesses him and his bride, and assures him that after happiness on earth they will join her in Heaven. Miss Peggy Webling, in her *Frankenstein* produced in Preston in 1927, presents a Monster who is childlike and submissive, though repulsive in appearance. With no knowledge of his strength and no understanding of life and death, he crushes a dove in his hand and throws it into the lake, where, much to his delight, it floats. He takes

Katrine, Frankenstein's crippled sister, out in a boat and tries to make her float like the dove. Finally, after he has had life, death, and immortality explained to him, he leaps in remorse from a crag to join Katrine in Heaven, where, he prays, God will have pity on him. The Lord Chamberlain's Examiner found the crushing of the dove the only feature in this play which might offend the sensibilities of the audience. The scenario writer for the first Frankenstein film adopted this incident (but not the ending) with the substitution of a flower for the dove and a little peasant girl for Katrine.

Some of the adapters of the story have emphasized, as did Mary Shelley, the serious scientific interest and enthusiasm of Frankenstein. They are stressed in the play by Gladys Hastings-Walton, produced in Glasgow in 1933, which follows more closely than any other version the original novel.[5] The author's prefatory note associates the original story with the early nineteenth-century horror of the machine and justifies a revival of it in the twentieth century because of contemporary industrial conditions for which, she asserts, machines are responsible. In the films, *Frankenstein, The Bride of Frankenstein, The Son of Frankenstein,* and *The Ghost of Frankenstein,* the setting is modern. Frankenstein uses, as he thinks, electricity but really, as his son discovers, cosmic rays to bring his creature to life. The son, persuaded by his scientific curiosity about his father's work to revive the Monster from a coma, subjects him first to a thorough physical examination, taking a blood-count, testing his blood-pressure and his basal metabolism, and finding all his processes to be supernormal. The blame for the Monster's savagery is placed, not alone on his ignorance or on Man's inhumanity to Man and Monster, but on the accident that Frankenstein used a criminal's brain in creating him. Something of this motive of scientific curiosity and activity is to be found in almost all the versions. Only in the French play of Merle and Antony and in its English translation are the experiments transformed into sheer black magic and the motives degraded to a desire to secure a willing slave.

Some may think that the modern screen versions reduce

---

5. Yet she calls Mary the daughter of Robert Goodwin.

the story to absurdity. Yet Mr. Willis Cooper and the other scenario writers were probably quite serious. Not so Mr. D. O'Meara, Mr. Herring, MM. de Saint-Georges and Simonin, the Brothers Brough, and "Richard Henry." Their versions were frank burlesques; Peake even burlesqued himself in *Another Piece of Presumption,* full of puns, allusions, and parodies of *Presumption,* which opened at the Adelphi on October 20, 1823. Frankenstein was variously transformed into Frankenstich, a tailor who in accordance with the proverb makes a Man out of nine of his journeyman tailors, into Frank-in-steam, an impecunious, body-snatching medical student, into a Parisian sculptor who hopes to bring to life his statue of Aesop, into the Student Senior Wrangler of Brazenface College in the University of Krackenjanzen, into the gay inventor of a mechanical man. The Monster appeared as a Hobgoblin, as the "Blue Demon of the Strand and the Cut," as the composite product of "the Promethean bodkin of Mr. Frankenstich," as a resuscitated bailiff, dug writ in hand by Frank-in-steam from the grave where he had been buried in a trance, as the dwarf who impersonates the statue of Aesop, as a mechanical man worked by springs. His end comes in "an awful Avalanche of Earthenware, a Tremendous Shower of Starch, and an Overwhelming Explosion of Hair Powder," in an avalanche of turnips, in the explosion of a Margate steamboat—or in reformation. The two Christmas entertainments got very far away from their source. Said Otto of Rosenberg to the audience in 1849:

> You must excuse a trifling deviation
> From Mrs. Shelley's marvellous narration.
> You know a piece could never hope to go on
> Without Love—Rivals—tyrant pa's and so on.
> Therefore to let you know our altered plan
> I'm here to represent the "nice young man"
> And in the hero's person you'll discover
> On this occasion the obnoxious lover.

But the Brothers Brough had made more than this one "trifling deviation." They had introduced Zamiel (from *Der Freischütz*), seedy in appearance and out of work, a Fancy Dress

Ball, a final ballet in Undine's Palace. Yet they did not discard all the conventions. At the Ball the Monster appears in blue fire and when Frankenstein remonstrates, "You naughty boy, go home," he responds:

> I oughtn't to suppress
> My raging organ of destructiveness.
> Zamiel. Of course we wish him not to.
> Frank. Pray, who's we?
> Zamiel. The Authoress of Frankenstein and me.
> He knows the sort of thing that we require,
> So he'll proceed to set the place on fire.

But Undine puts out the fire, and the Monster is finally tamed by the "magic flute" of Education! "Richard Henry" in 1887 also added complications as well as scenic effects: Frankenstein brought to life not only his Monster but the terra-cotta model from which it was made; there were a Vampire Visconti and Mary Ann, a Vampire maiden of low degree—in fact, a whole Vampire Club; the finale was a Planet Ballet. And in this version the part of Frankenstein was taken by a woman, Miss Nellie Farren, one of the leading comediennes of the day, who lightly danced through the play, singing the "Shivering Song" and "It's a funny little way I've got."

Only a few of the fifteen dramatic versions are to be seen in print: *Presumption*, Milner's 1826 *Frankenstein*, the two French melodramas, and the French burlesque. Others may be read in manuscript in the Lord Chamberlain's Collection at the British Museum or at St. James's Palace, or in the Larpent Collection at the Henry Huntington Library in California. Several—those unlicensed dramas performed in some of the minor theaters—must be reconstructed from playbills, advertisements, and reviews in newspapers and magazines.

That *Frankenstein* through the century was a box-office success cannot be doubted. Although some of the melodramas and burlesques lived only for a few nights, *Presumption, Le Monstre et le Magicien,* and Milner's *Frankenstein, Frank-in-steam, Frankenstein; or the Model Man,* and *Frankenstein; or the Vampire's Victim* all played to crowded houses for long runs. According to the newspapers, in Paris extra police were necessary to handle the crowds, or, in the words of a contemporary verse "Pot-Pourri," *Le Monstre,*

> dix gendarmes par personne,
> Afin d'empêcher de siffler.

Although the success of "Richard Henry's" play was threatened on the first night by a riot of pittites, aggrieved because some of the space usually allotted to them had been given to the stalls, on January 7 it was "drawing crowded houses and promises to rank amongst the most brilliant of Gaiety successes." The popularity of at least the earlier Frankenstein films is obvious.

There are other signs of widespread interest and favor beside numerous versions, long runs, crowded houses, and favorable reviews. The tribute of imitation was paid to *Frankenstein,* on the stage by *Wake Not the Dead,* a drama based on a German tale in which a nobleman brings his wife back to life, only to find her a Monster, and in French prose in a tale called *Le Fils de Sorcier,* purporting to be based on a Maltese folk-tale. It was well toward the middle of the century and the end of Mary Shelley's life before the echoes in the periodical press of the presumptuous scientist and of "———" died away, echoes in the form of serious allusion, verse and prose parody, adaptation for political or ecclesiastical satire. *Punch in London* in 1831, for instance, suggested that Mr. O. Smith (T. P. Cooke's successor) be created Lord Frankenstein, since he did not think it "fair that the Marquis of L——— should continue to *play the devil* by himself." *The Episcopal Gazette* in 1832 announced a performance of *Presumption; or The Fate of Episcopals* by the desire of John Bull. *The Man in the Moon* in 1847 drafted a sixth act to *Hamlet* in which ——— enters through a trap with a strong sulphurous smell and drinks and sings with the Ghost.

The stage history of *Frankenstein* offers one way of taking the pulse of a portion, at least, of the theatergoing public of the last hundred and twenty years. The rate and quality of that pulse and its response to the stimulus of mystery and horror seem to have changed little. Many a periodical writer of the 1820's mourned over the depraved taste of his times as evinced by the popularity of *Frankenstein*, *The Vampyre*, and *Der Freischütz*. What a writer in *The Opera Glass* for October 23, 1826, said of producers and public could probably, *mutatis mutandis*, be said today—that

> "true-blue" was long the favourite colour of the theatres, the monster's blue for a long time preventing the managers looking blue at the state of their benches. . . . [They] summoned to their aid a host of small wit, and of still smaller sense, succeeding so pre-eminently in the amalgamation of the proportions, that each god retired with a satisfactory growl from his one-shilling elevation, and acknowledged that the mixture was as exactly fitted to his taste as though it had been burnt brandy instead of burnt resin.

The history is also a kind of tribute to the imaginative powers of a young girl of barely nineteen, spurred to creative activity by the high talk about the nature of the principle of life that went on at Diodati in 1816. It is small wonder that Mary Shelley's publishers and the editors of the annuals considered that the best way in which she could sign her novels and tales and poems was "By the Author of Frankenstein." Sir Timothy's prohibition of the use of the Shelley name was no detriment to her reputation.

APPENDIX V

Unpublished Poems by Mary Shelley

From the Shelley-Rolls collection in the Bodleian Library
(MSS. Shelley adds. c.5)

1.
Tempo e' piu di Morire
Io ho tardato piu ch' i' non vorrei

> Sadly borne across the waves
> Hark! a voice from many graves,
>   Whispers—"Come!

"We for thee too long have waited,
"Haste, before thou art belated,
    "To our home!"

And the voice of my life's Lord,
Voice heard soon & aye adored,
    Cries still—"Come!
"Canst thou stay, my gentle Bride,
"I no long[er] at thy side,
    "In our home?

"Dark was this wild world to thee,
"Till I, in youthful extasy,
    "Cried—Come! Come!
"Gladly we together fled
"And across the sea we sped
    "To our home.

"Tender love & constancy
"Formed our nuptial revelry
    "And welcome.
"Ah! those days too quickly flew,
"Till, enforced, I bade adieu
    "To our home.

"Storm & Ocean bore me here,
"Thou remainest, Mary dear,
    "Yet. Ah! Come!
"Life is but a sickly dream,
"Swiftly cross the turbid stream
    "To my home.

"Never more will human love
"Woes requite which thou must prove,
    "Why not come?
"Never more in forest sweet
"Will be built a fair retreat
    "For thy home.

APPENDIX

"Hope and joy from thee are gone,
"And thou wanderest aye alone,
    "Dearest, come!
"Ere worse betide than all you fear,
"Ere Evening shadows gather near
    "My lone home.

"Onc[e] again in storm tossed bark
"Speed across the Ocean dark
    "Sweet! Ah! Come.
"Now as then thy husband's arm
"Will bear thee from every harm
    "To his Home."

1833

2.
La Vida es sueño

[1]

The tide of Time was at my feet
   Flowing with calm & equal motion;
With gladdened heart my eyes might greet
   The coming of the sunlit ocean,
Till at its full, a fatal storm
Wrapt in grim shade the mighty form.

2

Then backward rolled the ebb of Time,
   While I with eager steps pursue,
And though the hour had lost its prime,
   Still as the dim beach wider grew,
I passed along the utmost verge
Of the inconstant fleeting surge.

3

Back & more back the waters rolled,
   And faster yet the waves receded—
And now, alas! my hopes grew cold,
   And the vacant prospect heeded,

For blank and desart shewed the strand,
As sad I paced the barren sand.

4

When, lo! upborne by fairy pinions,
   Occasion [?] came, Enchantress coy,
And brought from the serene dominions
   Of Hope & love, a dream of joy;
I closed mine eyes, & laid me down,
And thought no more of Ocean's frown.

5

Where is my Dream? Again the roar
   Of Time's vast flood salutes mine ear,
And I stand lonely as before
   On the waste sands, so sad & d[r]ear
And hope has vanished from the scene,
And is as if it ne'er had been!

                              1834

3.
(Printed here because the manuscript differs from the text as set to music by H. H. Pearson and as printed by Jones, *The Letters of Mary W. Shelley*, II, 159 n)

O listen while I sing to thee;
   My song is meant for thee alone;
Thy thought imparts its melody,
   And gives the soft impassioned tone.

I sing of joy—& see thy smile,
   That to the swelling note replies;
I sing of love—& feel the while
   The gaze of thy love-beaming eyes.

If thou wert far, my voice would die
   In murmurs faint & sorrowing;
If thou wert false—in agony
   My heart would break—I could not sing.

> Then listen while I sing to thee,
>   My song is meant for thee alone;
> And now that thou art near to me
>   I pour a full impassioned tone.
>
> March 12, 1838

From Lord Abinger's collection

1.
> Alas I weep my life away
> And spend my heart in useless sorrow,
> As sadly wanes the lingering day
> Bringing a yet more hopeless morrow.
>   (Entry in the journal for September 14, 1831)

2.
> Struggle no more, my Soul with the sad chains
> Which time & fortune have thrown over thee
> Yield thy last life to the eclipse that stains
> With shadows dark its once bright tracery.
>   (Entry in the journal for September 16, 1831)

APPENDIX VI

Persons Real and Fictitious Referred to in the Book

Ada: daughter of Byron and Lady Byron
Adrian: chief character in *The Last Man*
Albé: nickname given to Byron by the Shelleys
Alfred: son of Lionel Verney in *The Last Man*
Alithea: wife of Mr. Neville, beloved by Falkner in *Falkner*
Allegra: daughter of Byron and Claire Clairmont
Alleyn, Marcott: English artist in "The Bride of Modern Italy"
Annabella: Anne Isabelle, Lady Byron

Baxter, Christy: girlhood friend of Mary
Beatrice: mistress of Castruccio in *Valperga*
Castruccio: Prince of Lucca, in *Valperga*
Claire: see Clairmont
Clairmont, Charles: Mary's stepbrother
Clairmont, Claire: Mary's stepsister, originally called Jane
Clairmont, Mrs. Mary Jane: Mary's stepmother, Godwin's second wife
Clara: see Shelley
Clara: daughter of Lord Raymond and Perdita in *The Last Man*
Clarice: heroine of "The Mourner"
Clermont, Mrs.: Lady Byron's governess
Clerval, Henry: Frankenstein's friend in *Frankenstein*
Clorinda: see Saviani or Saville
Constance: heroine of "The Dream"
Derham, Fanny: friend of the Villiers in *Lodore*
Derham, Francis: friend of Lord Lodore; father of Fanny in *Lodore*
Diana: mother of Mathilda in *Mathilda*
Dmitri: Albanian Klepht in "The Evil Eye"
Edward: see Villiers
Eliza: see Westbrook
Elizabeth: see Lavenza or Raby
Emilia: see Viviani
Emily: name for Emilia Viviani used by Shelley in *Epipsychidion*
Ethel: see Villiers
Evadne: Greek girl beloved by Adrian and Raymond in *The Last Man*
Evelyn: son of Lionel Verney in *The Last Man*
Euphrasia: heroine of "Euphrasia"
Euthanasia: heroine of *Valperga*
Falkner, Rupert John: main character in *Falkner*
Fanny: see Derham or Imlay
Faro, Hernan de: character in *Perkin Warbeck*
Felix: character in *Frankenstein*
Fitzhenry, Mrs. Elizabeth: sister of Lord Lodore in *Lodore*
Frankenstein, Victor: scientist in *Frankenstein*

APPENDIX 237

Gamba, Piero: Teresa Guiccioli's brother
Giacomo: friend of Alleyn in "The Bride of Modern Italy," wooer of Clorinda
Gisborne, John: friend of the Shelleys
Gisborne, Maria: wife of John Gisborne, formerly Mrs. Reveley, courted by Godwin
Godwin, Mary Jane: Godwin's second wife
Godwin, William: father of Mary Shelley, husband of Mary Wollstonecraft
Godwin, William, Jr.: son of William and Mary Jane Godwin
Guiccioli, Teresa: Byron's mistress
Guinigi: character in *Valperga*
Harriet: see Shelley
Hogg, Thomas Jefferson: friend of Shelley
Hunt, John: brother of Leigh Hunt
Hunt, Leigh: friend of the Shelleys, poet and essayist
Hunt, Thornton: son of Leigh Hunt
Idris: sister of Adrian, wife of Lionel Verney in *The Last Man*
Imlay, Fanny: daughter of Mary Wollstonecraft, half-sister of Mary
Jane: see Clairmont or Williams
Jervis, Miss: Elizabeth Raby's governess in *Falkner*
Katherine: wife of Richard of York in *Perkin Warbeck*
Lavenza, Elizabeth: Frankenstein's bride in *Frankenstein*
Leigh, Augusta: Byron's half-sister
Lewis, M. G.: author of *The Monk*
Lodore, Lord: character in *Lodore*, father of Ethel
Malville, Edmund: character in "Recollections of Italy"
Martha: character in *The Last Man*
Mason, Mrs.: friend of Mary, former pupil of Mary Wollstonecraft
Mathilda: heroine of *Mathilda*
Mavrocordato, Prince: Greek patriot who taught Mary Greek
Medwin, Thomas: Shelley's cousin
Merrival: astronomer, character in *The Last Man*
Monna Gegia de' Becari: character in "A Tale of the Passions"
Moore, Thomas: Irish poet, friend and biographer of Byron
Moxon, Edward: publisher
Murray, John: publisher

Neville, Gerard: character in *Falkner*
Neville, Horace: character in "The Mourner"
Noel, Lady: Lady Byron's mother
Novello, Mary: daughter of Vincent Novello, wife of Charles Cowden Clarke
Novello, Vincent: organist and composer, friend of Mary
Ollier, Charles: publisher
Owen, Robert Dale: son of Robert Owen, active in public life in the United States
Pacchiani, Francesco: acquaintance of the Shelleys
Payne, John Howard: American actor and playwright, in love with Mary
Peacock, Thomas Love: friend of Shelley; novelist
Pepe, Benedetto: character in *Valperga*
Percy: see Shelley
Perdita: sister of Lionel Verney, wife of Lord Raymond in *The Last Man*
"Pirate, the": nickname for Trelawny
Procter, Bryan: friend of Mary; writer using pseudonym "Barry Cornwall"
Raby, Edwin: character in *Falkner*
Raby, Elizabeth: daughter of Edwin Raby, foster daughter of Falkner in *Falkner*
Raby, Oswi: father of Edwin Raby in *Falkner*
Raymond, Lord: character in *The Last Man*
Reveley, Henry: Mrs. Gisborne's son
Reveley, Mrs. Maria: friend of the Shelleys; later Mrs. John Gisborne
Richard of York: pretender to the throne in *Perkin Warbeck*
Rosina: heroine of "The Invisible Girl"
Ryland: character in *The Last Man*
Santerre, Lady: mother of Lady Lodore in *Lodore*
Saviani, Clorinda: heroine of "The Bride of Modern Italy"
Saville, Horatio: character in *Lodore*
Saville, Clorinda: wife of Horatio Saville in *Lodore*
Shelley, Sir Bysshe: Shelley's grandfather
Shelley, Clara: daughter of Shelley and Mary
Shelley, Harriet Westbrook: Shelley's first wife
Shelley, Percy: son of Shelley and Mary

Shelley, Sir Timothy: Shelley's father
Shelley, William: son of Shelley and Mary
Stacey, Sophia: friend of Shelley and Mary in Florence
Timothy, Sir: see Shelley
Trelawny, Edward John: friend of the Shelleys and Byron; "the Pirate"
Verney, Lionel: character in *The Last Man*; "the last man"
Villiers, Edward: character in *Lodore*
Villiers, Ethel Fitzhenry: wife of Edward Villiers, daughter of Lord Lodore in *Lodore*
Viviani, Emilia: friend of the Shelleys; subject of *Epipsychidion*
Walton, Robert: character in *Frankenstein*
Westbrook, Eliza: Harriet Shelley's older sister
William: see Shelley or Godwin
Williams, Edward: friend of Shelley, drowned with him
Williams, Jane: common law wife of Edward Williams, later of T. J. Hogg
Wollstonecraft, Everina: sister of Mary Wollstonecraft
Wollstonecraft, Mary: first wife of Godwin; mother of Mary Shelley; author of *The Rights of Women*
Woodville: character in *Mathilda*

Bibliography

I have made no attempt to name the many books and articles which I have read about Mary Shelley and her family and friends. I have listed below the chief printed sources used in this book, aside from Mary Shelley's own writings. They are grouped and arranged chronologically in their groups. The descriptive comments point out their particular value for this study. Information about unpublished material and about Mrs. Shelley's works (my principal sources) is given in the notes and in Appendix II. Bibliographical details about books and articles referred to only once or twice are given in the notes.

Shelley and Mary, 4 vols. Privately printed, 1882.
    Only twelve copies were printed. It contains the journals and correspondence then in the possession of Sir Percy and Lady Jane Shelley, selected by them for printing and private circulation only. It formed the basis of Mrs. Marshall's biography of Mary Shelley and of Dowden's life of Shelley. The journals and the Shelley letters have since been published. It is still the only printed source for some of the other correspondence.

Mrs. Julian Marshall. *The Life and Letters of Mary W. Shelley*, 2 vols. London, Richard Bentley & Son, 1889.
    The first biography, based on *Shelley and Mary*, and idealizing Mary. It was followed by other briefer, not very

significant biographies by Helen Moore (1886), Lucy Maddox Rossetti (1890), Richard Church (1928), and Muriel Spark (1951).

R. Glynn Grylls. *Mary Shelley. A Biography.* London, Oxford University Press, 1938.
 The latest full biography, utilizing unpublished letters and passages from the journal. Some errors, but generally authoritative.

Frederick L. Jones, ed. *The Letters of Mary W. Shelley,* 2 vols. Norman, University of Oklahoma Press, 1944.
 Although there are still some unpublished letters and a few in scattered printed sources apparently unknown to Professor Jones, this is the most considerable, fully annotated, and nearly complete collection.

Frederick L. Jones, ed. *Mary Shelley's Journal.* Norman, University of Oklahoma Press, 1947.
 Fully annotated reprinting from *Shelley and Mary.*

Richard Garnett, ed. *Tales and Stories by Mary Wollstonecraft Shelley.* London, William Patterson & Co., 1891.
 An edition, with a critical introduction, of most of the tales printed in the Annuals.

Maria Vohl. *Die Erzählungen der Mary Shelley und Ihre Urbilder.* Heidelberg, C. W. Winter, 1913.
 A critical study, making most of the familiar identifications between fictional characters and real persons.

Sylva Norman. "Mary Shelley: Novelist and Dramatist," in *On Shelley.* London, Oxford University Press, 1938.
 A brief critical essay.

T. J. Hogg. *Life of Shelley,* 2 vols. London, Moxon, 1858.
 Valuable for its inclusion of some fragments of Mary Shelley's projected life of Shelley.

Edward Dowden. *The Life of P. B. Shelley,* 2 vols. London, Kegan Paul, Trench & Co., 1886.
 The first really authoritative biography. Sympathetic to Mary.

Walter E. Peck. *Shelley: His Life and Work,* 2 vols. Boston and New York, Houghton Mifflin Co., 1927.

Important for its full (though sometimes mistaken) use of material from Mary Shelley's works for biographical purposes.

Newman Ivey White. *Shelley*, 2 vols. New York, Alfred A. Knopf, 1940.
The definitive biography to date.

Ethel C. Mayne. *Life and Letters of Anne Isabella, Lady Noel Byron*. New York, Charles Scribner's Sons, 1929.
This book contributes much to an understanding of the characters of Byron and Lady Byron and of the circumstances of their marriage and separation.

E. J. Trelawny. *Adventures of a Younger Son*. London, Colburn and Bentley, 1831.
The autobiography which Mary Shelley saw through the press and used for material in *Falkner*.

H. Buxton Forman, ed. *The Letters of Edward John Trelawny*. London, Oxford University Press, 1910.
Containing most of Trelawny's letters and also a number of Mary's in the footnotes.

H. J. Massingham. *The Friend of Shelley: A Memoir of Edward John Trelawny*. New York, D. Appleton and Co., 1930.
Valuable for details about Trelawny's relations with Byron and the Shelleys. Definitely hostile to Mary.

R. Glynn Grylls. *Trelawny*. London, Constable, [1950].
The latest biography, using some unpublished material. Sympathetic to Mary.

Kegan Paul. *William Godwin: His Friends and Contemporaries*, 2 vols. London, Henry S. King & Co., 1876.
Important for its inclusion of passages from Mary Shelley's notes for her projected biography of Godwin.

Ford K. Brown. *The Life of William Godwin*. London & Toronto, J. M. Dent & Sons; New York, E. P. Dutton & Co., 1926.
The most recent biography.

R. Glynn Grylls. *Claire Clairmont: Mother of Byron's Allegra*. London, John Murray, [1939].
   Valuable for additional details about Mary as well as for being the only biography of Claire.

Enrica Viviani della Robbia. *Vita di una donna (L'Emily di Shelley)*. Firenze, G. C. Sansoni, 1936.
   A full, scholarly, and sympathetic biography of Emilia Viviani, important for the account of her relations with the Shelleys.

Index

The names of the most important characters in Mary Shelley's fiction who represent real persons are included in the index and are enclosed in quotation marks. For identification of real and fictitious persons mentioned in the book, the reader is referred to APPENDIX VI.

Abinger, Lord, v, vi, vii, 50n, 62n, 89n, 106n, 109n, 118n, 172n, 207, 208, 210, 213, 217, 235
"Adrian, Earl of Windsor," 15, 26, 34, 37, 38, 41, 68-75, 78, 80, 81, 102, 112, 116, 153, 183, 186, 235
Aeschylus, 24n, 154
Alfieri, Vittorio, 92n, 154, 158, 160
Allegra, *see* Clairmont
"Alleyn, Marcott," 26, 64-66, 132, 137, 235
Allsop, T., 8, 9, 109n
Annuals, the, xiii, 30, 157; Mary's contributions to, 172-175
Another Piece of Presumption, 228
Antony, *see* Béraud
Appleton's Journal, 156, 207
Apuleius, 154
Arnold, S. J., 221

Athenaeum, The, 173
Austen, Jane, 144

Bailey, J. O., 29n, 153n
Baker, Carlos H., 70, 211n
Baxter, Christy, 5, 203, 236
"Beatrice," 61, 63n, 110, 149, 150, 186, 192, 236
Beddoes, T. L., 63n, 152
Bentley, Richard, 169, 171
Belle Assemblée, La, 63, 175, 208
Béraud, Antoine ("Antony"), 226, 227
Blackwood's, 61, 106, 144, 145-146, 150, 151, 152
Blake, William, 42
Blessington, Lady, xiii, 7, 22n
Bodleian Library, v, vi, 50n, 207, 210, 213, 231
Book of Beauty, The, 173, 174, 207
Bowring, Sir John, xii, 68, 160
Bride of Frankenstein, The, 227

Bride of Modern Italy, The, 26, 63n, 66, 207; picture of Shelley in, 64-66; picture of Emilia Viviani in, 65, 132-134
British Museum, v, 4n, 19, 229
Brooks, Kenneth A., 156n
Brough, R. B. and William, 220, 228
Brougham, Henry, 41
Brown, Ford K., 3n, 9n, 243
Bulwer, Edward L., xiii, 157
Byron, Ada, 120, 235
Byron, Anne Isabelle, Lady, 235, 243; as Cornelia, Lady Lodore, 113, 120-122, 130, 170; as Perdita, 103, 113
Byron, George Gordon, Lord, vi, xii, xiv, 3n, 8, 10, 15, 18, 20, 22, 26, 27, 35, 66, 67, 107, 128, 145, 173, 177, 188, 203, 204, 235; his opinion of Shelley, 112; Mary's opinion of, 107-109, 140; in Mary's novels, 107-123, 127; as Castruccio, 104-105, 109, 110; as Falkner, 80, 109, 122-123, 172; as Lodore, 20, 109, 110, 117-122, 170; as Raymond, 69, 72, 102-103, 109, 110-117; traits in other characters, 109-110

WORKS: *Cain*, 107; *Childe Harold*, 108, 114-115 (quot.), 117, 119 (quot.), 191; "Darkness," 152; *Don Juan*, 107; *Lara*, 108; *Manfred*, 108, 123 (quot.), 172; *Memoirs*, 113; *Siege of Corinth*, 116n; "The Sketch," 121

Cabinet Cyclopedia, 20n, 24, 32, 75, 167, 171, 208; inception, 159; reception of, 160-161; Mary's pleasure in, 160-161; merits of, 195; quotations from, 19-20, 195-196

Cacciatore, Vera, vii
Campbell, Alexander, 168
Campbell, Thomas, 152
Casquet of Literature, The, 174, 207
"Castruccio," 33, 43, 60, 61, 109, 110, 137, 148, 186, 188, 236
Cervantes, 196
Choice, The, 9, 55, 157, 210, 212; quotation from, 56
Church, Richard, 242
Clairmont, Allegra, 18, 65n, 72, 120, 203, 204, 235; as Louisa Biron, 129; as Clara Raymond, 72, 103, 129
Clairmont, Charles, 83, 105-106, 141, 236
Clairmont, Claire (originally Jane), vi, xii, xiv, 5, 13, 15, 18, 22, 24, 42, 52, 54, 62, 65n, 83, 85, 108, 115, 122, 128, 130, 134, 135, 141, 144-145, 167, 176, 203, 235, 236, 244; as Beatrice, 104-105, 110; as Miss Jervis, 105, 172; as Perdita, 72, 103-104, 112; "The Pole," 173n, 209; "Reminiscences," 4n, 20
Clarke, Charles Cowden, 4n
Clarke, Mary Cowden, *see* Novello
Clermont, Mrs., 236; as Lady Santerre, 121, 130
Cobbett, William, 41, 143
Colburn, Henry, 150, 167, 168
Coleridge, Samuel Taylor, 9n, 137, 173, 182, 191
Condorcet, Jean Antoine, 33, 35, 39, 47
Cooke, T. P., 146, 219, 220, 223-225
Court Magazine, The, 106, 173n, 209
Curran, Amelia, 12, 51n

Dacre, Charlotte, 144
Dante, 24n, 34, 215n, 217n

INDEX

Darwin, Erasmus, 27
Davy, Sir Humphrey, 26
"Derham, Fanny," 46, 47, 86, 87, 91, 99, 236
"Derham, Francis," 40, 47, 79, 99, 118, 236
"Derham, Mrs. Francis," 86, 98
"Diana," 90, 96-97, 236
Dillon, Lord, 10, 158
Disraeli, Benjamin, xiii, 223
Dowden, Edward, 241, 242
Dracula, 218
Drama, The, 222, 223, 224
Drawing-Room Scrap-Book, The, 157, 173, 210
Dugué, Ferdinand, 226

Edgcumbe, Fred, vii
Edinburgh Review, The, 144
Ehrsam, T. G., xi n
English Annual, The, 106
Essays, Letters from Abroad, and Translations (Shelley), 209; Mary's notes and preface to, 54, 179; publication, 163-164, 204; inclusions, 163
"Euthanasia," 34, 62, 63n, 87, 91, 104, 110, 137, 149, 150, 186, 192, 236
Examiner, The, 175, 176, 181, 208; Mary's letter in, 143; Trelawny's article in, 167

"Falkner, Rupert John," 14, 15, 34, 42, 75n, 80, 122-126, 182, 186, 193, 237
Falkner, 14n, 98, 124, 128n, 138, 142, 170, 186, 206; publication of, 171, 204; reviews of, 172; plot of, 181-182; style of, 172, 193; treatment of education in, 34; attitude toward religion in, 40; social and political problems in, 42, 45; biographical elements in, 172; Shelley in, 80, 172; Byron in, 109, 122-123, 172; Trelawny in, 123-126, 172; Claire in, 105; quotations from, 122-123, 124-125, 130-131
"de Faro, Hernan," 126, 236
Finch, Robert, 189
Forman, H. Buxton, 55n, 73n, 243
Frank, Pat, 153n
"Frankenstein, Victor," 16, 17, 26, 27-30, 32, 33, 83, 138, 182, 183, 187, 193, 222, 236
Frankenstein (burlesque by Richard Henry), 220, 228, 229, 230
Frankenstein (moving picture), 218, 227
Frankenstein (play by Gladys Hastings-Walton), 227
Frankenstein (play by Peggy Webling), 226
Frankenstein; or the Daemon of Switzerland, 226, 229
Frankenstein; or the Man and the Monster, 226, 229
Frankenstein; or the Model Man, 229
Frankenstein; or the Modern Prometheus, xiii, 3, 10, 83, 106, 129, 142, 150, 153, 178, 180, 181, 187, 191, 205-206; genesis of, 27, 66, 145; predecessors of, 144; publication of, 144, 203; reception of, 144, 145-146, 151; subsequent history, influence, and reputation of, 27, 29, 147, 148, 179, 230; dramatic versions of, 27, 146-147, 218-231; as expression of Mary's temperament, 15, 16-17; science and technology in, 16, 26-30, 32, 148; theories of education in, 34, 148; social and political theories in, 43; Shelley's ideas in, 57-58; plot of, 147,

Frankenstein (continued) 182-183; characterization in, 147, 148, 183; style of, 145, 146-147, 191-192, 193, 197-199; quotations from, 16, 17, 27, 28, 29-30, 34, 43, 83-84, 191-192, 197-199
Frankenstein; or the Vampire's Victim, 229, 230
Frankenstich, 228
Frank-in-Steam, 229
Fraser's, 157, 160, 170
Freethinker, The, 180n
Freischütz, Der, 218, 220, 221, 228, 231
Furnivall, Dr., 10

Gamba, Piero, 8, 237
Garnett, Richard, 25, 64, 174n, 242
Gaskell, Mrs. D., 188
Gatteschi, Signor, 167, 176, 177
Ghost of Frankenstein, The, 227
Gilfillan, George, 179
Gisborne, John, xii, 138n, 155, 175, 214, 237
Gisborne, Maria, xii, 7, 23, 42, 53, 76, 89, 96, 107n, 140, 155, 157, 171, 175, 189, 214, 215, 237, 238; Mary's description of, 139; as Ethel Fitzhenry, 138-139; as Elizabeth Raby, 138-139
Godwin, Mary Jane Clairmont, 83, 84, 85, 86, 141, 236; as Mrs. Derham, 98-99, 237
Godwin, Mary Wollstonecraft, *see* Wollstonecraft
Godwin, William, xiii, xiv, 3, 6, 9, 15, 18, 20, 22, 25, 35, 83, 84, 87, 95, 99, 102, 106, 128, 138, 139, 141, 144, 149, 155, 159, 165, 166, 167, 168, 177, 181, 189, 198, 204, 209, 214, 236, 237, 243; attitude toward Shelley, 93; theories on education, 23-24, 33, 85-87; Mary's love for, 89-90, 93; her love reflected in her stories, 91; Mary's interpretation of his character, 88-95; as Mathilda's father, 11, 90-93, 155; as Lionel Verney's father, 90, 94-95; as Countess of Windsor, 131
Godwin, William, Jr., 83, 105, 106, 141, 167, 209, 237
Gore, Catherine Frances, xiii
Gosse, Edmund, 97, 103, 113n
Gray, Austin K., 111n
Grylls, R. Glynn (Lady Mander), vii, 4n, 54n, 56n, 105n, 123n, 138n, 151n, 159n, 180, 242, 243, 244
Guiccioli, Teresa, 8, 103, 111, 118, 237
"Guinigi," 33, 42-43, 47, 61, 237

Hastings-Walton, Gladys, 227
Helvetius, Claude Adrian, 34, 35
Henry, Richard, 220, 228, 229, 230
Herring, Mr. (author of *Mr. Herring's Presumption*), 228
Hill, R. H., vii
Hogg, Thomas Jefferson, 18, 19, 40, 50, 66, 112n, 128, 130, 138, 151, 161, 162, 163, 188, 208, 237, 242
Holcroft, Thomas, 88
Holmes, Edward, 7
Hood, Thomas, 152
Hunt, John, 25, 237
Hunt, John H., 3n
Hunt, Leigh, xii, 3n, 4, 7, 8, 13, 17n, 25, 50, 53, 93, 94, 115, 128, 143, 149, 150, 155, 156, 162, 188, 189, 191, 204, 218, 219, 237
Hunt, Thornton, 4, 10, 57, 112n, 237
Huntington Library, v, 7n, 229
Huxley, Aldous, 153n, 181

INDEX

Imlay, Fanny, 5, 83, 84, 96, 128, 203, 237; supposed love for Shelley, 99; as Fanny Derham, 86, 99-102; as Evadne Zaimi, 102-103
Imlay, Gilbert, 83, 98
Indicator, The, 155, 156
Italian Sisters, The, 174, 181n
Irving, Washington, xii

"Jervis, Miss," 46, 105, 139, 185-186, 188, 237
Jones, Frederick L., vii, 24n, 63n, 159n, 180, 242
Juvenile Souvenir, The, 158

Karloff, Boris, 147, 224
Kean, Edmund, 25, 158
Keats House and Museum, v, vi, 156n
Keats-Shelley Memorial, v, vii
Keepsake, The, 55, 156, 157, 173, 174, 175, 207, 208, 210
Keepsake Français, Le, 174
Kelsall, T. F., 63n, 159
Kemble, Fanny, 126n
Knight's Quarterly Magazine, 144
Koszul, A., 158

Ladies Monthly Museum, The, 153
Lamb, Charles, xii, 8
Last Man, The, xiii, 10, 26, 90n, 105, 129, 131, 154, 166, 168, 180, 181, 186, 206; inception of, 66-67, 150; publication of, 150, 204; reception of, 151-153, 167; other works on same theme, 152-153; science and technology in, 30-31, 32-33; theories of education in, 34; social and political problems in, 35-36, 36-38, 41, 151; attitude toward religion in, 40; Shelley in, 57, 67, 68-75, 81, 151; Byron in, 102-103, 109, 110-117; Claire in, 103-104; Fanny Imlay in, 102-103; Mary in, 15-16, 68, 72, 112; Godwin in, 94-95; dramatic scenes in, 183-185; style of, 151, 153, 192, 193; quotations from, 15-16, 32-33, 41-42, 68-69, 70, 71, 94-95, 111, 114, 115, 116, 141-142, 184-185, 192, 193-194
Last Man, or Omegarus and Syderia, The, 152
Leigh, Augusta, 118, 122, 123, 237
Lewes, George Henry, 53
Lewis, Matthew Gregory, 66, 144, 145, 237
Liberal, The, 63, 150, 156, 175, 207
Literary Chronicle, The, 150, 151, 173
Literary Gazette, The, 110n
Literary Souvenir, The, 158
"Lodore, Lord," 13, 14, 15, 78, 86, 91, 109, 110, 117-122, 130, 193, 237
Lodore, 10, 98, 138, 142, 172, 186, 206; publication of, 169, 204; Mary's intention in, 169; reviews of, 169-170; treatment of education in, 34, 86-87; social and political problems in, 45; biographical element in, 13, 76-77, 78, 86-87, 153, 170-171; Shelley in, 66, 75n, 77-80, 118, 119, 121, 134-136, 170; Byron in, 109, 117-122, 170; Fanny Imlay in, 99-102, 170; Eliza Westbrook in, 121-122, 129-130, 170; Emilia Viviani in, 132n, 134-136, 170; style of, 193; quotations from, 46, 101-102, 117-118, 121

"Lodore, Cornelia Santerre, Lady," 13, 14, 20, 34, 45, 46, 77, 78, 96, 113, 120-122, 129-130, 135, 169, 186
London Magazine, The, 63, 66, 151, 157, 175, 207, 208
Lord Chamberlain's Collection, the, v, 229
Lovell, Ernest J., Jr., 112n
Luther, Martin, 47

"Malville, Edmund," 64, 237
Mander, Lady, *see* Grylls
Marchand, Leslie A., vii
Marshal, James, 88
Marshall, Mrs., xi, xii, 22n, 93n, 241
Mason, Mrs., 96, 129, 165, 237
Massingham, H. J., xii, 108, 117n, 127, 243
"Mathilda," 11-13, 14, 58, 90, 92, 93, 96, 193, 215-217, 236, 237
Mathilda, 26, 90n, 156, 207, 211-217; date of, 154, 212-214; MSS of, 212-213, 214-215; plot of, 92, 215-217; autobiographical element in, 11-13, 56, 93, 154, 211-212, 215; Shelley in, 12, 57, 58-60, 81, 154; Godwin in, 90-93, 155; Mary's references to, 215; opinions of, 155, 214; style of, 193; quotations from, 11, 12-13, 58, 59-60, 91, 97
Mavrocordato, Prince, 35, 137, 204, 237
Mayne, Ethel C., 113n, 243
Medwin, Thomas, 4, 10, 121, 128, 133, 188, 214, 237
de Mengaldo, Chevalier, 66, 145
Merimée, Prosper, xii, 24n
Merle, Jean-Toussaint, 226-227
Metropolitan Literary Journal, The, 210
Milner, H. M., 146, 226, 229

de Monnier, Mme., 19
"Monster, the," 16-17, 29, 34, 43, 183, 187, 193, 197, 222, 223-224, 225
Monstre et le Magicien, Le, 226, 229
Monthly Review, The, 151
Moore, Helen, 242
Moore, Thomas, 52, 109, 143, 167, 237
Moxon, Edward, 53, 161, 162-163, 177, 237
Murray, John, 19, 109, 160, 166, 167, 168, 237
Murry, J. Middleton, 158

Napoleon, 39, 114-115, 117
New Edinburgh Review, The, 178n
New Monthly Magazine, The, 170n, 178n
Nitchie, Elizabeth, 169n, 189n
Noel, Lady, 238; as Lady Santerre, 121
Norman, Sylva, 19n, 44, 158n, 199, 242
Norton, Caroline, 7, 174
Novello, Mary Victoria (Mrs. Charles Cowden Clarke), 4, 7, 238
Novello, Vincent, xii, 7, 25, 129, 150, 238

Ollier, Charles, 149, 164n, 171, 238
O'Meara, D., 228
Opera Glass, The, 220, 231
Owen, Robert Dale, xii, 4, 7, 238

Pacchiani, Francesco, 204, 238; as Benedetto Pepe, 137
Paganini, 25
Pascal, Blaise, 32
Paul, Kegan, 84n, 88n, 99n, 139n, 208, 243
Payne, John Howard, xii, 7, 8, 20, 25, 129, 238

INDEX 251

Peacock, Thomas Love, 48, 138, 143, 145, 150, 152n, 162, 188, 238
Peake, Richard Brinsley, 146, 174, 219, 222, 228
Pearson, Henry Hugh, 210
Peck, Walter E., 102n, 242
"Pepe, Benedetto," 137, 238
"Perdita," 72, 102n, 103, 112, 113, 115, 116, 238
Perkin Warbeck, The Fortunes of, 42, 129, 169, 206; sale of, 168; publication of, 168, 204; reviews of, 168-169; autobiographical material in, 75; Trelawny in, 126
Petrarch, 195
Pierpont Morgan Library, v, vi, 197n
Pitt, George Dibdin, 152
Pocket Magazine, The, 66n
Poetical Works (Shelley), 209, 210; publication of, 162, 204; Mary's preface and notes, 53-54, 161-162, 179; interpretation of Shelley in preface and notes, 53-54, 81-82; reviews of, 162, 163; inclusion of *Queen Mab*, 162-163; trial of Moxon, 163; quotations from preface, 81-82
Polidori, John William, 5n
Posthumous Poems (Shelley), 50, 63, 66, 132, 150, 154, 176, 204, 209; Mary's editorial work, 50, 161; preface by Mary, 51; recall of edition, 51, 161
Powell, Benjamin E., vii
Presumption; or the Fate of Frankenstein, 146, 198, 218, 219, 220, 220-225, 229
Procter, Bryan, xii, 50, 129, 140, 159, 170, 238

Quarterly, The, 144, 145

"Raby, Edwin," 80, 130, 238
"Raby, Mrs. Edwin," 46, 80, 96, 131
"Raby, Elizabeth," 45, 46, 87, 91, 96, 98, 105, 129, 130, 131, 138-139, 181, 182, 186, 238
"Raby, Oswi," 80, 130-131, 238
Radcliffe, Anne, 144
Rambles in Germany and Italy, 9n, 10n, 159, 209; origin of, 177; reasons for writing, 176-177; publication of, 177, 179, 204; comments on contemporary society in, 36, 38-40, 41, 43-44, 46-48; reviews of, 177-178; quotations from, 31-32, 36, 48, 190-191
"Raymond, Lord," 35, 36, 37, 41, 69, 70, 71, 72, 73, 102, 103, 109, 110, 110-117, 183, 193, 238
"Raymond, Clara," 40, 72, 103, 129
Recollections of Italy, 63-64, 73, 208; quotation from Shelley in, 64
Redding, Cyrus, 51n
Rennie, Eliza, 19, 166
Reveley, Henry, 31, 188, 238
Reynolds, Frederick Mansel, 174
Robinson, Henry Crabb, 3, 179
Rossetti, Gabriele, 4, 160
Rossetti, Lucy Maddox, 242
Rousseau, Jean Jacques, 33
Russell, Bertrand, 187

St. James Royal Magazine, 151
de Saint-Georges and Simonin, MM., 228
"Santerre, Lady," 120-122, 129-130, 238
Saturday Review, The, 180
"Saviani, Clorinda," 64-66, 132-134, 136, 137, 238
"Saville, Clorinda," 66, 77-78, 134-136, 137, 238

"Saville, Horatio," 13, 66, 77-78, 79-80, 134, 135, 137, 170, 238
Sgricci, Tommaso, 25, 189
Shelley, Sir Bysshe, 131, 189, 238
Shelley, Clara, 9, 72, 92, 129, 203, 211, 238
Shelley, Harriet Westbrook, xi, xii, xiv, 5, 6, 57, 203, 238; as Clorinda Saviani, 65; as Cornelia, Lady Lodore, 119, 121, 122, 129-130, 170
Shelley, Hellen, 131
Shelley, Lady Jane, v, xi, xii, 21
Shelley, Mary Wollstonecraft, outline of life, 203-205; biographies of, 241-242; personal appearance, 3-5; opinions of her, xi-xii, 5-7, 10, 18, 22, 25; contradictions in, xiv, 10; personal traits, 8-10; loneliness, 13-17, 21; attitude toward convention, 17-20; attitude toward second marriage, 20; social and political liberalism, xii, xiii, 26, 35-48; attitude toward education, 33-35, 39-40; attitude toward religion and the church, 40-41; attitude toward "women's rights," 45-46; interest in the arts, 25-26; interest in science and technology, 26-33; reading, 23-24; self-portraits: as Mathilda, 11-13, 93, 212; as Lionel Verney, 15-16, 68, 72, 112, 131, 141-142, 153; as Ethel Villiers, 13, 77, 86-87, 99, 136; as Elizabeth Raby, 87, 91, 96, 98; as Mrs. Raby, 80, 131; traits in other characters, 13, 16-17, 72, 75, 86-87; relationship to Shelley, xii, 10, 11, 148, 211-212; relationship expressed in journal, 54-55, 67; in poems, 55-56; in fiction, 11-13, 15, 57, 58, 67, 69, 72-73, 74, 75, 77, 212; interpretation of Shelley in her writings, 15, 49-82, 161-164; use of quotations from Shelley, 57, 62n, 64, 73-75; her pencil sketch of Shelley, 51n; interpretations of other persons, xiv, 107, 83-140 (for details, see under Byron, Claire Clairmont, Gisborne, Godwin, Fanny Imlay, Pacchiani, Viviani, Eliza Westbrook, Mary Wollstonecraft); on writing Shelley's biography, 49-51, 53, 161; on projects of others to write his biography, 51-53; fragments of a biography of Shelley, 50, 51, 54, 56-57, 61, 64-66, 76, 81, 208 (see also under *Falkner*, *The Last Man*, *Lodore*, *Mathilda*, *Valperga*); attitude toward own work, 141, 142, 165-166, 169, 176, 177; motives for writing, xiii, 44, 141, 154-155, 159-161, 165-166; reputation as a writer, 179-180; general estimate of her writing, 179, 200; faults as writer, 180-181; dramatic structure in novels, 181-185; characterization in fiction, 183, 185-187; use of characterizing phrase in fiction and letters, 187-189; observations on human nature, 189-190; descriptions of individuals in journal and letters, 188-189; range of style, 194-196; descriptive powers, 190-194; revisions, 196-199; poetic style, 199; as a translator, 24

INDEX 253

QUOTATIONS FROM: journal, 10, 13, 15, 17-18, 19, 45, 49-50, 54, 55, 56, 67, 77, 90n, 125-126, 145, 148-149, 155n, 164, 166n, 171n, 189, 190, 212; letters, 10, 12, 17n, 23, 25, 42, 52, 53, 62, 76, 89, 94, 99, 106, 109, 110, 111-112, 118, 136n, 137, 143-144, 146, 149, 158, 160, 161-162, 162-163, 165, 168, 169, 170, 171, 175, 176-177, 188, 189, 190, 215, 219

PUBLISHED WORKS
  Novels, 24, 205-206 (see also under *Falkner, Frankenstein, The Last Man, Lodore, Perkin Warbeck, Valperga*)
  Novelettes and tales, vii, 30, 43, 47, 75n, 76, 109, 110, 126, 131, 138, 150, 154-156, 159, 172, 173-175, 181, 186 207-208 (see also under *The Bride of Modern Italy*)
  Poems, 55, 156-157, 199, 210, 234-235 (see also under *The Choice*)
  Plays, 25, 158-159, 174, 209-210, 218
  Books of travel, 159, 209 (see also under *Rambles in Germany and Italy, Six Weeks' Tour*)
  Articles, 19n, 24, 63, 66, 76, 157, 175-176, 208-209 (see also under *Recollections of Italy*)
  Biography, 87-88, 159-161, 208 (see also under *Cabinet Cyclopedia*)
  Editorial work, 106, 161-164, 167, 209 (see also under Shelley's *Poetical Works, Posthumous Poems, Essays from Abroad* and Trelawny's *Adventures of a Younger Son*)

UNPUBLISHED WORKS, 55, 172, 206, 207, 210, 213, 217, 231-235 (see also under *Mathilda*)

UNFINISHED WORK IN MANUSCRIPT, 30, 206, 208

LOST WORKS, 58, 142-143, 155, 158-159, 205, 207, 208, 209

PROJECTED WORKS, 87, 166-167, 209

Shelley, Percy Bysshe, vi, xiii, xiv, 8, 9, 13, 18, 20, 22, 23, 25, 26, 31, 35, 40, 42, 47, 48, 49, 54, 67, 87, 89, 93, 101, 106, 128, 137, 140, 143, 144, 145, 150, 156, 173, 178, 203, 213, 215, 242, 243; as Adrian, 15, 57, 68-75, 78, 81, 102-103, 112, 153, 161; as Alleyn, 64-66, 132n; as Francis Derham, 79, 118; as Euthanasia, 62-63, 104-105, 110; as Idris, 112n, 131; as Malville and his friend, 64; as Edwin Raby, 80, 172; as Saville, 20, 66, 77, 79-80, 132n, 134-136, 161, 170; as Villiers, 77, 79, 99, 136, 161, 170; as Woodville, 12, 57, 58-60, 81, 154; traits and ideas in other characters, 61, 75, 76, 79, 80, 118; quotations from poems, 5, 6, 8, 11, 43, 48, 60, 69n, 101, 135; quotations from letters, 5, 6, 22, 48, 93, 166

WORKS: *Adonais*, 74, 75n; *Alastor*, 73; *The Cenci*, 92n, 158; *Charles the First*, 158; *A Defense of Poetry*, 163; *Epipsychidion*, 65, 78; Essay

Shelley, Percy Bysshe (*cont.*)
on Devils, 163; *Essay on Love*, 76; *Hellas*, 62; "Indian Serenade," 75n; *Julian and Maddalo*, 60, 74, 112, 211; *Mont Blanc*, 73, 143, 191; poems for *Proserpine* and *Midas*, 158; *Prometheus Unbound*, 28n, 74; *Queen Mab*, 161-163; *The Revolt of Islam*, 61, 69; *St. Irvyne*, 144; "Stanzas Written in Dejection near Naples," 75n; translation of *Symposium*, 76, 163; "Ode to the West Wind," 67; *The Witch of Atlas*, 72; *Zastrozzi*, 144

Shelley, Sir Percy Florence, v, xiii, 8, 18, 21, 49, 129, 130, 148, 166, 177, 204, 205, 212, 214, 238

Shelley, Sir Timothy, 45, 51, 53, 56, 101, 148, 152, 161, 162, 204, 205, 231, 239; as Oswi Raby, 80, 130-131, 172; traits in other characters, 131

Shelley, William, 12, 56, 72, 92, 203, 212, 217n, 239; as Euthanasia's brother, 129; as Frankenstein's brother, 129

Shelley and Mary, 4n, 8n, 10n, 92n, 149n, 151n, 152n, 155n, 159n, 165n, 241

Shelley-Rolls, Sir John, v, vi, 50n, 207, 210, 213n, 231

Sisters of Charity, The, 174

Six Weeks' Tour, History of a, 163, 209; publication of, 143, 203; reception of, 143, 159, 177; biographical information in, 54; style of, 191, 194; quotations from, 42, 194-195

Smith, Horatio, 146

Smith, O., 225, 230

Smith, Robert Metcalfe, xi n, xii

Son of Frankenstein, The, 227

South Atlantic Quarterly, The, 218n

Spark, Muriel, 242

Spirit and Manners of the Age, The, 175, 176, 209

Stacey, Sophia, 4, 239

de Staël, Mme., 39, 160, 166, 196

Stanhope, Col. Leicester, 116-117

Studies in Philology, 211n

Taaffe, Count, 188

Talfourd, T. N., 163

Thomas, Mrs., 197, 198

Toynbee, A. J., 62

Trelawny, Edward John, vi, xii, xiv, 4, 8, 10, 17n, 18, 20, 22, 35, 40, 51, 52, 53, 87, 113, 116, 128, 151, 163, 165, 170, 188, 204, 239, 243; in Mary's novels, 107, 123-127; as Falkner, 80, 123-126; as de Faro, 126; traits in other characters, 126-127; *Adventures of a Younger Son*, 124-125 (quotations), 167, 170, 209

Valperga, xiii, 60, 89, 137, 144, 152, 155, 156, 159, 168, 180, 206, 214, 215; inception of, 148-149; publication of, 149, 204; Godwin's opinion of, 149; Mary's opinion of, 149; Shelley's opinion of, 149; reception of, 61-62, 110, 150, 151; treatment of education in, 33, 34; attitude toward war in, 42-43; plot of, 181; characterization in, 186; style of, 192-193; autobiographical element in, 63n; Shelley in, 57, 61, 62-63, 104-105;

Byron in, 104-105, 109, 110; Claire in, 104-105, 110; quotations from, 33, 47, 192-193
Vampyre, The, 218, 220, 231
"Verney, Lionel," 15-16, 31, 32, 34, 38, 68, 69, 72, 96, 110, 112, 116, 131, 153, 183, 190, 236, 239
"Verney, Mr.," 90, 94-95
"Villiers, Edward," 45, 77, 79, 80, 99, 136, 170, 239
"Villiers, Ethel Fitzhenry," 13, 77, 79, 80, 86, 91, 96, 99, 120, 136, 138-139, 169, 170, 239
Viviani, Emilia, vi, xiv, 57, 204, 236, 239, 244; as Clorinda Saviani, 65, 132-134, 136; as Clorinda Saville, 66, 77-78, 134-136
Viviani della Robbia, Enrica, 133n, 137, 244
Vohl, Maria, 242

Wallack, James William, 146, 219, 223, 224
"Walton, Robert," 16, 17, 32, 182, 222, 239
Wasp, The, 151
Watts, A. A., 158
Webling, Peggy, 226

Westbrook, Eliza, xiv, 57, 239; as Lady Santerre, 121-122, 129-130, 170
Westminster Review, The, 19n, 76n, 175, 176, 208, 209
White, Newman Ivey, vii, 60, 80n, 99n, 102n, 130n, 134n, 137n, 211-212, 243
Williams, Edward Ellerker, 8, 155, 204, 214, 239
Williams, Jane, 5, 19, 62, 89, 106, 109n, 118n, 128, 155, 167, 204, 214, 215, 239
Winter's Wreath, The, 158, 174, 210
Wollstonecraft, Everina, 188, 239
Wollstonecraft, Mary, xiii, 6, 22, 45, 83, 100, 138, 141, 203, 217n, 239; ideas on education, 23, 33, 84-85; Mary's admiration for, 95-96; Mary's sense of loss, 96; Mary's description of, 97-98; as Diana, 90, 96-97; as Lionel Verney's mother, 97
"Woodville," 12, 26, 57, 58-60, 72, 75n, 80, 81, 216, 239
Wright, Frances, 170

"Zaimi, Evadne," 72, 74, 102-103, 115, 236